What Others Are Saying About

"This is an extremely powerful sto mentor and brother, Timothy. Tim and Miriam have been instrumental in my spiritual journey, and I admire how they connect and build bridges between Christians and Muslims. This book is the story of love. As a former Muslim, I learned the biblical emphasis on love from Tim, Miriam, and other Christians, and this helped me change from Islam to following Jesus. Jesus our Lord put Tim and Miriam on my path to feel and understand our God in different ways than I could have imagined. I highly recommend this book, particularly to Muslim people wherever they may be. Our Muslim friends should read it without any bias, just to see how these lovely stories happened in peoples' lives. I am one of those people."

"HASSAN"
The BMB (Believer from a Muslim Background) from the Middle East who is the primary character in chapter 50 of this book

"I've enjoyed reading Tim and Miriam's book, *Loving Your Muslim Neighbor*. Words that have come to my mind are accessible, easy to read, relatable, personal, gripping, humorous, honest, authentic, informative, varied (they've befriended Muslim people in many different settings), and down-to-earth (no evangelical hype here, just real relationships!).

"These two are truly an 'unlikely couple' to engage in 'loving their Muslim neighbor,' which makes their story a delight. A mid-life crisis of a Midwestern pastor plunges them into the deep end of relating with Muslims as friends and neighbors. They invite the reader to walk with them as their hearts attune to God's purposes and their minds acquire the skills of communicating his love.

"Tim and Miriam lead with love, with relationship. They communicate unconditional welcome and embrace. The result is fresh and winsome. It opens new possibilities for relating with Muslims (and others) in neighborhoods, schools and parks. Their experience teaches us that there are no 'professionals,' only followers of Jesus who love him and others.

"And, by the way, they don't sweep the hard stuff under the rug. They deal with real issues that stand in the way of communicating with Muslims. Their responses are born out of relationship, not academics, which gives the book its unique tone and value.

"Read this book to be encouraged and to be educated, but ultimately to be transformed. I am pleased to recommend *Loving Your Muslim Neighbor*."

REV. DR. MICHAEL F. KUHN
Author of *Fresh Vision for the Muslim World, Finding Hagar,* and *God is One*

"*Loving Your Muslim Neighbor* is a must-read for everyone who loves and serves the Author of the parable we all know and love—The Good Samaritan. To reach the Islamic world with the gospel seems to be a daunting, impossible task filled with profound risks. To engage the unfamiliar 'neighbor' is intimidating and uncomfortable, particularly when the unfamiliar is beset with a reputation of resistance and terrorism. Through their stories of simple obedience to love their neighbor, Timothy and Miriam make the unfamiliar familiar. Their stories are permeated with proof of God's faithfulness and provision as they have taken, and still take, risks to love their neighbors. Their stories reveal how not-so-daunting the task really is when we allow Christlike love to bridge the relational gap to some of the most unreached peoples of the world."

EMILY FOREMAN
Missionary to North Africa, former wife of a martyr, and author of *We Died Before We Came Here: A True Story of Sacrifice and Hope*

"I wish I had written this book!

"As one who has been seeking for 57 years to see Muslim peoples from around the world pass from death to eternal life, I am constantly encouraged by Tim and Miriam. I am ready to shout to anyone and everyone who has some of the Savior's heart for Muslims, dwell on the pages of *Loving Your Muslim Neighbor*. It's not only the best guide I've ever seen, it's a delight to meet Muslims through Tim and Miriam's experiences.

"Tim and Miriam's book isn't theory, nor does it pretend to be a full explanation of varying Islamic theologies. It's a demo of what any of us can do if we are moved with compassion, as the authors are. Watch out! Reading this book may be contagious!"

REV. DR. GREG LIVINGSTONE
Founder of Frontiers and Consultant for World Outreach of the Evangelical Presbyterian Church

Author of *You've Got Libya: A Life Serving in the Muslim World*, *The Muslim World: A Presbyterian Mandate*, and *Planting Churches in Muslim Cities*

"A refreshing look at what every believer can do as a witness amongst this largest unreached people group in the world! Tim and Miriam are joyfully doing what comes (super)naturally to them by the Holy Spirit. We've been friends for a long time, and I still remember the exhilarating conversation I had with Tim in my aged truck, encouraging him to lift up his eyes on this delightful harvest field of formerly inaccessible nations which God is bringing to our shores (Acts 17:25–27). This helped to launch him from pastoring to missions. I pray God will launch many more 'recovering pastors' like us!"

PASTORS SYD AND LIZ DOYLE
Cross Cultural Church Planters and Founders of Nations Light Ministries

"I really appreciate this book to counter the many books that make us afraid and even demonize the Muslims among us. It breaks down the myth that Muslims are not approachable or amenable to the gospel. The early church addressed the issue of Jews versus Gentiles, but God interfered and opened the gospel for the Gentiles. If that did not happen, all of us would not have come to Christ. Let us not treat the Muslims as those unworthy of the gospel. Muslims desperately need the Lord. I believe this book introduces the way of love, not the way of hate. BMBs all agree that the God of the Bible being a God of love is one of the most attractive things that drew them to following Christ. God is love, and this is the message of the gospel. I encourage you to read this book and use it as a study tool."

REV. DR. ABU ATALLAH
BMB and author of *From Cairo to Christ*

"Tim and Miriam were in pastoral ministry for many years but increasingly felt burdened to reach out to others beyond their own flock. Their book, *Loving Your Muslim Neighbor*, is a sequence of delightful stories and an autobiographical journey that chronicles that process. Their stories are short, easy to read, yet bold, gentle, and loaded with practical instruction, as well as grace and truth. Tim and Miriam are quick to share their heart struggles and failures, in addition to the many practical things they have learned about loving Muslims. They did not begin as experts in Islam. They did start, however, with Jesus's heart of love for anyone in need.

"One of my favorite stories was Tim and Miriam's response to the Christian pastor from Gainesville, Florida, who sponsored the International Burn a Qur'an Day in 2010. This caused much distress among Muslims worldwide, as well as the intervention of our own US Secretary of State. Tim and Miriam responded by sponsoring an I Love Muslims Day on a university campus. Needless to say, Muslim students were intrigued and came to this very successful event.

"In this day when Islamophobia and fear garner increasing media attention, Tim and Miriam's book is a refreshing interlude. It is also a wonderful example of our Lord Jesus in 'going everywhere and doing good.'

"I can't more highly recommend Tim and Miriam's book. Read it! It is a refreshing stream in today's relational desert!"

ED HOSKINS, MD, PHD
Author of *A Muslim's Heart* and *A Muslim's Mind*

"*Loving Your Muslim Neighbor* is more than a 'how to' book about Christian- Muslim relationships. It's a 'why not?' book. Christians: Why not engage in honestly loving your Muslim neighbors whom God has 'sent' to live in your country? This book isn't a missions manual for the local church but rather an invitation for ordinary Christians to engage with ordinary Muslims in loving and respectful ways, inviting them to become followers of Jesus. The numerous down-to-earth personal stories that Tim and Miriam share in this book are written just as they speak—with winsome honesty and self-reflection. I have personally seen Tim and Miriam's genuine love and compassion in action for any 'neighbor' they encounter (not only Muslim neighbors). Their 'neighbor encounters' usually involve inviting Jesus into the conversation. As evidenced in this book, Tim and Miriam have truly lived out their calling to seek out their Muslim neighbors and serve them in love and truth. The format of short chapters and reflection questions at the end of every chapter invites the reader to do the same. My deep heart's desire is that all Muslims would have the opportunity to encounter a loving

Christian who shows them who Jesus is in their words and deeds. This book should inspire you to say, 'With God's help, I can do that, too!'"

KAYE ANTHONY
Long-term Christian worker who has been loving and inviting Muslims to follow Jesus in the US, Europe, North Africa, but mostly in Central Asia, for thirty-five years, currently working in Bible translation.

"This book is the perfect 'Loving Muslims for Dummies'—if you understand that a 'dummy' is simply a non-expert beginner on the path to excellence. Jesus said the wise person is the one who hears his words and puts them into practice. That describes Tim and Miriam, and this book is a distillation of wisdom procured through that process. Tim and Miriam do not present themselves as scholars or experts. They share their mistakes and failures. And, in story after story, as they take Jesus's command to love their (Muslim) neighbors seriously, we learn wisdom about the complex issues that scholars debate. This profound guidebook that is grounded not in theory but in real friendships with Ahmeds, Omars, and Salimas will give you the map and fuel you need to start your own journey."

REV. PHIL LINTON
Director, EPC World Outreach

"Tim and Miriam truly do love Muslims. Tim is kind, patient, and honest with Muslims—all essential to having a fruitful ministry. Having journeyed in mission with Tim while he was still in the pastorate all the way to the present, it has been a joy to see him grow from reaching out to Muslims himself to where he is now equipping others to help Muslims trust in Jesus. This book will equip you to witness in Spirit and in truth and to share your trust in Jesus with Muslims so that they, too, may become reproducing disciples."

MERT HERSHBERGER
Former North American Coordinator of Praying Through the Arabian Peninsula and current Lead Minister with International Fellowship for Everyday Saints

"What is most striking about *Loving Your Muslim Neighbor* are the riveting stories about Muslims whom Tim and Miriam have met. For example, there is Abdul from Lebanon, who was bereaved, sick, and all alone in an American city. There is a desperate Syrian woman, who with her four small children lived in squalid conditions in a Middle Eastern refugee camp. There is Khalil, the Saudi student on a US university campus who had prayed on the bus that he'd meet a friendly American. And there is Ali, who learned to love John 3:16 so much that it was on his lips when he died in an Iraqi hospital. Nearly every Muslim person they run across is approachable, warm, and hospitable.

"The book, however, is more than stories: we learn that there are 250,000 Muslims in greater Detroit. Tips are given on how to evangelize and how not to do it. There are questions for pondering, cultural clues for witnessing, and recommended books for reading. Most important, this non-academic text shows that it is possible to love our Muslim neighbors. One cannot read it without sensing the authors' passion to share the good news."

WARREN LARSON, PHD
Senior Research Fellow and Professor, Zwemer Center for Muslim-Christian Relations, Columbia International University

"One of the most asked questions I receive is, 'I have a Muslim neighbor, (or co-worker), and I just don't know how to begin a friendship with them. Where can I start?' If you've ever found yourself asking this question, this book is for you. (If you haven't asked yourself this question, then Timothy and Miriam, with love and grace, lead you in asking it!)

"Timothy and Miriam have given us a window into their journey doing this very thing: starting conversations and building friendships with Muslims they've encountered. From self-described 'newbies' to those with much experience to share, they give us a humble, vulnerable, and compassionate example to follow in loving others as Jesus has loved us. For those wanting very practical help, they give many simple conversational tools to help start and deepen spiritual conversations.

"What beautiful, precious stories! These stories are filled with Muslims responding wholeheartedly in wanting friendship and relationship with Timothy and Miriam (even at times providing rescue for them in difficult spots!). A relationship is the place where Muslims can see your faith come alive, one that points them to Jesus. Each Muslim needs a friendship with a Jesus-follower."

"ELIZABETH"
A long-term worker in the Muslim world (Southeast Asia)

"This book chronicles the amazing journey of one couple as they have sought to love their Muslim neighbors. Several key insights flow out of their story: the impact of love and friendship, the providence of God, the power of the gospel message to transform lives, the humility necessary to be good learners, the joy found in obedience, and the importance of attitude change that leads to action. The appendices provided offer practical help with such titles as 'Glossary of Terms,' 'Conversation Starters,' and 'Cultural Do's and Don'ts.' Read this book to learn, to be challenged, and to be inspired as you observe their path of obedience in reaching out to Muslim people. I pray this book helps thousands of Christ-followers to 'go and do likewise.'"

TIMOTHY K. BEOUGHER, PHD
Associate Dean, Billy Graham School of Missions, Evangelism and Ministry; Billy Graham Professor of Evangelism and Church Growth, The Southern Baptist Theological Seminary; Senior Pastor of West Broadway Baptist Church in Louisville, Kentucky

Author of *Overcoming Walls to Witnessing; Evangelism for a Changing World; Accounts of a Campus Revival: Wheaton College, 1995;* and *Richard Baxter and Conversion*

"Tim and Miriam are the real deal. Their love for Jesus and their love for people are evident and infectious. The book you are holding isn't theory apart from practice. *Loving Your Muslim Neighbor* is the outworking of years and years of fruitful ministry in the United States and around the world. Having traveled with them to the Middle East, I've seen firsthand how Jesus shows up through the very practices they describe. They showed me that people respond to the disarming, noncoercive love of Jesus received through the ministry of his body, the church. In a world that is increasingly polarized by fear and hatred, this book is a guide to becoming a people formed by the Holy Spirit to love our Muslim neighbors as ourselves."

REV. CHRIS WINANS
Lead Pastor, Cornerstone Evangelical Presbyterian Church
Brighton, Michigan

Published in the United States of America by Credo House Publishers
a division of Credo Communications LLC, Grand Rapids, Michigan
credohousepublishers.com

The events and conversations in this book have been set down to the best of the authors'
ability. Some names—including the authors' names—have been changed to protect the
privacy of individuals.

ISBN: 978-1-62586-181-8

Cover design and interior typesetting by Jonathan Lewis
Editing by Donna Huisjen

Canvas texture on cover: iStock.com/jessicahyde
Watercolor texture on cover title: Image by Rosa Palma from Pixabay
Additional cover texture: Photo by Annie Spratt on Unsplash

Printed in the United States of America
First edition

"For the entire law is fulfilled in keeping this one command:
'Love your neighbor as yourself.'"
GALATIANS 5:14, NIV

"For the commandments . . .
are summed up in this word:
'You shall love your neighbor as yourself.'"
ROMANS 13:9

"If you really fulfill the royal law according to the Scripture,
'You shall love your neighbor as yourself,'
you are doing well."
JAMES 2:8

LOVING
YOUR
MUSLIM
NEIGHBOR

Stories of God Using an Unlikely Couple
to Love Muslim People . . .
and How He Might Use You to Do the Same

Timothy and Miriam Harris

credo
house publishers

This book is gratefully dedicated to:

Each of our family members, friends, and coworkers who has supported us and prayed for us during these thirteen years of outreach to Muslim people. We can never thank all of you enough. We especially dedicate this book to our cousin, Valorie. Cancer did not take her home, Jesus did. She is the one who kept encouraging us to write this book.

Global workers who have left all—families, homes, safety, comfort—to go to least reached Muslim people groups all over the world so they might hear the good news for the first time. Great is your reward in heaven, dear missionary friends. May you hear your "well done" even now.

Believers from a Muslim background who have given up everything to follow Jesus—their honor, their family, their education, their job, their possessions, and for some . . . even their very lives. Your dedication to the Savior humbles, inspires, and encourages us to press on and not give up.

The missionary martyrs who loved Jesus more than their own lives and followed the Lamb to their deaths so that Muslims might enter the kingdom of God and live forever. May your first love be our first love. You are the overcomers.

Each of our Muslim friends in the US and around the world who has shown us kindness and hospitality and love. We have you in our hearts. We only want you to know and follow the Jesus of the Bible and be with us in heaven forever. No matter what you decide, we will always love you.

Our Lord—the Lord of the harvest who loves Muslim people more than we could ever imagine and proved His love through the greatest sacrifice possible. Thank You Father, Son, and Holy Spirit. May Your name be hallowed. May Your kingdom come. And may the Lamb who was slain receive the reward of His suffering.

"Not to us, O Lord, not to us,
but to your name goes all the glory
for your unfailing love and faithfulness."
Psalm 115:1, NLT

Contents

Introduction

God Is Moving in the Muslim World!
But You Won't Hear It on the Nightly News

We met Kareem in 2017 when we were Christmas caroling in a Muslim neighborhood in Michigan. As we approached his well-kept home on an unusually warm December afternoon, we were singing our Christmas carols with the joy of the Lord! Kareem's mother happened to be outside the house with his sisters. When she saw and heard us, we noticed that she immediately began to cry. What had we done? We knew the vast majority of Muslims—even in the US—don't celebrate Christmas. But we didn't anticipate that our carols about Jesus's birth could elicit such a sad response!

As this Muslim woman invited our group of about ten carolers into her large, attractive home, we quickly found out why she was touched by our song. She and her husband informed us that their sixteen-year-old son, Kareem, was in the battle of his life against lymphoma. The whole family needed encouragement, and the Holy Spirit's choice of our particular Christmas carol had touched her heart.

Kareem's parents graciously seated us in their spacious living room and encouraged us to sing more Christmas carols for the whole family. As we did, their Arab hospitality was on display as they brought us all manner of refreshments. You would have thought we were members of this generous Lebanese Muslim family, but we had never met them before that day!

Before we left, we took several pictures together. We also had a time of prayer for Kareem—prayers offered up to the Father in the name of Jesus—which this Muslim family clearly appreciated.

One year later, we took another group Christmas caroling in that city, and we remembered Kareem and went to his home. Again, his parents welcomed us in, gave us Arabic sweets, and listened to our songs. We discovered that Kareem was fighting cancer in a hospital in our town an hour away.

I was blessed to visit Kareem three times in that hospital, the first time with a cancer survivor who understood what he was going through and could bring unique encouragement. On my second visit, it was readily apparent that Kareem's organs were shutting down and that, apart from a miracle, he didn't have long to live. I prayed and shared Jesus's loving words from Revelation 3:20 with Kareem:

> *"Look! I stand at the door and knock.*
> *If you hear my voice and open the door, I will come in,*
> *and we will share a meal together as friends."*
> REVELATION 3:20, NLT

I told Kareem that I felt Jesus was knocking on the door of his heart and encouraged him to invite Jesus into his heart. His response? He said in a very weak and tender voice that I will never forget:

> *"Jesus, come into my heart."*

That was Friday. I saw him one more time before he died on the following Tuesday.

On that Tuesday, I was able to share the Revelation 3:20 "God-story" with several of Kareem's Muslim relatives and friends in a hospital waiting room.

They treated me like family.

———

God is moving in the Muslim world.

He really, really is.

Yes, more Muslims have become followers of Jesus in the last fifteen years than in all the previous fourteen centuries of Islam . . . *combined!*

But you won't hear this on the nightly news, or even in churches.

Most Christians *don't hear* about how our awesome and glorious God is reaching Muslim people around the globe with His redeeming love through avenues such as seeing Christian satellite TV and websites, reading the Bible in one's own language, receiving an answer to a prayer offered by a Christian, finding practical help from believers in a time of need, and most of all—enjoying a relationship with a genuine follower of Jesus.

Most Christians *don't know* a Muslim person. In thirteen years of ministry to Muslims in the US—and traveling to nine different Muslim majority countries—we have met so many Muslims who are a whole lot like us: they just want to make a living, raise children and grandchildren, and live in peace. They are generally kind, hospitable, decent people like Kareem's family. But so many Christians don't know this.

Most Christians *have never met* former Muslims (BMBs—believers from a Muslim background), as we have. We have been blessed to meet Syrian refugees who have abandoned everything to gain Jesus and whose stories sound like something from the book of Acts in the Bible: dreams and visions of Jesus; healings; food multiplying; money appearing; and yes, persecution.

There is so much good news happening in the Muslim world. If only Christians could hear about it! Perhaps then we wouldn't be hearing comments such as these:

- *"I don't want to hear anything about Muslims in our church."*
- *"I don't think we need to assimilate to Muslims; they need to assimilate to us."*
- *"If I see a Muslim woman in the mall, I'm not going to speak to her unless she speaks to me first."*
- *"I don't want to visit a mosque with you, even for evangelism. I don't want to be spiritually contaminated."*
- *"I don't want to eat their food or visit their restaurants with you."*
- *"They want to take away our rights, our Constitution. They want to put in Sharia law."*
- *"I have a duty to be concerned about my grandchildren and their safety."*
- *"I wish we would just nuke the whole Middle East and be done with it."*

The fact is that Muslim people have come to North America—to big cities, and even to smaller towns. They come as immigrants who pay their own way to find a better life. They come as international students to our college campuses for a better education. And they come as refugees attempting to escape real, horrific, life-threatening danger from extremists. We need to think about how we are going to respond to these Muslim people who come here:

Will we be like Jonah?
Will we run, . . . hide, . . . and hate as he did?

Sadly, so many Christians in our churches are much like Jonah: either angry or afraid of Muslims, especially since 9/11, and also since the rise of ISIS. We have all turned on our televisions and seen news about radical Islam and terrorist attacks. These stories are not coming just from the Middle East. They originate in places like Australia, France, Denmark, Canada, and within the US. These events trigger *fear* and *anger* as our natural responses to Muslims. They can even create in our minds unfair and untrue stereotypes of *all* Muslims as terrorists.

As followers of Jesus, we must ask ourselves:

As Muslims come to North America, will we be like Jonah,
or will we be like Jesus?

Will we be like the One who came to seek and to save the lost?

We believe we must be prepared to be a light to the Muslim people who are coming to our lands. Many of them have lived in the terrible darkness of war, disease, poverty, starvation, and incomprehensible loss. We also need to be somewhat informed about their religion (Islam), their prophet (Muhammad), and their book (the Qur'an).

In this book, *Loving Your Muslim Neighbor*, we have two primary goals:

1. *Attitude:* We want to share our journey with you of how God has grown a love in our hearts for Muslim people—how He has changed our attitudes toward them. When you have *God's* heart for Muslims, it changes everything. We hope and pray that reading this book will help you grow to love Muslim people as well, and to move from being even the least bit angry or afraid of Muslims to being compassionate and confident witnesses to them.
2. *Action:* In this book we provide some practical evangelistic tools and strategies for you to reach out to Muslim people with the good news of Jesus. Attitude change is vital, but we invite you to

take action steps as well—however large or small—in loving your Muslim neighbor.

Our sincere desire is that this book of God-stories of our experiences with Muslim people—and our accompanying teaching points and questions to ponder—will help to accomplish these two goals.

Each of our stories reveals how God sovereignly put us—a very unlikely couple—in places and situations with Muslims in ways that have beautifully changed our lives. These stories about real people and real events—from the Midwest to the Middle East—have given us just a tiny glimpse into God's John 3:16 love for Muslim people.

We invite you to prayerfully open your heart and mind as you read our stories—and learn from what God has taught us—in the pages of this book.

Let's grow together in *loving our Muslim neighbor.*

QUESTIONS TO PONDER

- When you hear the word *Muslim,* what are the first words that come to your mind?
- When Jesus, our Good Shepherd, hears the word *Muslim,* what words do you think are the first to come to His mind?

"I have other sheep, too, that are not in this sheepfold.
I must bring them also.
They will listen to my voice,
and there will be one flock with one shepherd."
JESUS IN JOHN 10:16, NLT

"And people will come from all over the world—
from east and west, north and south—
to take their places in the Kingdom of God."
JESUS IN LUKE 13:29, NLT

"Dear brothers and sisters,
the longing of my heart and my prayer to God is for [Muslims] to be saved.
I know what enthusiasm they have for God, but it is misdirected zeal.

For they don't understand God's way of making people right with himself."
PAUL IN ROMANS 10:1–3A, NLT
(WITH OUR SUBSTITUTION OF THE WORD "MUSLIMS")

CHAPTER 1

✝ ☾

Why Muslims?—The *Call*

"Oh No! A Mid-Life Crisis!"

———

I was a very burnt out pastor in 2006.

The calling to get into evangelism or missions full time was bursting inside me. I felt like a missionary trapped inside a pastor's body—and I couldn't get out!

We were pastoring a lovely group of people, but I just had to get out of the four walls of the church and be with unbelievers—first and foremost, unbelievers from other cultures. Every mission trip to Mexico, Haiti, the Ukraine, Russia, or Sri Lanka that I went on just confirmed this calling more and more.

Also, every book I read about vision, gifting, and ministry passion was another confirmation of the "arrowhead"—the direction—toward evangelism and missions that I had received in college in 1977. There had, however, been a big problem: God would not release me to that calling! For almost thirty years He simply would not give us a firm leading, along with an inner peace, about leaving pastoral ministry. There were no specifics to grab hold of from Him: no people group, no country, no organization. There was no defined tip to the arrowhead of this strong evangelism and missions calling.

I don't get depressed very often, but I was depressed. It became increasingly difficult to get out of bed and go into my church office every day, and Miriam had to help me do that. I had no energy, and there was nothing in pastoral ministry that excited me or gave me life except for preaching.

I asked my elders at our small church for a ten-week sabbatical to figure things out. I had been there as their pastor for over twelve years, and they kindly granted it to me. A few weeks before that sabbatical started, a piece of mail came across my desk at the church that caught my eye . . . and then compelled my heart. There was a seminar coming to Dearborn, Michigan, about reaching out to Muslims with the gospel. When I saw that brochure, somehow, I knew—*I knew*—I *had* to be at that seminar.

The four-day seminar in June of 2006 was called "Legacy," and it totally changed our lives. In that long weekend God supernaturally planted a love for Muslim people in my heart. I couldn't explain it then, and I can't explain it now. God used every speaker to touch me and call me to outreach to Muslim people. Muslims were not really "on our radar" at that time, but in that seminar they became front and center.

As Miriam and I drove around Dearborn those four days, I couldn't help but notice all the Arab Muslim people sitting on their porches in the early evenings with their children or grandchildren playing in the front yard. I yearned to know them. There was something about them that drew me. There was something fascinating about them and their culture (I am not speaking of Islam but of the Arab culture). Even then, I began to long for these Muslim people from Lebanon, Iraq, and Yemen to come to know the Jesus of the Bible.

For dinners during the Legacy seminar, we went out to local Middle Eastern restaurants and ate mostly Lebanese food. We absolutely loved that food and felt so comfortable with the Arab Muslim servers and clientele. I was getting more and more "hooked" on reaching Muslims for Jesus! (Can God use *food* to alter the course of your life? In our case, the answer was a resounding *yes*—especially if it is Lebanese food!).

At the seminar on Thursday, we were told that on Friday night we would have several options to choose from: attend the yearly Arab Festival, take a tour of a local mosque, or go out to eat at a Middle Eastern restaurant. But there was one more option. A man named Mike, who goes door-to-door every Saturday in Dearborn sharing the gospel, stood up and asked if anyone would like to come with him on Friday night to do that. There were about two hundred people at that seminar on reaching Muslims for Jesus. I figured that the majority of them would want to go talk to Muslim people about

Jesus! But to my utter surprise, only two of us raised our hands to go door-to-door to share the good news with them.

Nevertheless, on Friday night only Mike and I went into the Muslim neighborhoods of Dearborn to share Jesus (I'm not sure what happened to the other guy who raised his hand, but he didn't show up!). We knocked on several doors, but people did not come to the door or were not at home. As we kept walking, we saw a large Arab man, Abdul, sitting on his front porch. He invited us into his home, and what happened next astounded me. After a time of conversation about the good news, Abdul—a Lebanese American Muslim—prayed to receive Jesus!

Yes, God had a plan. He knew just how to "hook" me into Muslim ministry that long summer weekend in 2006: through a compelling seminar, a large Muslim man named Abdul, delicious food, and a beautiful people I had never met before—Arab Muslims.

I went home at the end of that seminar and told Miriam:

> *"This is it. I found it!*
> *I found the tip of the arrowhead of missions and evangelism*
> *that I have been looking for all these years.*
> *It's Muslims!"*

Of course, Miriam was elated. Wouldn't any wife be excited if her husband came home and said he was leaving his job to reach out to Muslims? On the contrary, my dear wife responded with:

> *"Oh no! A mid-life crisis!"*

But to her everlasting credit, Miriam started on that journey with me, and I can never thank her enough. Within a year we resigned from pastoring that beloved little church and launched full time into simultaneously raising support and reaching out to Muslim people.

I was ecstatic about this new change in our lives and the fulfillment of a vision I had had for nearly thirty years to reach the nations. Miriam was who she has always been—an impressively strong and solid woman who has joined me in ministry wherever God has called us.

This was no exception.

———

QUESTIONS TO PONDER

- If someone were to ask you to define your ministry vision or calling in life right now, how would you answer?
- If you could do anything for the Lord and His kingdom and were not limited by time or money, what would you do?
- Why do you think God sometimes gives a person a vision and calling but then waits so long to fulfill it?

> *"For still the vision awaits its appointed time;*
> *it hastens to the end—it will not lie.*
> *If it seems slow, wait for it;*
> *it will surely come; it will not delay."*
> HABAKKUK 2:3

CHAPTER 2

The Lebanese Muslim: *"Who Could Pass Up an Offer Like That?"*

**I Thought, *"This Muslim Ministry Stuff Is Easy!"*
Little Did I Know . . .**

We saw him sitting on the porch of his little house in Dearborn, Michigan. He just looked lonely.

Really, really, *lonely.*

After we went into his house to share the gospel with him, we found out why. This second-generation Lebanese Muslim man, Abdul, had lost his wife to a heart attack while she shoveled snow in front of that home. His mother had been murdered in a robbery of their store. His brother had been killed in a snowmobile accident. And his only grandchild had died of SIDS (sudden infant death syndrome).

After getting to know Abdul a little better, my outreach partner for the night, Mike, shared the gospel with him. (I listened because Mike was the expert in door-to-door outreach in the Muslim neighborhoods of Dearborn, and I was the total rookie). Abdul courteously listened, but it was obvious that, for some reason, what Mike was sharing wasn't impacting him. It just wasn't "taking." Mike closed his presentation, and then I began to make small talk with Abdul—something that comes naturally to me as an extrovert.

"Abdul, you're a big man. Did you ever play football?"

"Yeah, I played here in Dearborn at Fordson high school."

"Do you ever watch football on TV?"

"Yeah, I watch the Lions." (We commiserated.)

"Have you ever seen someone hold up a sign during a football game that says, 'John 3:16'?"

"Yeah, what is that?"

I quoted that supremely wonderful verse, John 3:16, to Abdul. When I finished the last word— *"life"*—he said one simple word:

"Really?"

I'll never forget it. It was like the Holy Spirit came into the room!

Abdul's one-word comment was a combination of an exclamation of surprise and an open-ended question begging for more information.

To be honest, I really didn't know what I was doing. I had witnessed to many, many people through the years, but this whole Muslim thing was utterly new to me. Nevertheless, I pressed forward.

"Abdul, wouldn't it be so good if you went to bed tonight and you didn't have to be afraid of where you would be if you died in your sleep?"

I had no idea Abdul was in very poor health when I asked him that question, but the Holy Spirit did. And I had no idea that so many Muslims fear hell and have no assurance of salvation, . . . but the Holy Spirit did.

After a little more discussion, I asked Abdul if he would like to pray with us based on the truths of John 3:16 that he had just heard. I'll never forget what he said as he answered me with his own question:

"Who could pass up an offer like that?"

I prayed alone with Abdul, since Mike did not feel comfortable engaging in what is commonly called "the sinner's prayer." (I totally understand his reasoning: many people pray this prayer as a form of "fire insurance" from hell, not as a sincere commitment to following Jesus.)

I was amazed. I was on cloud nine. My first time out witnessing to Muslim people, and this man had said "yes" to Jesus! I'm ashamed to admit it, but a thought came into my mind:

"This Muslim ministry stuff is easy!"

(Oh, what a naïve—and prideful—thought! Little did I know . . .)

Though we lived more than an hour away, for the next year and a half we had the joy of meeting fairly often with Abdul. One day I called, and he did not answer. I called his son and heard the painful news: Abdul had been hospitalized for two weeks and had died.

Our hearts hurt over the loss of this big, lovable Arab man.

But our hearts also rejoiced that our compassionate and omniscient God had led us right to Abdul's home that night in June of 2006.

God knew when He would call Abdul out of this earthly life . . . and when to send us to him.

MINISTRY TO MUSLIM PEOPLE:
It Won't be Easy, But It Will Be Worth It!

Dear readers, we want to caution you in the beginning of this book: if you want to reach Muslim people for Jesus, please disavow yourself of any thought that it will be "easy."

This is not to discourage you!

There will be times of "joy unspeakable and full of glory" as you seek to help Muslims see Jesus for who He really is and enter His kingdom. You will have occasions when your friendship with a Muslim will be so enjoyable: the food, the culture, the hospitality. And there will be times when your Muslim friend will begin to "get it." They will begin to ask the right questions, and your heart will soar with excitement and anticipation of what the Lord might do in their hearts.

We pray that there will be those times when you will get to watch God open the heart of a Muslim friend and see them be born again. To see them enter the kingdom of God is a miracle like the birth of a baby—and oh, the joy! There is nothing like it!

But while you will experience these times of deep fulfillment, you will also likely experience times of painful frustration and exhaustion. You may enter innumerable conversations with your Muslim friends that will seem to go nowhere as far as the good news is concerned. You will in all probability be perplexed as to what to do or say next. You might spend time in prayer pleading with the Lord of the harvest to move within your Muslim friend's heart. You might wonder whether He is listening, because, as far as you can tell, nothing—absolutely nothing—is happening.

So please, don't reach out to Muslims because you want to be among the "spiritually elite."

Don't reach out to Muslims because you want an "adventure." That motive will not help you persevere when this kind of outreach is less than exciting or seems to have come to a screeching halt as far as your Muslim friend becoming a follower of Jesus is concerned.

Don't reach out to Muslims because your friend is doing it, or because it seems "trendy" right now.

Reach out to Muslims because you love Jesus, who said,

"Love your neighbor."

Ministry to the people of Islam for whom Jesus died *won't* be easy, but it *will* be worth it!

QUESTIONS TO PONDER

- The renowned British preacher John Henry Jowett once said, "Ministry that costs nothing, accomplishes nothing." From what you have read above, in what ways might you experience frustrations, difficulties, troubles, and hardship in ministry to Muslim people?
- Knowing that there will be real joy and fulfillment in outreach to Mus-

lims, how can you *prepare* for the hardships that Jesus and the New Testament writers also speak about?

> *"Our ministry . . . as servants of God . . .*
> *troubles, hardships and distresses."*
> 2 CORINTHIANS 6:3–4, NIV

> *"I suffer hardship."*
> 2 TIMOTHY 2:9, NASB

> *"Endure hardship . . . discharge all the duties of your ministry."*
> 2 TIMOTHY 4:5, NIV

> *"That's why I take pleasure in my weaknesses, and in the insults,*
> *hardships, persecutions, and troubles that I suffer for Christ.*
> *For when I am weak, then I am strong."*
> 2 CORINTHIANS 12:10, NLT

CHAPTER 3

Why Muslims?—The *Confirmation(s)*

The Dream of a Song, the Vision of a Plane, and the Missionary Who Called Me a Coward

---

A fter the life-changing seminar in Dearborn and having the privilege of watching Abdul put his faith in Jesus in that summer of 2006, my calling of full-time ministry to Muslim people was a certainty.

Or was it?

I had wanted to be in full-time missions and evangelism so badly! Once we were finally called to leave pastoral ministry and reach out to Muslims, we both experienced a new freedom. I felt life and energy return to my soul.

But something surprisingly happened in the beginning of 2007 to dampen all of that.

Terrible fear and anxiety began to creep into my thoughts at the prospect of resigning from my pastoral position at the church. I got cold feet. No, I got frozen feet, thinking:

"What if we don't make it in this ministry?
What if people don't support us?

What will happen to us?"

I was scared. It was mostly about financial security. I knew we had to raise financial support, and even as a pastor I had felt uncomfortable talking about money matters in front of the church (or even participating in taking up the offering!). How could I ask people now for money—for us? Fear had me in its grip.

Thankfully, God was kind and patient with me despite my lack of faith. He gave me not one, but three confirmations that our calling to reach out to Muslims full-time was indeed from Him.

CONFIRMATION #1
The Dream of a Choir Singing "Trust and Obey"

One morning during this season of anxiety and fear, I woke up and went downstairs to my office, which doubled as a spare bedroom in our home. I was still drowsy, and I lay down on the bed and fell asleep. As I was waking up from that little nap, I heard music that I can only describe as peacefully and delightfully otherworldly. It sounded like a choir, and they were singing an old Christian song, "Trust And Obey." I thought that surely Miriam must have had on the radio, or it was playing on a CD or on the TV. I went upstairs to find the source of this captivating music, but Miriam and our youngest son were still asleep. All was quiet up there.

As I continued to wake up, I realized that God had graciously given me a dream of a choir singing to confirm His calling to the Muslim world.

Here are just a few lines from that old song:

When we walk with the Lord in the light of His Word,
What a glory He sheds on our way!
While we do His good will, He abides with us still,
And with all who will trust and obey.

Refrain:
Trust and obey, for there's no other way
To be happy in Jesus, but to trust and obey.

But we never can prove the delights of His love

Until all on the altar we lay;
For the favor He shows, for the joy He bestows,
Are for them who will trust and obey.
(*"Trust and Obey,"* lyrics by John Henry Sammis, 1887)

That simple tune helped me in my lack of faith . . . for a while. But then the doubts crept back in. I needed a second confirmation.

CONFIRMATION #2

The Vision of a World War II Troop Carrier Airplane

On another morning I was sitting on a couch in my office having a time of Bible reading and prayer. Suddenly, I saw a vision of a World War II airplane and a group of people lined up to get into it. Miriam and I were in that line. Looking ahead, I could see that Jesus was in the doorway of that plane, handing out parachutes and plans for where each person was going to jump. When we got to the door, I brazenly said to Jesus,

"I'm not getting on that plane until You tell me where we're going!"

His response?

"I'm not telling you where you're going until you get on that plane!"

I was scared. I was afraid our parachutes would not open and we would die. At that point, Jesus said something to me that was so strongly convicting—but also so tender:

"I packed your parachutes."

My heart was moved. That vision—a second confirmation—helped me again with my lack of faith . . . for a while. And then, as embarrassing as it is to say, I allowed doubt and unbelief in our Provider to once again fill my mind.

CONFIRMATION #3
The Voice of a Missionary Who Called Me a Coward

Poor Miriam. She had to live with this man who was on an emotional rollercoaster. This was nothing new to her, since I am the emotional, up-and-down one, and she is generally the strong, stable one.

One night Miriam came home from her work of cleaning houses. I was sitting at the kitchen table hunched over my laptop, head in my hands, trying to write a letter of resignation to my church elders. I just couldn't do it. I was too afraid. I had been asking everyone what they thought I should do—and still, I couldn't decide.

Miriam went into the living room and turned on a Christian television station. The program was about evangelism, and the speaker was quoting the renowned missionary to China, India, and Africa C. T. Studd. His words, though I had heard them once before, rocked me on that winter evening:

> *"To your knees, man! And to your Bible!*
> *Decide at once! Don't hedge! Time flies!*
> *Cease your insults to God, quit consulting flesh and blood.*
> *Stop your lame, lying, and cowardly excuses.*
> *Enlist!"*

That was it.

There was no more need of confirmation or of asking the opinions of others.

I immediately and resolutely went back to my laptop and wrote our elders my letter of resignation.

In October of 2007, our church gave us a wonderful sendoff into Muslim ministry. This was nearly thirty years—and three confirmations—after my original calling to evangelism and missions!

Jesus—and C. T. Studd—had left me no choice but to forge ahead and *love my Muslim neighbor.*

THE IMPORTANCE OF MENTORS IN MINISTRY TO MUSLIM PEOPLE

After we officially resigned from pastoring our church in early 2007, there was an interval of several months before our last Sunday on the job in October of that year. On days off from my church duties, we would reach out to Muslims in our area and also travel to Dearborn to spend time with missionaries there to learn as much as we could from them about how we could reach out to Muslim people.

Some of the missionaries who lived there were unbelievably helpful to us. They were so kind and patient with us (notably Douglas, Scott, and John). We knew nothing about outreach to Muslims! They mentored us in those early months—and far beyond.

If you are fairly new to reaching out to Muslim people, you can read books like those we have listed in Appendix 7. But there is much to be learned that cannot come from a book. Besides his sermons, Jesus taught his followers by simply having them be "with him" (Mark 3:14). That way they could feel His heart and watch His life.

We encourage you to find experienced people—mentors—who have been doing outreach to Muslims for years—and be "with them." Watch how they interact with Muslim people. Make sure they undeniably love Muslims and treat them with respect (1 Peter 3:15). Make sure that they are investing their lives in them—building relationships with them and serving them (1 Thessalonians 2:8). And make sure they are unashamed of the gospel (Romans 1:16).

Mentors like that will be invaluable to you as you learn more and more about *loving your Muslim neighbors.*

QUESTIONS TO PONDER

- What mentors or coaches might help you confirm and answer your calling . . . and then grow in it?
- Have you battled anxiety and fear in attempting to follow a ministry

calling from God in your life? What has God promised you in His Word regarding His provisions for you?

"Don't be afraid, for I am with you.
Don't be discouraged, for I am your God.
I will strengthen you and help you.
I will hold you up with my victorious right hand."
ISAIAH 41:10, NLT

"And he said to them,
'When I sent you out . . . , did you lack anything?'
They said, 'Nothing.'"
LUKE 22:35

CHAPTER 4

✝ ☪

The Palestinian Grad Student: *"Tim, I Swear to You, I Love Jesus More Than You Do!"*

How Would *You* Respond?

———

O ne late night in 2007, I was at the apartment of Omar, my new Muslim friend and an international student from Gaza in the West Bank of Israel (he would say Palestine).

Omar was zealous for Islam. Very zealous. I usually enjoyed being with him, but on this night he was in preaching mode—as in preaching at me. We were not really in a discussion, but rather it was a monologue—a monologue that was intended to convert me to Islam. Finally, at one point in his long speech, he declared emphatically to me—poking me in the chest for emphasis:

"I swear to you, Tim,
I love Jesus more than you do!"

What was I to say?

What would *you* say?

———

DO MUSLIMS *BELIEVE* IN JESUS? DO THEY *LOVE* JESUS?

A Muslim will always tell you that they believe in Jesus—that they *must* believe in all the prophets, including Jesus, or they cannot be Muslims! Jesus is mentioned in ninety-three verses of the Qur'an, but who is that Jesus? Who is the Jesus that Muslims emphatically say they love? Let's take a very brief look at the comparison between a few Muslim and Christian beliefs about our Savior:

Jesus in Islam (from the Qu'ran)	Jesus in Christianity (from the Bible)
born of the virgin Mary	born of the virgin Mary
a Word from God, His Word	Word of God
worker of miracles	worker of miracles
a revered prophet	Son of God and God the Son
never died on a cross	died on a cross for our sins, rose
coming again	coming again
Bottom line: Jesus is *prominent*	Bottom line: Jesus is *preeminent*

Our Bible tells us:

"Christ is the visible image of the invisible God.
He existed before God made anything at all and is supreme over all creation.
Christ is the one through whom God created everything in heaven and earth.
He made the things we can see and the things we can't see—
kings, kingdoms, rulers, and authorities.
Everything has been created through him and for him . . .
he is first in everything."
Colossians 1:15–18, NLT

As you reach out to Muslim people, the following quote is helpful in understanding how the people of Islam view Jesus:

"Muslims have a great respect for Jesus,
but the view that Jesus is Divine, or the Son of God,
is to them, the highest blasphemy."

"The Qur'an says God is not a man, therefore he cannot have a son,
and God is so transcendent and 'other' than humankind,
that He would never stoop to enter our world."
(https://www.awm-pioneers.org/)

Warren Wiersbe, one of our favorite Bible teachers, wrote about false teachers in the first century who did not

". . . deny the importance of Jesus Christ.
They would simply dethrone Him,
giving Him prominence but not preeminence."
(https://www.preceptaustin.org/colossians_111-16)

Though Wiersbe was talking about the false teachers infiltrating the ancient church of Colossae, we think this a perfect description of the beliefs of our Muslim friends about our Lord Jesus.

And before we judge them too quickly, harshly, or proudly, perhaps it would be good for all of us to ask ourselves a vital question: "Is Jesus Christ *prominent* (high profile, well thought of) in my life, or is He *preeminent* (consummate, incomparable, peerless, supreme, unequaled, unrivaled, unsurpassable) in my life?"

Returning to where we left off in the story above, my Palestinian Muslim friend Omar declared, "I swear to you that I love Jesus more than you do!" How did I respond? That night, I said:

"Omar, I swear to you
that you don't love Jesus more than I do
because you have a different Jesus!"

I'm afraid I acted like a kid on the school yard. Instead of comparing my dad to another kid's dad, I was comparing my Jesus to Omar's Jesus. It was as though I were boasting:

"My Jesus is better than your Jesus!"

Please hear me: if I had it to do over again, I would answer much differently—less defensively, and in a way that would slow down competition and speed up heart-to-heart dialogue. I think now I would say something like:

"Omar, that is great!
You love Jesus.
I love Jesus.
Let's talk about . . . Jesus!"

Please learn a lesson from my mistake at a time when we were so new to Muslim ministry.

Don't respond defensively and wind up building higher, thicker walls between you and your Muslim friend when you are challenged about what you believe. Don't let your ego or competitive nature get the best of you. Answer humbly but with godly confidence and boldness, trusting that the Holy Spirit is at work and will help you in the conversation. Let the pressure be on Him. Don't take it on yourself. Don't think you always have to *"win."* (see Appendix 5, "Suggested Guidelines for Interacting with Your Muslim Friend.")

If you think you have to "win" every conversation with a Muslim as you talk about your differences, you will put way too much pressure on yourself instead of relying on the Holy Spirit. You will rely on your knowledge of Scripture or Islam, your apologetics, your explanations, your giftings, and your personality. It will all be about . . . *you!*

Muslims need to see a heavenly peace in us regarding what we believe. When you argue from a defensive posture, you will inevitably express—at least nonverbally—frustration, pride, anger, judgment, or even a lack of faith in the gospel. And you won't be listening. You won't be learning what is in the heart and mind of your Muslim friend.

The next time you feel defensive in a conversation with a Muslim person, you might just take a spiritual and emotional time-out inside yourself, ask for the Holy Spirit to help and guide you, and then say,

"Let's talk about . . . Jesus!"

Ultimately, we believe that is a wise and peaceful way to *love your Muslim neighbor.*

QUESTIONS TO PONDER

- Are you naturally competitive? Do you feel a need to always "win"?
- What is the difference between respectfully attempting to help your Muslim friend understand a point about Jesus and His gospel vs. trying to win an argument?
- Even if you "win" an argument, how might you lose?

"Show proper respect to everyone."
1 PETER 2:17, NIV

"But the wisdom from above is . . .
peace loving, gentle at all times."
JAMES 3:17, NLT

CHAPTER 5

"Look, Ahmed, All These People, Going to the Hell-Fire!"

The Pain of a Muslim Zealot—
Do We Have the Same Pain?

I became convicted by the Lord about an experience with Omar. As we mentioned in the last chapter, Omar and I became friends in 2007, and we had many lively discussions about faith issues at his apartment—sometimes until 2:00, 3:00, or 4:00 o'clock in the morning. (Get used to late nights if you want to do a lot of ministry to Arab Muslims!)

Omar related a story to me about how he had walked by an American restaurant with a fellow Muslim international student friend. As they passed by, they looked in the restaurant window at those who were eating there. Omar said to his friend with real concern in his voice,

> *"Look, Ahmed, all these people, going to the hell-fire."*

When Omar shared this story with me, I asked him for an explanation of his intriguing comment. He explained that in his mind—in his way of thinking and understanding Islam—because the people in that restaurant were not Muslims, they were in real danger of hell.

I could see that this thought pained him, and I respected him for it. He cared about the eternal destiny of those people, and because of that care it was difficult for him emotionally.

Now, as followers of Jesus we can disagree all we want with Omar's theology, and we should. Islam is not God's way to eternal life. But how can we disagree with his heart for people to escape the pain of hell? Do we have that same heart? Most of us can almost certainly confess that we are not there yet.

Let us ask the Lord that we might have even a little bit of the *heart* for lost people of the renowned missionary to China, Hudson Taylor (1832–1905), who said,

> "Would that God would make hell so real to us that we cannot rest;
> heaven so real that we must have men there,
> Christ so real that our supreme motive and aim
> shall be to make the Man of Sorrows the Man of Joy
> by the conversion to him of many."

Let us ask the Lord that we might have even a little bit of the *pain* for lost people of Richard Wurmbrand (1909–2001), a Romanian pastor who was imprisoned and tortured for Christ for fourteen years by the Communists:

> "In the first days after my conversion,
> I felt that I would not be able to live any longer.
> Walking on the street, I felt a physical pain
> for every man and woman who passed by.
> It was like a knife in my heart,
> so burning was the question of whether
> or not he or she was saved."
> (Tortured for Christ)

> "All these people, going to the hell-fire."

Omar, a Muslim, had a real concern about this. *Do we?*

Dear readers, the subject of hell—here, and also in chapter 13—is painfully uncomfortable for most of us to talk about. But because it is a subject very much on the minds of many (if not most) Muslims, and because our Savior addresses it so often, we felt compelled to include it in this book.

Having said this, if our desire to see Muslim people escape hell is the only motivation for sharing the gospel with them, we will probably put terrible pressure on ourselves. How can we function during the day or sleep at night if hell is always on our minds? We would develop a most unbiblical view of evangelism, one that is much too dependent upon us and not dependent enough on the Holy Spirit. We can share the gospel through Spirit-led words and actions, but we cannot save anyone.

While not abandoning the biblical reality of hell as one motivating factor for our evangelism, let us first and foremost share Jesus with Muslim people to bring praise and glory to God (Ephesians 1:3–14), to bring satisfaction to Jesus (Isaiah 53:11), and to bring joy to Muslims, who can begin now to have a reconciled relationship with our heavenly Father (Romans 5:10; 2 Corinthians 5:18–21; Colossians 1:19–22)!

QUESTIONS TO PONDER

- Do you hear anything, or very much, about hell in the church you attend or by preachers you follow on TV, radio, or the internet?
- Why do you think fewer and fewer Christians talk or think about hell, as compared to Christians in the past?
- Can the concept of hell cause us to comprehend and appreciate the sacrifice of Jesus in a deeper and more significant way? If so, how?
- What should be our highest motivation for sharing the gospel of Jesus with a Muslim—or any other person?

"Christ's love has moved me . . .
His love has the first and last word in everything we do."
2 CORINTHIANS 5:14, MSG

"He is so rich in kindness and grace that
he purchased our freedom

with the blood of his Son and forgave our sins."
Ephesians 1:7, NLT

CHAPTER 6

What Causes a Muslim to Risk It All and Follow Jesus?

The Top Five Reasons—Number One Is . . .

——

We drove as fast as legally possible—and then some—to make it to the end of Omar's graduation ceremony from a local university in April of 2007.

It was difficult because we had told our Palestinian international student friend that we would be there as his "family" for his graduation. But, alas, it turned out to be the same day as our church's congregational meeting—the very meeting where we were to announce our resignation from pastoring our church to go into full-time Muslim ministry. The calendar conflict could not be resolved.

We spoke to our well-wishing parishioners after our difficult announcement and then raced off to try to make it to part of Omar's graduation. We didn't make it. The parking lot of the university's basketball arena was empty except for a few cars and a few people scattered around them. We drove over toward those cars, and among those few people were Omar and his Palestinian fellow graduates! He was so happy to see us and encouraged everyone to don their caps and gowns for pictures with us. We were, after all, his family.

With appreciation, Omar emailed about our relationship with him after his graduation:

"Dear brother Tim,
"I hope you and your family are doing well.
    "Do you know, the most precious thing that I'll lose is your friend-
ship . . . it has affected me, and you touched me. I wish I could be
beside you to learn from you and enjoy your friendship. You are great
man Tim, and you are knowledgeable and always look for the truth. I
appreciate your style. You and your wife, Miriam, are very kind and
polite. Days ago, I mentioned you before my friends and said that you
were the only Americans that impressed me with your morals.
    "Unfortunately, I'll leave.

"Regards,
Omar"

———

What causes a Muslim to potentially risk losing what is so precious to them to gain Jesus:

    family, community, job, education, possessions?

What causes a Muslim to risk this kind of possible suffering to follow Jesus:

    isolation, imprisonment, torture, rape,
    and—in somewhat rare situations—even death?

This is not a pleasant subject, but it is a necessary one. For a Muslim to make an intentional choice to leave Islam and become a follower of Jesus will almost always require some kind of cost. We learned early on that it is critical that we warn our seeking Muslim friends of this so that we would not be guilty of "sugarcoating" the gospel.

In thinking about the possible cost(s) for a Muslim to follow Jesus, we want to discover how this momentous change in their lives takes place. Are there common factors we can all learn from?

There are more recent studies, but we found a study undertaken by Dudley Woodbury, Professor of Islamics at Fuller Seminary, and others, to be the most helpful (article in *Christianity Today* magazine, October 2007). Between 1991 and 2007, about 750 Muslims who had decided to follow Christ filled out an extensive questionnaire on why they had become followers of Jesus. The respondents—from thirty countries and fifty ethnic groups—represented every major region of the Muslim world.

THE TOP FIVE REASONS MUSLIM PEOPLE BECOME FOLLOWERS OF JESUS (IN INVERSE ORDER)

#5 The Love of God—in the Qur'an, God's love is conditional. By contrast, God's love for all people (even His enemies) in the Christian faith was definitely eye-opening for these former Muslims. They were also moved by the love expressed through the life and teachings of Jesus.

#4 The Bible—Muslims are generally taught that the Torah, the Psalms, and the Gospels originally came from God but that they later became "corrupted" (changed). These former Muslims said, however, that the truth of God found in Scripture became compelling for them and key to their understanding of God's character.

#3 Dissatisfaction with Islam—many expressed dissatisfaction with the Qur'an, which they felt emphasizes God's punishment over His love. Others cited Islamic militancy (even Muslim-on-Muslim violence) and the failure of Islamic law to transform hearts and society.

#2 The Power of God (Answered Prayers, Healings, Dreams and Visions of Jesus)—these followers of Jesus from a Muslim background experienced God's supernatural work when Christians prayed for them. When help from a Muslim spiritual leader, as well as a pilgrimage to Mecca, could not heal two Muslim girls, God used the prayers of Christians to bring healing. Others spoke of deliverance from demonic powers. And one in four former Muslims had dreams or visions of Jesus that led to their commitments to follow Him.

#1 The Lifestyle of Christians—former Muslims cited the love and lifestyle that Christians exhibited. One said there was no gap between the moral profession and the practice of Christians that he could see. Some noticed Christian women being treated as equals. Others spoke of seeing loving Christian marriages and simple lifestyles among believers.

We want to emphasize the obvious here: *relationship* with followers of Jesus is the #1 reason why former Muslims say they came to true faith in Jesus.

Dear believers, you are the light of the world. You are the city on the hill. You are the salt of the earth. Please grasp the significance of those statements of Jesus (Matthew 5:13–16) and pray for an understanding of how important you are in God's redemptive plan to bring Muslim people to Himself. What a privilege! What an honor!

Muslim people need to meet you, speak with you, watch you, ask you questions, eat with you, hear you pray, see your family, and enter your home. They need to see your lifestyle.

But here is a sad truth: *roughly one in four people walking the earth today is a Muslim, and . . .*

More Than 86% of Muslim People in the World *"Do Not Personally Know a Christian."*

(This statement is from Todd Johnson and Charles Tieszen, Department of World Missions at Gordon Conwell Seminary, in the October 2007 edition of *Evangelical Missions Quarterly*.)

There are somewhere near 1.9 billion Muslims in the world, and eighty-six percent of them do not know a follower of Jesus!

We find this statement to be shocking; sobering; and, as we said, just plain sad. One of the purposes of our ministry is to see this statistic change.

That is why, since 2007, we have personally reached out to Muslim people everywhere:

on a jet going to Amsterdam, in an airport in Paris,
sitting in a mosque in Moscow,
at a sidewalk coffee shop in Jordan, in a small restaurant in Bethlehem,
on the streets of Ashford Kent in England, in a taxi in the Arabian Peninsula,
in the enormous Grand Bazaar in Istanbul,
inside the stunning Sheikh Zayed Grand Mosque in Abu Dhabi and
the Mother Mosque of America (built in 1934) in Cedar Rapids, Iowa.

That is why we go to churches all over the US,

from San Antonio, Texas, to Kokomo, Indiana,
from Beavercreek, Ohio, to Reno, Nevada,

> from Montezuma, Iowa, to Memphis, Tennessee,
> from Brighton, Michigan, to Aurora, Colorado,
> from Corinth, Mississippi, to Wichita, Kansas,
> from Sacramento, California, to Lancaster, New York,
> from Tulsa, Oklahoma, to Montgomery, Alabama.

We travel to churches in these towns and cities to help Christians gain God's heart for Muslims, to give them practical evangelistic tools, and to encourage them to join us in reaching out to Muslim people through *personal relationship*.

Please Hear It Once Again:
Muslim People Most Often Come to Know Jesus through
***a Personal Relationship* with a Real Follower of Jesus.**

To reach Muslims, God is mightily using non face-to-face means, such as the internet, satellite TV (such as SAT-7 for Arabic speakers or SAT-7 Pars for Persian speakers), dreams and visions of Jesus, and reading or hearing something from the Bible. But listen to the words of our friend and pioneer missionary to Muslims for over fifty years, Greg Livingstone:

> *"A real person (Christian)*
> *must cross over a cultural/religious boundary*
> *to establish an openness based on trust,*
> *which then enables a Muslim*
> *to take the Christian's witness seriously."*

Personal, human, face-to-face contact is vital. *Relationship.* From what we have learned—from the beginning of our ministry to Muslim people until now—we can't emphasize this enough.

We invite you to reflect on the words of a former Muslim, Nabeel Qureshi:

> *"Effective evangelism requires relationships.*
> *There are very few exceptions.*
>
> *"In my case (growing up in Virginia),*
> *I knew of no Christian who truly cared about me.*

"Since no Christian cared about me, I did not care about their message.

"If they [Muslims] were to intimately know
even one Christian who lived differently,
their misconceptions might be corrected,
and they might see Christianity in a virtuous light.

"Only the exceptional blend of love,
humility, hospitality, and persistence can overcome these barriers,
and not enough people [Christians] make the effort."
(*Seeking Allah, Finding Jesus,* pp. 120–21)

Thankfully, one Christian did reach out with real friendship to Nabeel for several years. And thankfully, God used that relationship to draw Nabeel to Jesus as his Savior.

What causes a Muslim to risk it all to follow Jesus?

The primary answer, of course, is that God does His sovereign work in a Muslim's heart so that he or she can believe in His Son and be drawn to Him (Matthew 16:15–17; John 6:44, 65).

But, as we have seen, there are additional answers.

Most of all, we believe that God would take delight in using *you* to give to Muslims what they usually need the most in coming to know Jesus: a *relationship* with one of His committed followers.

That's what Omar told us he appreciated most when he finished his master's degree in the US and was on his way back home to the Middle East.

QUESTIONS TO PONDER

- Why do you think building a *relationship* with someone is so important in their journey to enter the kingdom of God?
- If you were to travel overseas for work or education for a period of time, what would you miss the most about home?
- What would you most appreciate receiving from the people of that foreign country?
- Besides giving a Muslim international student, refugee, or immigrant the gospel, how can you give them your life as well?

"So we cared for you. Because we loved you so much,
we were delighted to share with you
not only the gospel of God but our lives as well."
1 THESSALONIANS 2:8, NIV

Does a Person Have to be a *"Christian"* to Enter the Kingdom of God?

Is That What We Tell Muslim People?

———

I t was my birthday, and I was so excited! We were relatively new to Muslim ministry, but I was asked to be the speaker at an outreach event for Muslim people. What could be a better birthday present than an opportunity to share the good news with them?

The church basement was packed that November evening for the event—a dinner, enjoyable conversation, and then my talk. A combination of about 150 Jesus-followers and Muslims came, including many Muslim international students from Oman.

My talk was titled "I Am Not a Fan," based on the excellent book *Not A Fan* by Kyle Idleman. It was a challenging message that night, contrasting "fans" of Jesus with "followers" of Jesus. To further enhance the sports metaphor, I wore a hockey jersey. Each person—Muslim or Christian—received an outline with these and other points below.

"FANS" OF JESUS

These are people who sit in the stands and cheer for Jesus when things are going well, but who walk away in difficult seasons of life. They never thought that following Jesus would require pain or sacrifice or change!

Their lives are characterized by their wants:

- to be a spectator, escape hell, and get their "ticket" for heaven
- to have a comfortable, safe, good, and happy life
- to experience no big life changes, no hard choices
- to "believe" in Jesus (head) but not "follow" Jesus (heart and life)
- to know a nice Jesus—not a Jesus who asks you to give him everything
- to enjoy a life with God that costs nothing but offers everything.

To sum up, fans of Jesus want all the benefits of living in the kingdom of God without embracing His rule and Lordship.

"FOLLOWERS" OF JESUS

These are people who go after Jesus with a determination to know Him, be with Him, learn from Him, and love Him.

Their lives—when following Jesus wholeheartedly—are characterized by:

- abandonment—of what is safe, comfortable, and predictable
- obedience—go anywhere, do anything, say anything for Him
- sacrifice—counting the cost and willing to risk it all for Him
- surrender—an uncompromising, unconditional commitment to Jesus.

I told the Muslim people that night that it costs us nothing to be forgiven of all our sins through Jesus, but it might cost them everything to follow Him.

I warned them that if they got serious about following Jesus, they might lose the approval of their wife or husband, their parents, their brothers or sisters, or their friends, but they would have the approval of Jesus.

I explained that following Jesus wholeheartedly would involve radical risk, but also radical reward (they would receive Jesus Himself in their hearts now, and paradise with Him after this life!).

Even though this was by far not my best sermon in terms of delivery, I felt that the content of this message was quite good (thanks mostly to Kyle Idleman's book).

And, I felt *a tangible presence of the Holy Spirit in the room.*

The Muslims there were really listening as I spoke (sometimes at these events they talk to each other—a lot—while the speaker is presenting). When I finished speaking, I gave an invitation for people to pray silently to become true followers of Jesus, and there is no doubt in my heart and mind that some Muslims in the room prayed that kind of commitment prayer that night. Don't ask me how, I could just tell. I could feel it. They may not have told a soul that night, but they prayed. I believe their commitment was real. I believe they entered the kingdom of God, even if it was as secret believers at that time.

I was so happy, so fulfilled in the Lord after that meeting. *What could be better?*

But my elation was to be somewhat short lived. I had made one statement during my talk that evening that significantly disturbed a few of the believers in the room who also do outreach to Muslims. Here is that statement:

> *"I don't see in the Injeel*
> (or Injil, what Muslims call the Gospels)
> *where Jesus said you have to be a 'Christian' to go to heaven."*

After all the statements I had made—strongly challenging everyone to be followers of Jesus instead of fans of Jesus—that one statement got me into trouble with certain Jesus followers that night.

───────

We hope that statement won't get us in trouble with you also! Please . . . *keep reading through our book!* In the next chapter we will clarify what the word *Christian* means to so many Muslim people in the world and why it is such a stumbling block—an impediment to belief or understanding—to them.

In our ministry to Muslims, we realize that the *cross* of Jesus is, as Paul says, a stumbling block:

"We preach Christ crucified,
a stumbling block to Jews and folly to Gentiles."
1 CORINTHIANS 1:23

We are not ashamed of the cross or the gospel of Christ (Romans 1:16). But the words "Christian" or "Christianity" can—in our opinion—place a real and unnecessary

> barrier
> > hindrance
> > > obstacle
> > > > hurdle
> > > > > bar
> > > > > > impediment

between a Muslim person and their desperately needed entrance into the kingdom of God (more to follow on this point).

QUESTIONS TO PONDER

- Do you think a person has to become a "Christian" to enter the kingdom of God? Why or why not?
- Did Jesus—or any of the New Testament writers—ever say or write that?
- What *did* Jesus and the New Testament writers say are the requirements for entering God's kingdom?

These are critically important questions that you must wrestle with if you are going to be engaged in outreach to Muslims.

And these are questions we will address more in our next chapter.

"Truly, I say to you, unless you turn and become like children,
you will never enter the kingdom of heaven."
MATTHEW 18:3

"The time is fulfilled, and the kingdom of God is at hand;
repent and believe in the gospel."
MARK 1:15

CHAPTER 8

Which Do We Promote:
Christianity . . . or *Christ?*

Are We Trying to Convert Muslims to "Christianity"?

———

We entered a grand home in a country in the Arabian Peninsula through separate entrances.

While Miriam ate in a room for the women, I ate in a room for the men—customary in some Middle Eastern Muslim homes. When our visit ended that night in 2007, I asked Miriam how it had gone for her as we rode in a car to the place where we were staying. She said the first question the Muslim women had asked her was:

"Are all the people in America like the people on The Jerry Springer Show?*"*

Needless to say, Miriam was shocked!

———

This was our very first trip to that part of the world, and we had a lot to learn about Muslim people. In this case, we needed to grow in our understanding of how Muslims view the West (especially the US) and Christianity—how they often see the two as *synonymous*.

For that reason, in our conversations with Muslim people we do not promote "Christianity." We do not promote being—or even becoming—a "Christian." Let us explain before you think us to be heretics!

We know that "Christian" is a biblical word and thus believe it's an important one. We are not ashamed of the word when it's rightly understood in the biblical sense, and we use it when we are speaking with fellow believers (and often in this book). Having said that, the word "Christian" appears only three times in the entire New Testament (Acts 11:26, 26:28, and 1 Peter 4:16). Because it is a word used in the Bible, some of our friends say that we need to simply define it—or redefine it—as we use it with Muslim people. However, . . .

It is our firm opinion that redefining the word "Christian" for Muslims is a daunting task. Why? Because so many Muslim people in the world today equate the label "Christian" with a lot of external baggage that would shock and dismay us:

- "Christianity" = the atrocities of the Crusades
- "Christianity" = the economic exploitation of colonialism
- "Christianity" = America or the West
- "Christianity" = US military incursions into the Middle East (which many of them see as "Christianity" attempting to attack and conquer Islam)
- "Christianity" = Hollywood movies and television (which include violence, immorality, abortion, divorce, drunkenness, drug usage, swearing, lack of care or honor for the elderly, and some of the disgraceful things that have been part of *The Jerry Springer Show*)
- "Christianity" = rap singers from Western countries spewing f-words in their lyrics and rapping about doing drugs, beating women, and killing people . . . while sporting huge crosses
- "Christianity" = a famous American female singer belting out sexually explicit lyrics, dancing provocatively, and wearing a cross, . . . but not much else
- "Christianity" = unconditional support for Israel but hatred for Arab Muslims
- "Christianity" = a religion having three gods.

To be a "Christian" then, in the mind of numerous Muslims, is to be a polytheistic, wine-drinking, pig-eating, immoral, materialistic, imperialistic, Zionistic infidel!

If you were a Muslim person, wouldn't you think to yourself,

"If all of that is 'Christianity,' I don't want it!"

Just from these few examples of real misunderstandings (and there are more), can you see how "Christian" or "Christianity" are not positive words in the minds of many Muslim people around the world? Can you see how we need to strive to learn how Muslims think about words that we take for granted?

Depending upon which translation you use, the word "disciple" is found in the New Testament between 230 and 260 times—obviously far more than the word "Christian." We share with our Muslim friends that Jesus is calling all of us to believe in Him and His work on the cross, repent, be Jesus's disciples, and follow Him.

So, we promote being a *disciple* or a *follower of Jesus* to Muslims. If we must have a label to describe our faith in speaking with Muslim people, those are terms we most often prefer.

No "religion" can die for a person, cleanse their heart, and change them from the inside out. No religion can take away all their sins or free them from their fear of the Day of Judgment and hell.

But someone can. A person can. *Jesus* can.

Following Jesus can most assuredly set a Muslim person free. Trusting in Jesus's sacrifice on the cross can make a Muslim person clean on the inside. Forgiven of every sin. Stripped of all shame.

And that is why we don't promote Christianity as God's answer for Muslim people.

That is why we promote *Christ* . . . only Jesus, *the* Christ—God's answer for all of us.

QUESTIONS TO PONDER

- How can we help our Muslim friends make the necessary distinction between how they view Christianity (and Christendom) and the kingdom of God that Jesus and Paul preached about?

- What are practical ways you can promote Jesus to Muslim people without the trappings and baggage of Western cultural Christianity?
- In light of the subject of this chapter, please consider reading about the early church's dilemma regarding what to do with Gentiles who were becoming followers of Jesus. Did these converts have to become Jewish to follow Jesus and enter the kingdom of God? See Luke's account of the Jerusalem Council in Acts 15:1–35, its conclusions partially summed up in the words of James:

"It is my judgment, therefore, that
we should not make it difficult
for the Gentiles who are turning to God."
ACTS 15:19, NIV

"For I decided to know nothing among you
except Jesus Christ and him crucified."
1 CORINTHIANS 2:2

CHAPTER 9

✝ ☪

He Said, "I Want Jesus and Muhammad"

Betwixt and Between: The Painful Back-and-Forth of a Muslim Coming to Christ

———

I t was so painful to hear our friend, Abdul, say that on the phone. It was to be our last conversation before he died in August of 2007. After hearing this declaration in that final call, I was confused about his spiritual state. He had seemingly grabbed ahold of John 3:16, and we thought he had entered the kingdom of God. *But had he?*

Since then, we have read the biographies and autobiographies of a number of former Muslims who struggled mightily as they walked on their journey toward the Lordship of Jesus. Abdul's comment and thought process were not unique. Many Muslim people become enamored with Jesus but cannot let go of Muhammad and Islam—at least not easily (sometimes it takes *years*). They want *both* . . . or they go back and forth between them.

In relating to Muslim people in this place in their spiritual journey, we need to be so patient and understanding. They can be "betwixt and between." This has been defined as:

- not fully either of two things
- in a midway position, neither one thing nor the other
- in an intermediate, indecisive, or middle position
- conflicted and unable to decide between two options.

We have often wondered about where Abdul is now, but we know God touched him that June evening of 2006 in Dearborn, Michigan, in a real way. And now we entrust his soul to a faithful Creator and Redeemer.

We emailed and asked a former Muslim about this painful back-and-forth of fully following Jesus. This is how our friend, Fares, from Saudi Arabia, answered:

"Yes, I think it took about a year before I (grudgingly) came to the conclusion that the Quran is NOT the word of God . . . During that time I completely believed in the authority of the Bible and confessed Jesus as Lord, but I still hoped there was some way to 'save' some part of Islam. Accepting that everything you based your salvation on (and your parents' salvation and their parents' and so on) was untrue was a very bitter pill to swallow. I wanted to think that there was something redeemable; that Muhammad had the right message, but we just misunderstood it somehow.

"But there is no way to the Father, except by Christ Jesus, His Son. And both Muhammad and his Qur'an flatly denied that. A bitter pill indeed.

"I have seen this same struggle in many other BMBs I've met. It usually takes anywhere from six months to two years to finally begin letting go of the baggage and allowing Christ to remove the works-righteousness bondage of Islam. I want to stress, this is a process! More than twenty years later, I am still finding little thorns from my Muslim life that need to be plucked from my flesh as the Holy Spirit continues to renew my heart and mind.

"So, yes, please encourage those working with my family [Muslim people] to have patience. Speak truth in love, but remember that love is patient and kind. Allow Jesus room to 'make all things new.' I have found that He is very, very good at that. 'Grace and peace be upon you in Christ,'

"Fares"

As the Lord leads in His timing, let us not waver from promoting the Lordship of Jesus to our Muslim friends who are seeking Him. But let us also be gentle and patient with them as the Holy Spirit works in their hearts to reveal ultimate truth during their spiritual journey.

After all, most of us don't know the horrible pain and difficulty of being betwixt and between two faiths.

QUESTIONS TO PONDER

- How would you respond if your Muslim friend were to say, "I want Jesus *and* Muhammad"? What would you say and how would you feel?
- Like Fares, every new believer brings some kind of baggage to their new life in Jesus, whether from a Muslim or some other kind of background. What practical means can you use to help them grow in their journey of becoming more and more like Jesus?
- What kind of "birth pains" have you experienced watching a Muslim— or someone else—come to Jesus and grow in Him?

"My little children . . .
I am again in the anguish of childbirth
until Christ is formed in you!"
GALATIANS 4:19

CHAPTER 10

One Size Doesn't Fit All

Who Is Your Muslim Friend?
What Does *He* or *She* Believe?

I sat in the office of our friend Frank, the regional director for ISI—International Students Inc.—a fine ministry to international students on college campuses all across the US.

This was in about 2008, very early in our outreach to Muslim people, and Frank gave me some of the best advice anyone has ever given us for this kind of ministry:

> *"In your new work with Muslims,*
> *you can study the religion of Islam and learn what you can about it.*
> *There is benefit in that.*
> *But it's far more important for you to know about*
> *the Islam of your individual Muslim friend.*
> *What do they believe and practice?"*

We have never forgotten Frank's words of wisdom.

In Appendix 2, we have given you a simple and brief overview of the origins of the religion of Islam and a few of the core beliefs and practices of Muslim people worldwide. We hope that is helpful.

But, more importantly, we want to encourage you to heed Frank's sage advice. Do your best to find out what your *specific* Muslim acquaintance believes—what is in his or her heart and mind as an *individual* concerning Islam? Don't assume that you know, even if you have read up on Islam. Instead, attempt to discover what their own *unique* concept of Islam is, and how they live out their faith.

This will take time, effort, and patience on your part.

This will require developing a *relationship*.

First of all, we encourage you to learn about your Muslim friend's background and upbringing—just as you would do with any new acquaintance. If they are an international student, immigrant, or refugee, this means asking about:

- their family (this is hugely important)
- their country of origin
- why they came to the US or Canada
- what their very first experiences were when they arrived
- what they miss about home
- what difficulties they have encountered here
- what they like about living here
- what their goals are.

Show interest. Ask questions. Love. Listen. Learn.

After you have learned the answers to this kind of beginning-of-relationship questions, you're probably ready to delve deeper and make inquiries into the particular faith of your particular Muslim friend. (See additional helpful "conversation starters" in Appendix 3, including questions about faith.)

Muslims are much like people who self-identify as Christians or "followers of Jesus" (we prefer the latter term—as we have mentioned earlier and will discuss again later). Certain essentials of their faith are non-negotiables, while other beliefs and practices vary widely within their religion. So, you can't really find an answer to the broad question that we hear so often:

"Do Muslims believe in _____ ?"

They might. They might not.

One size doesn't fit all.

You are going to meet Muslim people in the US or Canada who are extremely devout and will do everything in their power to practice their faith as they did in their home country: modest dress, regular prayer and mosque attendance, eating only *halal* (it means "permissible"—like Jewish kosher) foods, living a highly moral life, etc.

You are also going to encounter nominal Muslims who barely practice their faith. Some are what might be called "high identity-low practice" Muslims. This kind of Muslim person might say to you,

> *"I was born a Muslim;*
> *I'll die a Muslim."*

but barely practice their faith! (On one occasion I went to the apartment of an international student from Saudi Arabia to watch the *Jesus Project* DVD with him. He greeted me at the door wearing a T-shirt advertising a local strip club he had visited. But as we watched this movie about the life of Jesus, he defended Islam!)

On another occasion we went to a Turkish restaurant in Michigan and had a delightful waiter, Hassad. When we asked him if he was a Muslim, he said he was a "default-Muslim," a term he defined as one who does not practice their faith but grew up in a Muslim majority country. That was a new term for us.

Early in our ministry we read a book written by young men who traveled widely as short-term missionaries around the world. While in Turkey, they had met a university student who described himself as a Muslim . . . *and an atheist!*

As you can see, just like Christians, every Muslim person is unique in their beliefs, practices, and self-identification regarding their faith.

So, men, as you attempt to discover information about the Islam of your hypothetical new international student, immigrant, or refugee friend "Faisal," you might kindly and humbly ask questions like these:

- Faisal, I would like to learn more about you. Would you mind if I asked you some questions about your religion?
- When you grew up, what did the faith of your parents and rela-

tives look like? What did they teach you about Islam and what it means to be a good Muslim?

- What does prayer look or sound like for a Muslim person? Are there specific prayers that you are required to pray?
- I've never been in a mosque. What happens there?
- What is the most important thing for me to know about the religion of Islam?
- In Islam, how can a person get to paradise after this life ends?

(Note: as you ask initial questions of your new Muslim friend about their faith, be careful that your questions don't drive them deeper into Islam by immediately challenging them about areas in which you feel they are misguided. Also, as you inquire about their faith, be careful that you don't make them think that you might want to become a Muslim by appearing overly curious about Islam! Ask the Holy Spirit for the right balance between showing loving interest in what they believe and challenging Islam in the beginning of the relationship. You will have time to confront Islam later—if the Lord so directs.)

Ladies, as you make the effort to understand the Islam of your hypothetical new international student, immigrant, or refugee friend "Aleena," perhaps you could ask some of the same questions as above, but also some of these:

- Aleena, what did your mother or female relatives teach you about the specific roles and duties of a woman in a Muslim family?
- What are the most important teachings in the Qur'an for women?
- Why do some Muslim women wear a head scarf—the hijab—and some do not?
- When you go to the mall, grocery store, or a restaurant here, do you ever feel like people are staring at you because of your hijab? Has anyone ever made a comment about it or mistreated you because of it?
- How can people from churches make Muslim women and their families feel loved and accepted?

Show interest.
Ask questions.
Love.

Listen.

Learn.

"One size doesn't fit all."

QUESTIONS TO PONDER

- How do you feel when people make assumptions about your spiritual beliefs without making the effort to find out the reality by speaking with you?
- How might listening well to a Muslim person fulfill Jesus's words to *love our neighbor?*

> *"My dear brothers and sisters, take note of this:*
> *Everyone should be quick to listen, slow to speak."*
> JAMES 1:19, NIV

CHAPTER 11

Is Pepperoni Pizza a Problem?

You're Going to Make Mistakes in Ministry to Muslims!

Even as a true extrovert, it was hard for me to go to a Muslim owned and operated barber shop. I always felt some anxiety going in.

Why?

Every time I walked in, everyone in the barber shop would turn and stare at me—the white guy with the white hair. Upon entering, I would immediately see five or six barbers from the countries of Jordan, Iraq, Syria, and Palestine, and usually anywhere from five to fifteen Muslim men from all over the Middle East and Africa getting their hair cut or waiting. I was a novelty there.

Early on in our ministry to Muslim people, I knew that if I wanted to reach them, I needed to go where they were, regardless of any anxiety I might experience. What better place than the local barber shop to build relationships with Muslim men and learn about their lives?

I started getting my hair cut in Muslim owned and operated barber shops beginning in about 2008. After the cut, I would usually stay afterward to talk to the barbers and the other clients. It was a perfect place to sit and learn about their families, where they came from, why they had left their countries to come to the US, what they missed about home, what they liked about the US, what they did for a living, and so much more.

I noticed that, when things slowed down in the middle of the afternoons, the owner of the barber shop would send one of his guys to get lunch for the rest of the barbers. One day, I volunteered to go and get lunch for them. Just down the street was a pizza place, and I was on my way.

Happily, I marched back into the barber shop with the pizzas for the guys! They expressed their sincere appreciation, and the boxes quickly disappeared into a break room in the back.

Years later, my favorite barber, a Jordanian, said to me,

> *"Mr. Tim, do you remember the time you bought pizzas for us?*
> *They were pepperoni!"*

I was so new to outreach to Muslim people at that time that it had not been sufficiently impressed upon my mind that they might not eat pork! It is not a *halal* (permissible) food for them in their religion.

Two points to learn from my "rookie" error:

- *You're going to make mistakes in ministry to Muslim people, but don't let that stop you!* It's guaranteed that you will make mistakes, and that's okay. Don't walk on eggshells. But whatever mistakes you might make, don't let them reflect a lack of Christ-like love. And don't let fear of mistakes inhibit your evangelistic efforts and zeal. Keep building relationships and keep sharing Jesus!
- *Most Muslim people are very gracious about your gaffes!* They generally know you are well-intentioned, and they appreciate the efforts you make to show simple kindness and build relationships with them.

The barber shop ministry has continued to this day. Through the years we have given Arabic-English Bibles to all the barbers as gifts. We have become friends on Facebook. We have had good faith discussions. We have prayed out loud for them in those barber shops. We have visited them in their home countries when they were there and we were on trips to the Middle East for ministry.

But since that day in 2008, we have not taken any more pepperoni pizzas to our Muslim friends!

(You can learn about cultural do's and don'ts in outreach to Muslim people from Appendix 4 of this book. These can be very helpful to avoid a faux pas like mine!)

———

QUESTIONS TO PONDER

- What kind of faux pas, flubs, foul-ups, gaffes, blunders, miscues, missteps, mistakes, or slipups have you made with a Muslim person (or someone else from a different faith or culture)? How did they respond?
- What can you do to possibly avoid mistakes like this in the future?

"Indeed, we all make many mistakes."
JAMES 3:2, NLT

CHAPTER 12

† ☾⋆

"I Just Wanted a Tour and a T-Shirt"

Open Doors into the Heart of a Middle Eastern TV Station

We were back in the Gulf—no, not the Gulf of Mexico—the Arabian, or Persian, Gulf.

It was a special and unique blessing for us to go there for up to six weeks at a time to do ministry in an international English-speaking church. Our times there were so full and rich—preaching three times each Friday; speaking at men's and youth retreats; doing premarital and marital counseling; visiting the apartments of many of the church members; meeting with Muslims from that country; and, of course, eating at many sumptuous Middle Eastern restaurants!

During one such trip to the Gulf in March of 2009, an American man in the church asked me if there was anything I would like to see or do in that wealthy, Middle Eastern city, indicating that he would be happy to be my tour guide. I mentioned that I would very much like to visit a prominent Middle Eastern TV station located there. He called to see whether we could arrange a tour, but the reply was that this would not be possible. I determined that we should just go there anyway and see what might happen (Miriam comments that I don't take no for an answer, at least not easily!).

When we entered the TV station, we were met by two guards, both Arabic speaking Africans. They spoke no English and did not understand what we wanted but kindly took us to an Arab woman dressed in the customary Muslim garb for that country. I mentioned that we had come seeking a tour and that perhaps we could buy a t-shirt if they had a gift store. She didn't know what to do with us and took us on to someone further up the chain. This poor Arab gentleman was also at a loss. He took us to one of the heads of security, who also was mystified in terms of how to proceed. He then took us to one final person—Sultan—a very distinguished looking Arab man dressed immaculately in a white, neatly pressed "thobe" (a floor length robe for men) and a *keffiyeh* (the traditional Middle Eastern headdress for men in the Gulf).

In a dignified way, Sultan asked how he could help us. I spoke up:

"I was just wanting to take a tour of your station and buy a t-shirt."

Sultan must have thought we were a little bit strange—or a little bit crazy—but if he did, he didn't act like it. Instead, he kindly and respectfully asked us to tell him about ourselves. I began by mentioning that I was from Michigan. With sudden excitement, he interrupted me and almost shouted:

"Michigan?!
I went to college in Michigan.
My wife is from Michigan.
Of course you can have a tour!"

It was that fast.

It was an open door from our God.

He quickly proceeded to tell his security man to get us a gift bag. The bag was huge, and it was filled with all kinds of things with the logo of this famous Middle Eastern TV station—including not just a t-shirt but a very nice golf shirt!

Sultan then told the security man to take us to the TV studio and give us a tour. As we passed through a checkpoint between the offices and the studio, the security man said to us with obvious bewilderment,

"How did that just happen?
It usually takes two weeks to get into this studio,
and you got in in two minutes!"

I saw the opening to plant a gospel seed and mentioned that we had prayed before this trip that God would open doors that no man could shut.

I don't think he knew how to answer that. (By the way, the tour was superb!)

I was blessed to see Sultan several more times during the course of the seven trips I made to that Middle Eastern country. Before one of those trips, Miriam suggested that we buy him a Michigan State t-shirt, since he had gone to school there. We wanted to bless him and thank him for the shirt and the other gifts he had given to me on the day we met. Miriam always has such good ideas from the Lord, and this was another one. Sultan loved that green and white Michigan State t-shirt!

On one occasion when we were in his city, Sultan invited Miriam and me to eat dinner with him in his home with his family. This was a real honor because the nationals in that country do not often invite Westerners into their homes. We arrived at his huge house and, after going in, saw a meal on a large table that would have fed fifteen people! After finishing that splendid dinner, Sultan asked me if I would pray for him and his family. I did not hesitate, but I knew very well that it was illegal in that country for a Christian to share his faith with a Muslim, and praying like that would surely be against the law. Putting that thought aside, I found it to be such a privilege and a joy to pray for this family. (Muslims need to hear how we pray in Jesus's name, in a personal way, to a God who is majestic but also approachable. We pray to a spiritual Father. This is so important. We call it "prayer evangelism.")

Sadly, we have lost touch with Sultan due to circumstances beyond our control (I am blacklisted in that country now, with no current possibility of returning). But there is no limit to prayer, and God knows exactly what He is doing with opening and closing doors.

We so desire to eat once again with Sultan and his family in heaven, where they would be able to hear these words of heavenly hospitality:

"Blessed are those who are invited
to the marriage supper of the Lamb."
REVELATION 19:9

QUESTIONS TO PONDER

- Are there Muslim friends or acquaintances you really long to see at the "marriage supper of the Lamb"? Why don't you take a moment right now and pray that God will draw them to Jesus and that they might enter the kingdom of God?
- Do you pray for "open doors" from the Lord for ministry opportunities?
- How have you seen God open doors that no one can shut?

"Pray for us, too, that God may open a door for our message,
so that we may proclaim the mystery of Christ."
COLOSSIANS 4:3, NIV

"A wide door for effective work has opened to me."
1 CORINTHIANS 16:9

" I went to Troas to preach the gospel of Christ
and found that the Lord had opened a door for me."
2 CORINTHIANS 2:12, NIV

"And when they arrived and gathered the church together,
they declared all that God had done with them,
and how he had opened a door of faith to the Gentiles."
ACTS 14:27

"What he opens no one can shut . . .
See, I have placed before you an open door that no one can shut."
REVELATION 3:7–8, NIV

CHAPTER 13

† ☾

I Asked Him, *"Do You Fear Hell?"*

The Muslim's Terrible Fear of the Day of Judgment and Hell

———

I was meeting with a Muslim grad student from our local university for dinner one night near the campus in the fall of 2009. Mahdi was a very kind, gentle, humble young man with family roots in Bangladesh. At some point, I took a risk and asked him,

"Do you fear hell?"

He looked down and said softly,

"Every day."

On another occasion in 2012, I was driving to Hamtramck, Michigan, with a Saudi Muslim international student friend to enjoy food from Yemen. We began discussing the fact that Muslim athletes were having to make difficult decisions about whether to eat during the daytime at the Olympics since it was Ramadan—a time when Muslims are to abstain from food and water from sunrise to sundown. There was a Muslim Olympic rower from England who had decided he could not let down the rest of his team or risk damaging his Olympic ambitions by fasting during Ramadan (he said he would make up for it later by feeding street children in Morocco). But Fareed, my Saudi friend, saw the issue differently. In fact, he was emphatic:

"Of course, they should fast!
The Day of Judgment is more important than the Olympics!"

To him, no medal or honor was worth displeasing God.

I asked him whether he feared the Day of Judgment and hell. He said with growing agitation,

"Everyone will have to go to hell for some period of time.
What would it be like to put your hand in the oven?
Of course, I am afraid of hell!"

In 2013, a Muslim restaurant owner from India overheard a private conversation I was having with a young man, Paul, who was very torn about his faith. He was, as we have talked about earlier, "betwixt and between." This, like several of our other stories, took place in the Arabian Gulf.

Paul had grown up in a Christian home but was trying to decide between Christianity and Islam. Actually, in his confusion, he wanted both. We met in a restaurant where I hoped we could have a private conversation. Miriam and I frequented this restaurant because we loved the Indian Muslim family who owned it, and we really enjoyed their food. Normally, we would have a private place, but this day the host seated us next to the owner's office—a place where she could overhear everything this young man and I were discussing. I knew I needed to be discreet, and so I just listened to Paul extol the virtues of Islam. I prayed silently, and God gave me the faith that somehow this was going to work out. At one point, the Muslim woman who owned the restaurant could not resist; she came out of her office to join us and enter the conversation. The three of us talked for well over an hour about Islam, Muhammad, the Qur'an, the Bible, Jesus, heaven and hell, good works, and grace.

This devoutly Muslim woman wistfully spoke of the possibility that she might go to hell—at least for a time. (Like Fareed, many Muslims we have met believe they will spend some amount of time in hell before Allah might mercifully allow them to go to paradise.)

I looked right at her and said firmly,

> *"Salima, God loves you and does not want you or your family*
> *to spend one second in hell!"*

She was stunned. Speechless. We talked some more about the place of good works or grace in our salvation before getting up to leave. As we did, I told her and the confused young man one last thing:

> *"We can do good works to get to heaven (as Muslims do),*
> *or we can do good works because*
> *we are already going to heaven (as followers of Jesus do)."*

Once again, Salima—a very kind, extremely intelligent, and quite devout Muslim person—was dumbfounded by the Holy Spirit.

Oh, may she and her family come to a true understanding of what the grace of God is about! *Jesus!*

QUESTIONS TO PONDER

- Please understand that your Muslim friend or acquaintance may well have an internal, gnawing, painful fear of hell. Wouldn't it be rewarding if you could experience the privilege of helping him or her move from that terrible place of fear to a humble assurance of one day being with the Lord forever (1 John 5:13)? How might the Holy Spirit assist you with this?
- Do you know of Muslim people who have this kind of fear? Take a moment and pray for them now (and for all people you know who don't have faith in the Jesus of the Bible), that they may escape the anguish and horror of the place that Jesus Himself spoke about so often:

"Father Abraham, have pity on me and send Lazarus to dip the tip of his finger
in water and cool my tongue, because I am in agony in this fire . . .
I beg you, father, send Lazarus to my family, for I have five brothers.

Let him warn them,
so that they will not also come to this place of torment."
LUKE 16:24, 27–28, NIV

"And these will go away into eternal punishment,
but the righteous into eternal life."
MATTHEW 25:46

"Why had . . . Christians never asked me what I thought of Jesus?
They thought I needed Jesus to go to heaven, right?
Were they content with letting me go to hell,
Or did they not really believe their faith?"
(former Muslim Nabeel Qureshi,
Seeking Allah, Finding Jesus, p. 90)

CHAPTER 14

† ☾

Patriotism or . . . Evangelism?

Our Trip to See Thousands of Muslims Pray—in Washington, DC

———

"America, I announce to you it is my intention
to invite your children to the worship of one God [Allah]."

The place was Capitol Hill, Washington, DC.

The date was September 25, 2009.

The man who spoke those words that day was a Muslim leader, Imam Abdul Malik of Brooklyn, New York.

We had felt that God wanted us to be at this event, so we and a few other likeminded friends crammed into a Ford Flex and drove all that rainy night to be in Washington, DC for this historic—and troubling—event.

The Muslims advertised on their event website that there would be 50,000 Muslims in attendance, coming on buses from nearly every state. After the all-night journey, we got to the Capitol front lawn at about 7:30 a.m. There were fewer than twenty Muslims there, and about the same number of Christians. But by the main prayer time at 1:00 p.m. the number of Muslims had grown considerably. Buses kept coming in, mostly from New York and New Jersey.

Later in the afternoon, we asked a Capitol Hill policeman what he thought the attendance of Muslim people was that day. He estimated 3,000— hardly the 50,000 the Muslims had hoped for. Nevertheless, it was a strange and surreal sight that morning.

Try to picture it if you can.

There was our nation's striking Capitol building, glistening in the sun, with Old Glory flying above it in pristine blue skies. And on the grass looking up toward that symbol of American democracy were 3,000 Muslims getting ready to pray on the Capitol grounds' front lawn. Getting ready to pray . . . to Allah.

We confess that, though we genuinely love Muslim people, our patriotic senses were being assaulted. We wondered:

- Wasn't our country founded on Judeo-Christian principles?
- Didn't most of our founding founders believe in the God of the Bible?
- Isn't our country at least a supposedly "Christian" nation?
- So, what were all these Muslims doing on our Capitol grounds praying to Allah?

That afternoon, loudspeakers belted out the reading of the Qur'an (in Arabic), the normal Friday prayers, and even the public conversion of a man and a woman to Islam as they recited the *shahada*—the profession of faith in Islam that says:

> *"There is no god but Allah,*
> *and Muhammad is His messenger."*

First Amendment or not, it was *emotionally* difficult for us to hear those words on the grounds right in front of the Capitol building, knowing the Judeo-Christian foundations of our country.

First Amendment or not, it was also *spiritually* difficult hearing those words on those loudspeakers and thinking about the eternal destiny of those two souls who were converting to Islam.

God gave our little team of five many opportunities to share His love with the Muslims there before the large prayer time started. As people walked in, we greeted them warmly and respectfully. We walked around, getting in meaningful discussions with Muslim attendees. (My T-shirt with the Lord's Prayer in Arabic piqued their interest!)

We gave away a few copies of Josh McDowell's challenging little book *More Than A Carpenter*, including giving one to a woman who was herself giving away free copies of the Qur'an to non-Muslims. She joyfully put it in her purse and said she would read it. Like most Muslims there, she was very kind and friendly.

We thank God that there were a few other Christians at this event who were witnessing, giving out tracts, and loving the Muslim people in a Jesus-like fashion. We rejoiced in their presence. One couple from Texas was there handing out tracts in the entrance to the grounds. They said they were on vacation, had heard about the event, and had to be there to share Jesus. With baby in stroller, they did it with a smile!

After the Muslim prayer event in Washington, DC, we heard via email from a Christian young man that had also been there with a friend. He wrote about their "servant-evangelism":

> *"We stayed and helped clean up.*
> *At least 100 Muslims came up and said,*
> *'Why are you doing this?'*
>
> *We said,*
> *'We drove over 1,000 miles*
> *to tell you that Jesus loves you!'"*

———

As Muslims were converging onto the Capitol grounds that day, Miriam was troubled, and she went alone for a walk . . . and a talk with God.

She heard from Him too. Here is what she wrote about her experience:

> *"Since God called us into this ministry,*
> *I have been struggling with a divided heart toward Muslims.*
> *I know God loves Muslims and He longs for them*
> *to know Him and His Son, Jesus Christ.*
>
> *"But the other part of me wants to defend America*
> *and is angry at them for 9/11 and for their agenda*

to spread Islam to the extent that all nations become Islamic . . . even America!

"Being in Washington, DC brought my thoughts into sharper focus.

*"I can either continue to be angry and hinder Muslims from hearing the gospel,
or I can see God using the Islamic agenda
(to spread Islam worldwide) for His purpose.*

*"His purpose is to bring Muslims into countries with freedom of religion
so that they can hear the good news of Jesus Christ (Genesis 50:20).*

*"Patriotism to our country is still important to me,
but our primary job is to work with God to get the message of the cross to
Muslims—and all lost people—and advance His kingdom."*

QUESTIONS TO PONDER

- What kinds of emotions did you have when you read about our experience of seeing Muslims praying on the Capitol lawn in Washington, DC?
- How concerned are you that Muslims might "take over" America and install their form of government?
- What can you learn from Miriam's time with the Lord that day in Washington, DC?

*"But our citizenship is in heaven,
and from it we await a Savior, the Lord Jesus Christ . . ."*
PHILIPPIANS 3:20

CHAPTER 15

† ☾

What Would You *Lose* So That Muslims Might Truly *Live*?

Your Clothes, Your Car, Your Health, Your Visa, . . . Your Life?

I f you choose to dedicate yourself to reaching people who don't yet follow Jesus—including Muslim people—you will certainly *lose* something. You might lose the approval of people, even your closest relatives or friends who may not appreciate your interest in loving your Muslim neighbor. You might lose some of your comfort when God puts you in awkward situations while being with Muslim people. You might lose some of your security if God calls you to a risky or dangerous place to engage with them.

Jesus does not call us to a life of approval, comfort, or security. He calls us to follow Him. And that will undoubtedly—at times—involve loss.

In this chapter, we don't want to be guilty of exaggerating the human role in evangelism through our losses. After all, salvation belongs to the Lord:

"And they cried out in a loud voice:

'Salvation belongs to our God, who sits on the throne, and to the Lamb.'
REVELATION 7:10, NIV

Nevertheless, God has chosen people like you and like us to bring His good news to those who don't yet know Jesus. And sometimes he uses our personal losses to create kingdom opportunities for unbelieving people to come closer to eternal life.

In the stories of this chapter we want to encourage you to ask yourself what you would be willing to *lose* to see Muslim people come to know Jesus . . . and *live*.

"And this is eternal life, that they know you,
the only true God, and Jesus Christ whom you have sent."
JOHN 17:3

WOULD YOU LOSE YOUR *CLOTHES* THAT MUSLIMS MIGHT LIVE?

During a trip to the Middle East in the early winter of 2009, a friend who went with me experienced a rather small loss: the airline lost his suitcase. It was a brand-new suitcase with new clothes. It was frustrating for him, but together we used this inconvenience to make the most of new opportunities to witness to Muslims.

After a few days we went to a local clothing store. As my friend shopped for new clothes, we engaged in a surprisingly meaningful conversation with the young Muslim salesmen in the clothing store. This included my friend's gripping testimony of a vision of Jesus at the foot of his bed when he finally surrendered his life to Him.

Because my friend lost his clothes—even his suitcase—a few Muslim young men heard about Jesus in a store that day in that Middle Eastern country. And perhaps they came a little nearer to entering the kingdom of God and truly living. If so, it was a small loss indeed.

WOULD YOU LOSE YOUR *CAR* THAT MUSLIMS MIGHT LIVE?

At the end of May 2009, we traveled by car to Washington, DC to pick up our son and move him home to Michigan for his wedding. While we were there, we attended a worship service. But when we came out of the church building, our car was gone. Stolen!

This began a series of maddening days for about a week: trying to work with the police, a towing company, our insurance company, an adjustor, a rental car business, and a car dealership for repairs after the car was found.

I stayed in DC while Miriam and our son drove home in a rental car. On two different nights while there, I was blessed to engage in conversations from midnight to 2:00 a.m. with Muslims from Morocco, Qatar, and Turkey in a tiny Middle Eastern restaurant. On another day I had the joy of speaking about Jesus to two African Muslims from Niger at a seafood restaurant.

We "lost" our van for a while, and it was quite frustrating. But, as you have seen, personal losses can become kingdom opportunities. During that time I had the privilege of being used of God to plant gospel seeds in the hearts and minds of six or seven Muslim men so they might begin to see Jesus for who He really is—the One who gives life.

WOULD YOU LOSE YOUR *HEALTH* THAT MUSLIMS MIGHT LIVE?

On that Sunday afternoon in 2009 when we were trying to locate our stolen van in Washington, DC, we were making many calls. In the midst of those calls, we got a call informing us that my eighty-three-year-old mother had been in a terrible car accident. Her pastor's wife said that Mom appeared to be mostly alright but was being removed from her car by the jaws of life. Mom was immediately flown from western Kansas to Denver, Colorado, where they rushed her into surgery for her badly damaged right foot. Surprisingly, the surgeon placed no hardware in her foot, and she was released to a rehab facility a few days later.

Mom experienced a traumatic accident and lost the ability to walk for a time, but she made the most of every opportunity to speak about Jesus with numerous people in the hospital and in the rehab facility—including Muslim people who worked there.

We know that Mom would gladly suffer personal loss if it might help Muslim people move closer to receiving eternal life.

WOULD YOU LOSE YOUR *VISA* THAT MUSLIMS MIGHT LIVE?

Miriam did not accompany me on this particular journey, but we had flown together to this Middle Eastern country several times before to speak in an international English-speaking church and minister there for up to six or more weeks at a time. In fact, this was my eighth trip to this particular country.

As always, it just seemed routine.

But when I went through passport control that time in September of 2013, something concerned the man in the booth about my passport. He called for another man, who pulled me from the long line and told me to sit down. After an hour, they brought me into a very small room, took my fingerprints, did scans of my eyes, and returned me to my seat to wait (no riveting story such as bright lights in my face or sweat pouring down my face during a harsh interrogation!). Over four hours later I was told,

> *"You cannot have a visa to enter the country.*
> *You are blacklisted and can never return.*
> *You have to leave—tonight."*

At the time I had no idea in the world why I would have been blacklisted. Maybe because I had just come from Egypt, and there was some tension between the two governments. Maybe because of my blog for Muslims, but I don't think so. I begged for an answer, but they would give me no reasons at all for my expulsion.

I was perplexed . . . and heartbroken.

That weekend was to have been the first time for the church to meet in a new building—something very novel for that part of the world. I was so blessed to be scheduled to preach the first sermon in that building. It was going to be from Genesis 1 on the question "What Can God Create from the Chaos of Life?" (good question for the situation I now found myself in!).

That church in the Middle East had been our "home away from home." We loved the people of that unique and incredible fellowship, and they loved us. They took such good care of us on every visit. Going there was a significant part of our ministry vision and schedule. (The future plan was for us to be there twelve to sixteen weeks of the year.) Our visits to minister in that church were without a doubt some of the most fulfilling and meaningful times of our lives.

I flew home that night, and Miriam and I began to process this new change in our lives. She had emailed me in the airport before I boarded the plane to fly back home,

> *"This is not the period at the end of the sentence."*

And it hasn't been.

Though we have not been able to return to that country and our beloved friends there—certainly a significant personal loss for us—we were asked to take part in a new ministry of recruiting global workers to Muslim countries around the world. And to the glory of God, we have done so, so that even more Muslims might have the opportunity to enter the kingdom of God and really live.

> *" I want you to know, my dear brothers and sisters,*
> *that everything that has happened to me here*
> *has helped to spread the Good News."*
> PHILIPPIANS 1:12, NLT

WOULD YOU LOSE YOUR OWN *LIFE* THAT MUSLIMS MIGHT LIVE?

Our friend Emily Foreman tragically lost her husband almost ten years ago as they reached out to Muslims in North Africa. He was a martyr, killed by members of Al-Qaeda. Emily writes in her moving book *We Died Before We Came Here,*

> *"We knew that God had called us to go where very few would go,*
> *and we were aware of the risks we'd have to face.*
> *From the beginning we counted the cost.*

> *"We also understood that 'safety' was not*

a New Testament concept but merely an American one.
Jesus never called his disciples to safety but rather to obedience.

"[Jesus] never denied that hardship would be part of the bargain,
but he also promised there would be great joy and peace in following him.

"Ultimately, it boiled down to one thing:
Was he truly worthy of our lives?
And there was no debating that."

Those who long to see Muslims come to know Jesus may experience painful—even staggering—loss, as Emily did. But those who long to see Muslims enter the kingdom of God may also experience glorious redemption, also as Emily did. You see, because of her husband's death more Muslims have come to Christ in that North African country than during his life there.

To Emily and her husband, Jesus was worthy of that staggering *loss*, so that Muslim people might follow Him and *live* forever.

QUESTIONS TO PONDER

- Where have you seen a personal loss become a kingdom opportunity?
- Can you think of biblical examples of this kingdom principle?
- What are you willing to lose that people might come closer to gaining eternal life?

"For whoever would save his life will lose it,
but whoever loses his life for my sake and the gospel's will save it."
MARK 8:35

CHAPTER 16

† ☾

Who Brought Muslims to America?

It's *Not* a Trick Question!

In a span of just over one year of our ministry in 2009, it was our joy to reach out to Muslim people from Saudi Arabia, Pakistan, India, Palestine, Lebanon, Syria, Bangladesh, Iran, Iraq, Yemen, Jordan, Senegal, Turkey, Algeria, Kuwait, and Egypt.

All of these connections took place right here in the US—in the Midwest.

In some of these cases, we built relationships and followed up by:

- giving them Arabic/English tracts and Arabic/English New Testaments (to Arabic speaking people, of course)
- giving them *The Jesus Project* movie DVD (in numerous languages)
- helping them install *The Bible App—YouVersion* on their phones so they could easily and quickly access the Bible in their language.

In other cases during that year, we had very brief encounters with Muslims, but we tried to plant seeds for the kingdom, praying that those seeds would grow and help them come just a little bit closer to knowing Jesus.

We engaged with Muslim people in the mall, restaurants, bakeries, fruit and vegetable markets, gas stations, universities, convenience stores, barber shops, and different mosques.

The point is that a person doesn't have to have a passport and visa or spend a lot of time or money to be an ambassador for God to the nations. Many of you can do it from right where you live. You can reach out to Muslim people from all over the world without ever leaving the US or Canada!

Here are some examples of this from my outreach to Muslim men during that year:

- "Mehdi" From Iran: *"Keeping the rules didn't change me."*
  This young college grad student has been to our home—a vital part of ministry to international students (as many as 75% of international students have never been invited into an American home). While talking with us there, he told us how he used to call people to prayer in the mosque as a boy, but then how he lost faith in Islam as a teenager and abandoned the religion. He said that doing all the prayers and keeping all the rules didn't change him on the inside. He told us,

  "If I ever adopt another religion, it will be yours."

- "Sefa" From Saudi Arabia: *"If Jesus is God, who did he pray to?"*
  I met with this international university student one night at his apartment for five hours. Sefa asked question after question about Christianity after we had pizza (no pepperoni!) and watched the *Jesus* movie. He asked why the Jews wanted to kill Jesus if they had so many prophecies about him, how God could die on a cross, how the Trinity could be real, and whether the Bible has been corrupted (changed). Before Sefa came here to study in a university, he was in Ohio to learn English. God used a couple there to befriend him, take him to church, and share Jesus with him. Those seeds grew, and we had the privilege of watering them.
- "Sheraz," a Pakistani-American: *"May God bless your family."*
  This brilliant and engaging student was applying for a prestigious Fulbright scholarship following graduation from the university

nearby. He was a kind, gentle, sensitive young man who volunteered to help us in our efforts to dialogue with Muslim university students. In a lunch together he asked God to bless our sons and the children they would one day have.

- "Nassim" from Lebanon: *"If I believed like you do, I would sin more."*
  Like many Muslims, Nassim believes that we Christians just put our sins on Jesus and then live however we want, since all our sins are forgiven. I assured him that true followers of Jesus do not do that! Since our hearts have been changed, we have a new desire and power to live holy lives (Titus 2:11–13). He remains convinced that he would sin so much more if he had no fear of judgment. He has yet to understand the biblical motivation of love for God for living a holy lifestyle.

- "Abdullah" from Palestine: *"I wish you were my neighbor."*
  We so love this Muslim man and his large family of fourteen. We have eaten at his restaurant many, many times through the years, and I have stayed with his relatives in the West Bank of Israel/Palestine on more than one occasion. Once I went to his new home to join him as he ended that day's fast during Ramadan. He turned to me after supper and said,

  "I wish you lived next door. I wish you were my neighbors!"

  He sounded like a Palestinian Mr. Rogers! How we ache and pray for this super devout Muslim man and his family to know Jesus. As of now, he has no interest whatsoever in our Savior, at least not outwardly.

- "Ameer" from Pakistan: *"Ask me hard questions."*
  We spoke for four hours in a Middle Eastern restaurant one evening! He was a brilliant and very articulate medical student who wanted me to ask him hard questions about Islam. After talking with him for so long that night, I was exhausted because he had preached at me so intensely. Miriam said I came home looking like "a deer in the headlights"—a man confused and bewildered. Ameer had that kind of impact on me early in our ministry, before I knew more about heart-to-heart vs. head-to-head dialogue.

- "Mohammed" from Yemen: *"It is good to read many things."*
  This gentle young man worked at a restaurant we frequented when

doing evangelism. He was always warm to us. Like the other men, we gave him the New Testament and several small books about the gospel, all in Arabic. When we gave him books, he said it was good to read them all. *"Why not?"* he exclaimed!

- "Abed" from Jordan: *"It's dangerous to say that God has a son."*
  Brash. Bold. Lots of bravado and male ego. These words typify the attitude of this man toward me. At his place of business, he loved to loudly preach Islam to me in front of his Muslim customers. Sometimes I would just listen. Sometimes I would answer his questions and challenge his statements. But he knows one thing for sure: I care for him.

- "Mohsen" from Iran: *"What about my relatives who never heard of Jesus this way?"*
  We ate at his restaurant for eight years or so and enjoyed a sincere friendship and warm conversations. Over those years, we gave him a whole Bible in English, a New Testament in Farsi, and drew the "Bridge to Life" gospel illustration on a napkin for him. Usually he was polite but seemed uninterested. On one occasion, he was dismissive of the gospel and brought up the issue of those who have never heard. Later, however, he shared struggles he was having in life, and we shared the gospel one more time. That time he had questions.

———

Who brought Muslims—like these men—to America?
The answer is simple: *God did!*

> [God] *"made all the nations, that they should inhabit the whole earth;*
> *and he marked out their appointed times in history*
> *and the boundaries of their lands.*
> *God did this so that they would seek him*
> *and perhaps reach out for him and find him."*
> ACTS 17:26–27, NIV

The apostle Paul helped us understand that in His sovereign plan *God Himself* has people living *where* He wants them at the *time* He wants them there. This includes Muslim international students, immigrants, and refugees who come to the US.

God has brought Muslims to us so they might hear of Jesus through our love, service, and verbal witness as we patiently and persistently plant seed after seed of the gospel.

Miriam and I wonder how many Muslims who come to America from other countries are hungry—hungry for an American to reach out to them with Jesus-like love?

Whether you are a mom or a manager or a mechanic—no matter what you are called to be and do—may Jesus fill you with His joy in following Him into cafés, grocery stores, malls, gas stations, and universities to plant the seeds of God's love in the hearts of Muslims whom *He* has brought to America.

As in some of the cases of the men I mentioned above, you may not see immediate results. That's okay. Keep planting! Someone else will water. God will do what He does best.

"My work was to plant the seed in your hearts, and Apollos' work was to water it, but it was God, not we, who made the garden grow in your hearts."
1 CORINTHIANS 3:6–7, TLB

QUESTIONS TO PONDER

- Could it be that Muslim people are in our communities "for such a time as this" because they could not easily hear the good news of Jesus in their countries?
- Could it be that you are one of God's appointed means to bring Muslims a little nearer to the kingdom of God, even if that sometimes means committing to a long and slow process?
- What is one small step you can take right now to connect with a Muslim immigrant, refugee, or international student near where you live so they can experience the love of a follower of Jesus?

"The foreigner residing among you
must be treated as your native-born.
Love them as yourself, for you were foreigners in Egypt.
I am the LORD your God."
LEVITICUS 19:34, NIV

"And you are to love those who are foreigners,
for you yourselves were foreigners in Egypt."
DEUTERONOMY 10:19, NIV

"Love your neighbor as yourself."
ORIGINALLY FOUND IN LEVITICUS 19:18;
LATER QUOTED BY JESUS, PAUL, AND JAMES AND FOUND IN
MATTHEW 19:19; 22:39; MARK 12:31, 33; LUKE 10:27;
ROMANS 13:9; GALATIANS 5:14; AND JAMES 2:8

CHAPTER 17

† ☾

"Muslims Are All the Same, Right? They're All Out to Get Us, Right?"

A Satirical Slant on a Real Event

———

Years ago, Miriam and I met a Muslim family in a restaurant, and guess what?

They didn't try to harm us!
Imagine that!
Can you believe it?

We were driving through Iowa and stopped to eat at a McDonald's. As we were going in, we saw a Muslim family sitting alone. I said hello, and for some reason (I don't know why) we sat near them. Before we knew it, they were giving us some of their food: chicken sandwiches, French fries, and colas!

These Iraqi immigrants even invited us—repeatedly—to come to their home.

Strange!

We thought all Muslims were out to get us. We thought they were in America only to take over, change our way of life, and install Sharia law. Don't they want to take over the world?

Aren't they all . . . *terrorists?*

We thought to ourselves,

> *"They can't honestly be nice. It must be an act.*
> *They must have a hidden agenda, something . . . nefarious."*

So, even though that Muslim family in Iowa seemed nice, it must have been fake. A façade. We were glad we didn't go to their house. Who knows what might have happened to us?

So be careful.

Muslims are all the same—*they're all out to get us.*

———

We hope you quickly realized that the story we have written above is satirical.

Satire is the use of humor, irony, exaggeration, or sarcasm to expose a lack of information or understanding on a certain subject. Satire is used to denounce a certain way of thinking. In this case we have attempted to use it to denounce misinformed and untrue stereotypes of Muslims in America.

We love Muslims—one of us out of sheer joy, the other out of sheer obedience.

We have met hundreds of kind, gentle, humble, hospitable, and peaceful Muslim people—from the Midwest to the Middle East.

We have been in their homes.

We have eaten with them, laughed with them, listened to them, and grown to love them.

Yes, there is terrorism in the world today—Islamic jihadists who are bent on "slaying the infidels wherever they find them." We must not be ignorant about their evil deeds or hide our heads in the sand regarding their agenda. But do you know—has anyone told you—that these Muslim radicals kill more Muslim people than anyone else? (If anyone understands the evil nature of the terrorists and suffers the most at their hands, it is the moderate Muslims.)

Sadly, however, too many Americans see the actions of Muslim extremists as reported on television or the internet and mistakenly make sweeping generalizations against *all* Muslim people.

Primarily because of the media, too many Americans have attitudes like those in the story above. We hope and pray that you will not allow the media to unduly influence and inform your opinions of Muslim people. One of our goals in this book and in our ministry is to be used of God to bring about a new point of view.

Please do not allow the media to cause you to think about Muslim people in ways that do not honor or imitate our Savior, Jesus. His way is always the way of love. His love casts out fear.

If you haven't yet done so, we hope and pray that you will get to know Muslim people as we have.

We guarantee that *they* will be blessed.

And so will you!

One more thing: we really *did* meet a kind Iraqi Muslim family in a McDonald's in Iowa one night. They really *did* give us some of their food. And they really *did* invite us—repeatedly—to stay the night with them since it was getting late. We felt we needed to press on down the road, but before we parted ways, we got our picture taken with that sweet Muslim family as a reminder of the beauty of their sincere generosity and hospitality.

Muslims . . . they're *not* all the same.

And they're *not* all out to get us.

QUESTIONS TO PONDER

- Pew Research Center estimates that there were about 3.45 million Muslims of all ages living in the US in 2017 and that Muslims made up only about 1.1% of the total US population. Why do you think so many Americans—including Christians—are afraid of Muslims "taking over" the US?
- When you see a Muslim person or family in a store, restaurant, mall, airport, or some other place, what is your first reaction? Why do you think you have that reaction?

"For the Holy Spirit, God's gift, does not want you to be afraid of people, but to be wise and strong, and to love them and enjoy being with them."
2 TIMOTHY 1:7, TLB

CHAPTER 18

"Aren't You Afraid They Will Kill You?"

"Yes! We're Afraid They Will Feed Us to Death!"

We asked a pastor from North Carolina to set up a tour of a mosque for us, since we were going to do our "Bridging the Gap" Muslim outreach seminar in his church a few months later. Our seminars almost always include a visit to a local mosque, and we like the local church to set up the visit to potentially begin a relationship. Pastor Rick mentioned that the mosque was less than a mile from his church and that, whenever he passed it, he felt a nudge from the Holy Spirit to go in and meet people there but just couldn't bring himself to do it. Finally, he mustered up the courage and left a message on my cell phone:

> *"I'm going down to the mosque.*
> *If I perish, I perish."*

He didn't perish! We had a well-attended seminar at his church and a fine time at that mosque. We still have a picture of Pastor Rick with the leader of the mosque. Both are smiling broadly!

A pastor in California—a large cowboy—told me that he was interested in reaching out to Muslim people. I had been in his city and had seen a street with several Muslim owned and operated restaurants and food markets. I encouraged Pastor Jim to go to lunch at one of those restaurants as a way of overcoming some of his anxiety about being with Muslim people. One day, he decided to "do it afraid" and go to one of those restaurants. When we asked how it went, he confessed:

> *"When I put my hand on the door of that restaurant to go in,*
> *I was shaking in my boots."*

Pastor Jim survived . . . and loved the food. Now that big cowboy goes every Wednesday to eat at one of the Muslim owned and operated restaurants near his church building. He even went a big step further and went to the mosque on his own to meet the leaders. Soon he was eating at another Middle Eastern restaurant—with the founder of the mosque!

Radicals. Extremists. Jihadists. Terrorists.

Yes, they certainly exist. The evil one uses them to create fear—even terror—in the hearts of people. Although they comprise only the smallest minority of Muslims, they are out there. As we said in the last chapter, we don't hide our heads in the sand about that sobering reality.

People often ask us in our seminars:

> *"Why don't moderate Muslim leaders and Muslim people*
> *speak out against terrorism?"*

The truth is, they do.

Just Google the words "Muslims speaking out against terrorism." You will not be able to read all the articles on the internet you will find about the multitudes of Muslim people and organizations speaking out vociferously against terrorism. The problem is that this doesn't catch your attention because most of our news organizations don't report it. In our opinion, too much of our news—particularly cable news—is sensationalistic, and moderate Muslims simply are not conspicuous in how they live. Like you, they just want to live quiet, peaceful lives. Because of that, they don't get media coverage.

Sadly, the adage is true: "hate sells." If the cable news station you watch or the news app you use on your phone talks about Muslims only in the area of extremism, jihad, and terrorist attacks, it makes perfect sense that you might see all Muslims in that light.

After years of reaching out to Muslims here in the US and in nine different countries in the Middle East, we can say that almost every Muslim we have ever met, or count as a friend, hates terrorism. They are embarrassed by it. They go to great lengths to tell you that terrorism has no place in Islam or the Qur'an (our answer to that is in Appendix 8).

We have learned over these years that we don't have to be concerned that the average Muslim person will kill us, and we don't want you to be anxious about that either!

Before we take our trips to the Middle East, some Christians ask whether we are afraid. What they are really asking is,

"Aren't you afraid they [Muslims] will kill you?"

We learned a humorous response from an experienced Christian traveler to the Muslim world:

"Yes, we're afraid they [Muslims] will feed us to death!"

Believe us, it's true! There is no way we can describe for you the

    kind

        abundant

            extravagant

                sacrificial

                    hospitality

of Arab Muslims that we have experienced in the Middle East, and here in the US as well.

When you sit down at their table, you'd better be hungry, or you'd better eat very, very slowly, because as soon as you eat some of your food and they see an open spot on your plate they *will* fill it. It does no good to protest. They want to bless you. It is a cultural obligation and a way of life. More than that, they are simply an extremely generous people.

Please, don't be afraid that the average Muslim out there will kill you.

They won't.

But be afraid—*be very afraid*—that they might *feed you to death!*

QUESTIONS TO PONDER

- Have you had fears about Muslim people like the two pastors mentioned in this chapter? If so, what are they? And where do you think they originate from?

> "I, yes I, am the one who comforts you.
> So why are you afraid of mere humans,
> who wither like the grass and disappear?"
> ISAIAH 51:12, NLT

CHAPTER 19

† ☪

"Where's Your Robe?"
He Shouted at Miriam

Standing Out Like a Sore Thumb
at a Middle Eastern Animal Market!

———

While on a trip in March of 2010 to minister in an international church in the Middle East, we decided to venture out into the host culture. We landed in the animal *souk* (a marketplace). Though we had heard that this was not a place that Western tourists would normally go, we wanted to explore and have an adventure!

The animal souk is basically a lot like going to your county fair and your local feed store all rolled into one. Since we both grew up in the country on farms, we like those things.

We saw lots and lots of animals—mostly sheep and camels—in pens. They were there, as well as their owners and prospective buyers. A highlight was watching the men load and unload camels from trucks using a crane. The camels didn't seem to like it by the sound of their extremely loud and strange noises!

There were many men present at the animal souk, but . . . no women, and more notably, no Western women.

We stood out like a sore thumb, especially Miriam in a short-sleeved shirt.

As we walked around the animal souk, men would approach us, wanting to talk—probably more to Miriam than to me. I took pleasure in talking to the men as best I could, but my Arabic consists of about ten phrases, and they weren't too proficient in English either. Nevertheless, we made do and laughed a lot together. I loved taking pictures with them, which most of them seemed to also enjoy. As I was engaging in conversation with some kind Muslim men from Sudan, a little pickup truck pulled up near us and slammed on the brakes, stopping suddenly.

The Arab driver shouted out his window at Miriam in English,

"Where is your robe?"

He wanted to know why her head and body were not covered in the normal clothing for Muslim women: the *hijab* (headscarf) and *abaya* (a loose-fitting robe like a dress or cloak). Miriam had no idea what to say, but what came out of her mouth was,

"I'm English!"

Somehow that satisfied him.

He gave her a thumbs up and speedily drove off!

———

We have loved going to the Middle East, but at times we have done some pretty foolish things—unwise things from a cultural perspective. This was one of those times. Please learn from our mistakes:

- Men and women: we know it's common sense, but find out more about where you are going in an unfamiliar place and culture before you actually go there!
- Women: be aware of cultural norms for clothing in the places you visit. A short-sleeved shirt can work in some places (like the walking path along the beach of that same Middle Eastern city), but not in a place where there are only men. A common rule to observe in Muslim majority countries is to show as little skin as possible.

- Men: be careful where you take your wife in a Muslim country. There are some places that are "men only," and you are subjecting your wife to an embarrassing and potentially difficult situation. Think ahead and protect her!

God graciously inspired "I'm English!" as Miriam's unintentionally humorous but effective response that day, but her husband should have taken better care of her in the first place by researching the place he was taking her to—by thinking ahead.

So sorry, Miriam!

QUESTIONS TO PONDER

- What do you know about cultural do's and don'ts with regard to relating to Muslim people? (After you think about that question, please take a look at our list in Appendix 4. We wish we would have known those things in the beginning of our ministry to Muslims!)
- Since cultural norms for Muslim people differ somewhat from country to country, how could you find out what they are for the country of origin of the Muslim people in your community so you can be a wise and prudent servant witness?

O simple ones, learn prudence; O fools, learn sense."
PROVERBS 8:5

"A wise man thinks ahead; a fool doesn't."
PROVERBS 13:16, TLB

CHAPTER 20

† ☾

"They Have Sharia Law in Dearborn, Michigan, Don't They?"

The Short Answer Is . . .

—

No, they don't. Not officially.

People ask us this question frequently as we travel around the country doing our "Bridging the Gap" Muslim outreach seminars. Sometimes they even tell us that this is true before they find out that we actually live in Michigan and have had numerous positive experiences in Dearborn sharing the gospel there with complete freedom.

Though Dearborn is home to huge segments of Muslim immigrants from Lebanon, Yemen, and Iraq, Sharia law (Islamic law) is not the official law of the city government there. Might Muslims practice it in their neighborhoods and in their mosques? Yes, but you need to understand that not all Sharia law is necessarily bad or anti-American.

For example, we can assume that Muslims are constantly going to their religious leaders—imams and sheikhs—to ask for their opinions on marital disputes, land issues, ethical decisions, etc. In that sense, Muslims are trying to live by Sharia because they are trying to understand what their religious law allows for them so they may adhere to it. That doesn't mean that all Sharia law rivals public civil law in the US; the situation is no different in this regard from Christians following the biblical mandates or the guidelines of their churches or visiting their pastors to settle grievances in the church instead of in a court of law (1 Corinthians 6:1–8). Of course, problems can arise in areas where Islamic law is not consistent with US civil law. Examples of this would be allowing polygamy or practicing Islamic punishments for stealing, adultery, etc.

Well-meaning Christians have sent us email links to Christian news websites about Dearborn. Many of these media sites warn that Sharia law has come to Dearborn and that we are losing our American freedoms.

If you read these Christian media reports, you would think that Dearborn is totally closed to the gospel. Nothing could be further from the truth! In fact, at the Arab Festival one year, a church gave out $10,000 worth of gospel literature from their booth and openly shared the gospel with Muslims who passed by. Another year, the esteemed author and speaker Josh McDowell handed out 3,600 copies of his Christian novel *The Witness* and several thousand copies of his book *More than a Carpenter*.

Please pray for the huge Muslim population of Dearborn; for workers there who give their all to reach their Muslim neighbors with the gospel; and yes, that the gospel message will be unhindered—in Dearborn, Michigan, and throughout our magnificent land.

But along with these prayers, we implore you to ask God to give you at least as much concern about losing eternal Muslim souls as you may have about the possibility of losing temporary American freedoms!

Below are some very positive stories of our personal involvement in Dearborn and the freedoms believers have there to share the good news with Muslim people.

GOING DOOR-TO-DOOR IN THE MUSLIM NEIGHBORHOODS OF DEARBORN—*WHAT A JOY!*

It was a true joy for us to help with flier distribution for Josh McDowell, as well as with tract distribution for other ministries in June of 2010 and 2011. We quickly discovered that practically every house in Dearborn had steps to climb before we could attach the door hangers. It was tiring in the summer heat and humidity, but worth every step to give these items to the Muslim people there. The fliers were coupons to receive Josh's free books at his tent in the Arab Festival, and the tracts contained a clear presentation of the gospel in Arabic and English.

What is it like in Dearborn in the Muslim neighborhoods? The area we covered was mostly filled with people of Lebanese descent. Their yards, flowers, and homes were so well kept. Immaculate. Lovely. And the people? Very friendly and warm to us—graciously receiving our materials.

As we said earlier, Josh McDowell gave away literally thousands of his books in English and Arabic at his booth at the Arab Festival. As we observed him, we noted that his style was warm and engaging as he related to Muslim people. His approach reminded us of scriptural phrases for all of us to emulate:

> *"[Make] Jesus Christ attractive to all."*
> (PHILIPPIANS 1:11, MSG)

> *"Make Christ more accurately known."*
> (PHILIPPIANS 1:20, MSG)

> *"Live in such a way that you are* a credit
> *to the Message of Christ."*
> (PHILIPPIANS 1:27, MSG)

WISHING MUSLIM PEOPLE A *"MERRY CHRISTMAS"*— CHRISTMAS CAROLING IN MUSLIM NEIGHBORHOODS!

On the first and second Saturdays of every December, we join with many other Christians in singing Christmas carols in the Arab Muslim communities of Dearborn. It has been our joy to regularly participate in the caroling since 2008. Our friends Syd and Liz do an excellent job of arranging these events.

As we freely go door-to-door singing Christmas carols in Dearborn, we also give gift bags with a few presents (printed in both English and Arabic) for the Muslim people to learn about Jesus: the *Jesus Film* DVD, a printed story of Jesus's birth from the Gospel of Luke, etc. Though Muslims don't generally celebrate Christmas, we can say that most of the Muslim people who open their doors to hear us sing carols are very friendly. Some even invite us in and serve us hot tea and dessert! We also ask their permission to pray for these Muslim people about anything they might request, and this has led to quality times of sharing about Jesus. (This kind of praying to the Father, out loud and in the name of Jesus, becomes a kind of prayer evangelism—a dynamic tool of the Holy Spirit).

On one memorable occasion, a Muslim family was having a birthday party for a young boy. All of the children who were at the party crowded onto the front porch in the cold to hear us sing. We gave them our song sheets to follow along, and there they were, singing the gospel with us— maybe the only gospel they had ever heard!

As we were leaving, the Holy Spirit inspired us to give them our song sheets so they could continue to read about the Son of God—the real reason for Christmas.

(While most of our carolers prefer to go to homes, Miriam and I also like to take groups to sing inside businesses such as Middle Eastern restaurants, coffee shops, bakeries, barber shops, food markets, and even "hookah" shops—stores that sell pipes for smoking fruit-flavored tobacco. It is fun to see many Muslims take out their cell phones to take videos of us singing! Who knows who might see those videos and be impacted for Jesus, as they post them on social media or send them home to their families and friends in Lebanon, Iraq, or Yemen. God's ways of spreading His good news are astonishing!)

MUSLIM-CHRISTIAN DEBATES IN DEARBORN: NOT BEING A "HATER" BUT INSTEAD HUGGING THE MUSLIM DEBATER!

We have never been big on the idea of Muslim-Christian public debates, but we have attended at least three in Dearborn—one in a mosque, one in a church, and one at a community college. We have found them to be very educational, and not as volatile or mean-spirited as we had imagined. We believe, in fact, that such debates (when done with a Jesus-like spirit by the believers) might be the only way some Muslims will clearly hear the fundamental truths of the gospel.

At the end of one debate we attended in June of 2012, I felt the Lord nudging me to approach the Muslim debater and tell him that I love Muslims, give him a business card about our blog, and ask whether I could give him a hug. He was very surprised by my request but sheepishly smiled, received my hug, and posed with me for a picture.

Don't ask me how, but, somehow, I believe that hug broke down a barrier in his heart for Jesus. Pray for Mahmoud. He has to diligently study the Bible for these debates (oh, the wisdom of God!). May the Holy Spirit work through His Word to bring this debater to his need of a Savior.

PRAYING IN A MOSQUE IN DEARBORN: OUT LOUD—WITH A MICROPHONE—IN JESUS'S NAME!

Also in June of 2012, I participated in a tour of a mosque to observe a Muslim prayer time with a group of Jesus followers. Miriam and I had met the Iraqi imam (leader of the mosque) four years earlier. This time after he spoke and prayed in the prayer room, he asked whether any Christian tour guests would like to say a prayer in the mosque, using the microphone. Wow, did I ever! I believe the Lord gave me a prayer to honor Him in front of the imam and the other Iraqi Muslims who were there. I don't remember all of what I prayed, just two or three phrases that I prayed fervently:

> *"Father, thank You for sending Jesus to us—*
> *who I believe with all my heart to be Your Son.*
> *And thank You for bringing people here from Iraq*
> *to be our neighbors so we can love them.*
> *In Jesus's name, Amen."*

HOW DID SO MANY ARAB MUSLIMS MOVE TO DEARBORN, MICHIGAN?

Dearborn, Michigan, is a place we love, and as you can tell from our stories above, we feel very comfortable there. From what we understand, the total of all Muslims in the greater Detroit area—including non-Arabic speakers—is around 250,000. (Keep in mind that not all Muslims are Arabs and not all Arabs are Muslims.)

How did Arab Muslim people come to make Dearborn their home?

Henry Ford hired Arab men from overseas to work on his assembly line in Dearborn. That began a flow of Arab Muslims to Dearborn that mushroomed through the decades. Immigrants from Yemen, Syria, Lebanon, and Iraq were all part of the first wave of those who came to work in Ford's factories. A second great wave of Arab Muslim immigrants came in the 1980s, when whole villages in southern Lebanon departed their homeland due to an occupation by Israel. The third wave of Arab Muslims to immigrate to Dearborn consisted of the southern Iraqis in the 1990s after their failed attempt to oust Saddam Hussein.

Because of these three people migrations to Dearborn, it is not uncommon today to see businesses there with lettering in both English and Arabic above their doors. At a stoplight, you may well see a woman driver in the car next to you wearing a hijab (the headscarf commonly worn by many Muslim women).

QUESTIONS TO PONDER

- How would you feel about going to Dearborn, Michigan, for an outreach to Muslim people?
- What kind of outreach might be most effective for you there as an outsider?
- What had you heard about Dearborn, Michigan, before reading this chapter?

> *"My dear friends, don't believe everything you hear.*
> *Carefully weigh and examine what people tell you."*
> 1 JOHN 4:1, MSG

CHAPTER 21

✝ ☪

"Why Don't You Have an 'I Love Muslims Day'?"

Countering a "Pastor" Who Was Sponsoring an International "Burn a Qur'an Day" on 9/11

I was *livid*.

I sat across from Solomon, my long-time accountability partner, eating some good Middle Eastern sandwiches—chicken shawarma—at one of our favorite Lebanese restaurants in Michigan.

A pastor in Florida had just announced that he would burn 200 Qur'ans on the 2010 anniversary of the September 11 attacks. He was calling the event "International Burn a Qur'an Day," and it was getting a lot of publicity. Our President, Secretary of State, and Secretary of Defense—as well as the United Nations, NATO, and the Vatican—all weighed in with their statements and requests for this alleged pastor to not follow through on his terrible intention.

Miriam and I had talked about this. We were perplexed and frustrated.

What was this "pastor" thinking? Why would he deliberately do such a thing? Was he trying to have his moment in the sun—his chance to become famous?

Maybe.

We believe that he wanted to prove his theory that Islam is not a peaceful religion by burning the Qur'an and seeing the violent reactions he assumed would follow.

- But didn't he know that radicals would seize upon his horribly misguided action and use it to attack and kill innocent Christians and possibly moderate Muslims?
- Didn't he know it could hinder the efforts of missionaries in Muslim majority countries—or even endanger them?
- And, we couldn't help but think, how would this action negatively affect our own ministry to Muslims here in the US?

Solomon is one of my main idea people. He is so wise in the Lord. After I poured out these questions to him in real anger and frustration, he calmly asked,

"Why don't you have an 'I Love Muslims Day' on September 11?
Why don't you show Muslims that all Christians are not like that pastor?"

And so, the vision for an "I Love Muslims Day" began to take shape. I went home and told Miriam about it, and she readily agreed that we should try to make the event happen at our local university. We knew in our hearts that the Lord was in it.

When we had begun investing our lives in the harvest field of Muslim people three years earlier, one of our primary ministry objectives had been to reach out to Muslim students at our local university. This included attending various events sponsored by the Muslim Student Association (MSA) there. As we did, both of us were seriously impressed by the MSA students. They were so kind, respectful, intelligent, goal oriented, well spoken, and committed to their faith. Over time, we built a good rapport with the MSA student president and many other Muslim leaders and students in this group.

After meeting them and seeing how hospitable they were to us and the non-Muslim students at their events, a desire in our hearts grew for Christian sponsored events at which Muslim and Christian students could sincerely and honestly dialogue about their faiths and build meaningful friendships.

That idea was growing in us when the "I Love Muslims Day" idea came about. God's timing was evident!

So, with joyful expectation, I emailed the idea to the student president of the Muslim Student Association at the university near us, telling him that the "International Burn a Qur'an Day" was:

". . . reprehensible and does not coincide with the teachings of the Jesus of the Bible that I know, love, and serve. I want to do something radically different on that day which better expresses the teachings and lifestyle of Jesus and His true followers. So . . . here is my idea.

"On Saturday, Sept. 11th, at a time good for the MSA, we would have an event called 'I Love Muslims!' Day at the university. It would be sponsored by various Christian groups on campus.

"The format would be to have a 15 or 20-minute presentation from the campus Christian groups called 'Top 10 Reasons Why We Love Muslims!' Then we can have food, the kind you guys have—halal Arab food and veggie pizza provided/paid for by the Christian groups. Christian and Muslim students can sit together in small groups (by gender if you like) and discuss the presentation. Some discussion might be serious and meaningful, and some might just be having fun together!

"That is the purpose of why I wanted to talk. I realize this is extremely short notice and that the beginning of the school year is fast upon us and very busy. But I believe 9/11 is a day of such importance in our country and I want it to be known at our university for something much more like the loving and powerful character of Jesus than the divisive actions of the church in Florida. I also realize that the event might be small, but I still think it could be significant. It can be a start! The Christian students need to get to know you guys and I want to do my best to bring you together. Who knows? Maybe it could be an annual event that would grow and grow and benefit all of us.

"My friend, what do you think? Feel free to call or email!"

The rapid email response from the MSA student president about our proposal strongly touched our hearts:

"I almost wish I could have had you tell me this in person so you could see my face beaming and so I could give a hug out of pure love.

"I want you to know our MSA community truly appreciates servants of God like yourself.

"I nearly teared up reading your proposal, and I almost wish I could simply forward the email to all of our Muslims on campus (which I'm considering actually, if you don't mind).

"I simply can't put into words my feelings for this kind of event."

The event happened—on October 25, 2010, instead of September 11 due to calendar issues for the MSA—and it was a memorable night!

We were able to enlist support from campus ministry leaders from different groups, train their students who wanted to come, and enlist prayer support in the larger Christian community. The event was sponsored by a combination of twelve campus ministries and churches.

"I Love Muslims Day" wasn't huge, but we weren't disappointed. To our knowledge, nothing like this had ever been done before at our university. About fifty-five Muslim Student Association students and about fifty-five Christian students came to the event location, a new campus dorm cafeteria. We put them together in small groups, gave them ice-breaker questions, and then had them eat together—Muslims and Christians.

Miriam had worked with the university and put together the menu of halal food for the night, which the Muslim students appreciated so much. It was extremely fulfilling—after all the work we had done—to see Muslim and Christian students eating together, sharing phone numbers, and discussing the faith-related questions that we had prepared.

While this event was not intended to be overtly evangelistic in the sense of doing a big gospel presentation, after dinner we did a PowerPoint presentation on the "Top 10 Reasons Why We Love Muslims." Here they are, in inverse order:

#10 - We are related through our forefather, Abraham.

#9 - We are interested in Middle Eastern history and culture.

#8 - Muslims take spiritual matters seriously and are open to discuss them with us.

#7 - Muslims have a high respect for God.

#6 - Muslims give value to community, loyalty, family, and hospitality.

#5 - Muslims value our Holy Book and Jesus.

#4 - Muslims strive to follow God's commands.

#3 - We love your food! [we needed some humor to inject in there someplace!]

#2 - We all want to spend eternity with God.

#1b - Jesus said, "Love your neighbor as yourself."

#1a - To us as followers of Jesus, I.S.L.A.M. stands for "I Sincerely Love All Muslims"—John 3:16.

We put all the words of John 3:16 on the last slide of our PowerPoint that night for all our Muslim friends to see as our #1 reason for loving them. Come to think of it, John 3:16 is pretty evangelistic now, isn't it?

———

The "I Love Muslims Day" event was not intended to be politically correct or to gloss over the very real and serious differences between Islam and Christianity regarding salvation, the Person of Jesus, the Bible, etc. It was simply an effort to show genuine Jesus-like love to Muslim college students with no strings attached. It was a sincere attempt to joyfully obey Jesus's directive to love our Muslim neighbors and see what God would do through this effort for His glory and renown.

Further, the "I Love Muslims Day" event was not intended as a "be all, end all" event. It was a small—but hopefully significant—beginning step of evangelism:

> *"There is a time for everything,*
> *and a season for every activity under the heavens:*
> *a time to plant . . . a time to build . . .*
> *a time to embrace . . . a time to mend . . . a time to love."*
> Ecclesiastes 3:1–8, NIV

Our sincere hope and prayer was that this night would open doors just a little bit to Muslim-Christian friendships and further dialogue on substantive issues of faith in the future, such as,

- "Who is Jesus and why did He come?"
- "How can we enter paradise/heaven?"
- "What does relationship with God look like in our daily life?"

Some of that further dialogue did happen, and Muslim and Christian students are still working together on community service projects, in part because of that event in October of 2010.

The response of the Muslim students to the "I Love Muslims Day" was so gratifying to see. They kept thanking us over and over again! They felt so loved. This had been our goal—hence the name of the event!

Years later, Muslim students still talked about that night.

QUESTIONS TO PONDER

- What can you and some Christian friends do for Muslim people in your area to make them feel loved—not ostracized—by followers of Jesus?
- What do you think of asking a Muslim person if they feel accepted in your community? How do you think they might respond?
- Sometimes people who call themselves "Christians" commit evil deeds—like that pastor who ultimately did burn copies of the Qur'an. People around the world were injured and even died because of this unloving and unwise act. How can you and others counter the evil deeds of so-called Christians toward Muslim people?

"Conquer evil by doing good."
ROMANS 12:21, NLT

CHAPTER 22

† ☾

Pens and Purses

A "Scavenger Hunt" in One of
the Richest Countries in the World

———

I n March of 2011 we found ourselves back in the Arabian Gulf in an extremely wealthy country—beyond question one of the richest in the world. (What a contrast to the tents and barren apartments of Syrian refugees in another Middle Eastern country we would visit just one year later.)

One day we went to a luxurious mall in this wealthy land, and I had the crazy idea that Miriam and I should go on a bit of a "scavenger hunt" there. Actually, it was more of a treasure hunt.

We walked by a store that sold only ink pens. In some wealthy Arab countries, men are known for their ultra-expensive cufflinks, watches, and ink pens. I went in and asked,

"What is your most expensive pen?"

After going to the back room to the safe, they brought out a gold (not just in color) Swiss pen with diamonds on it; its price was $30,000!

We had heard that women in that country carried purses that averaged in value from $2,000 to $6,000. To Miriam's considerable embarrassment,

I went into stores trying to find the most expensive purse in that mall. We found it: a purse made from the belly of an Asian crocodile for $39,000 (and that was almost ten years ago)! The Filipino salesman was kind enough to take our picture with it.

———

We pray that the incredibly wealthy people of that county in the Middle East—and all of us—will learn and heed Jesus's words:

"Sell your possessions and give to the poor.
Provide purses for yourselves
that will not wear out,
a treasure in heaven that will never fail."
Luke 12:33, NIV

———

QUESTIONS TO PONDER

You might think this is an out-of-place story to include in a book about connecting with Muslim people, but we want you to know that we did so to generate questions like these:

- Which is more disturbing to you, the abject, dire poverty of Muslim refugees who have had to flee for their lives to find safety and a new life, or the ridiculously wasteful spending habits of rich Muslims blessed with oil and gas under their desert sands?
- How would you reach out with the good news to poverty stricken Muslim refugees living in Jordan or Lebanon or Turkey—or even in Europe?
- How would you reach out with the good news to incredibly wealthy Muslim people living in the Arabian Gulf countries of Bahrain, Qatar, the U.A.E., Kuwait, and Saudi Arabia—or even in Europe?

God may call some of you who are reading this book to a life for Jesus and His gospel in one of those countries. You might be reaching out to Muslims who are either dreadfully poor or unbelievably rich.

Yes, we know, there are plenty of Muslims in America who need to hear the good news, too. (We have heard that, and so will you.) But in America, Christians and churches are everywhere, and Christian radio and TV stations abound. Not so in those countries.

So please, *pray about going.*

Every Muslim—rich or poor—needs a follower of Jesus who will *love them, their Muslim neighbor.*

> *"Therefore go and make disciples in all the nations . . .*
> *and be sure of this—that I am with you always,*
> *even to the end of the world."*
> MATTHEW 28:19–20, TLB

CHAPTER 23

Christians Visiting Mosques and Muslims Visiting Churches

Why Don't You Have a "Good Will Tour" in Your Town?

"I want you to bring Muslims and Christians together and watch what I will do."

In May of 2011, I believe that the Lord laid that impression on my heart.
Shortly after that, I woke up one morning with an idea for a practical way to make that happen: a "Good Will Tour."

This was the idea I sensed the Lord was giving me:

- Take followers of Jesus to visit and observe a Friday afternoon sermon and prayer time at a mosque.
- Take Muslims to visit and observe a Sunday morning worship service at a church.
- Take these two little trips during the same weekend—all to show "good will" toward one another.

(Like the "I Love Muslims Day," these events were not at all intended to meld our *theologies* together; the goal was to bring our *hearts* together.)

We went again to our friends in leadership of the Muslim Student Association at the local university. The Islamic Relations chairperson and the larger executive board of that campus group were enthusiastic about the Good Will Tour. On two different weekends—one in the fall of 2010 and one in the spring of 2011—we went to each other's places of worship and prayer and then enjoyed question and answer sessions afterward (Miriam even provided halal food for the Q & A time at one church for our Muslim visitors, which they appreciated and we all enjoyed).

For those of you who might question the value of such bridge-building events, please listen to the honest response of a follower of Jesus, Jeff, who took part with us by observing one of the Muslim prayer times:

> "I want to tell you how moved I was by the experience, and how it has affected me.
>
> "The service itself was foreign to me; however, the young man (a student) who gave the sermon (yes, that's what it is called), gave a stirring message (half in Arabic) on CHARACTER. It roughly paralleled what we in Christian circles might hear preached from the Sermon on the Mount (Matthew 5–7) or the Fruit of the Spirit (Galatians 5). The bowing and kneeling, though cumbersome, seemed an apt attitude of humility and adoration. (Just think, if we adopted that practice, we wouldn't have to be moving chairs around in the sanctuary all the time.)
>
> "We were greeted and welcomed by many, and invited to stay for a Q & A afterward. Others who came had to leave . . . so it was just Tim, Miriam and me. At first, we gathered with just 5–6 students plus a very articulate (and friendly) Muslim chaplain. But the crowd grew over the course of the next hour to more than 20.
>
> "The exchange and dialogue were non-stop. One question seemed to lead to another . . . to another . . . to another. You would be (pleasantly) amazed at some of their 'theology.' We dwelt at length on a concept of theirs called 'presence'; it's an idea much like what Brother Lawrence (the 17th-century French monk who wrote The Practice of the Presence of God) taught. It's being in the moment . . . in the constant awareness of God, His blessings, etc. . . . and how integral prayer is to maintaining that.

"I have a whole new respect for the Muslims. After that dialogue, they are more real to me. Maybe a better way of saying it is, they are real people—very 'cool people,' no less. I have to confess that I've related to them (even if in my own mind) according to the stereotypes; this experience served to humanize them for me. Please don't misunderstand, I'm still as firmly rooted and grounded in Christ Jesus as ever; and I'm not pulling up stakes on Biblical truth. But I am glad for this experience . . . for deeper understanding . . . for the beginnings of friendship with people I have to confess I didn't understand as well as I thought I did.

"I'll tell you this, they are articulate; they can speak very intelligently about their faith. And they are highly devoted to it; they take it seriously. I'm impressed by that. We might have a little something to learn from them on that score."

———

We know God has a heart to bring Muslims and Christians together—not to create syncretism, where there are no important distinctions made between our faiths, but to break down walls and build bridges so we can really listen to each other. We want to provide a place and an atmosphere where our faith can be expressed conversationally with one another in honest, personal, nonthreatening, and mutually respectful ways.

It is surprising what can happen when Muslims and Christians get together with humble hearts—hearts that want to *listen and learn* from each other, not to argumentatively debate each other!

———

ARE GOOD, KIND, DEVOUT MUSLIM PEOPLE GOING TO HEAVEN?

We appreciated the testimony of Jeff in the story above. Why? Because he had learned to love and respect *Muslim people* more than he had before his mosque visit, but also because he did not allow himself to be fascinated or captivated by *Islam*. He is staying rooted in Jesus and the timeless, objective truths of the Bible.

As you grow to love Muslim people more and more through building relationships with them, there is a *danger* you must be aware of: falling into a kind of universalism in your thinking. The evil one can easily put into your mind a question like, "How could God send such wonderful people to hell?" In his cunning way, he is returning to his question in the garden, "Did God really say . . .?" He still asks that question now regarding the reality of hell, the necessity of the cross, and faith in Jesus alone for salvation.

Please hear the words of our friend, Tom, who has reached out to Muslims for many years regarding this potential pitfall in your outreach to Muslim people:

"I keep running into believers who have embraced some shade of universalism. This includes former missionary colleagues, who would not say that they are universalist but who at the same time are inclined to believe that their very kind, generous, faith-driven Muslim friend must be in the Kingdom. Not because the Muslim friend has surrendered to Jesus as King and Lord and believes in His death, burial, and resurrection, but rather because the Muslim friend is such an amazing person who seems to love and serve God so well."

Dear readers, the old adage is true, "Good people don't go to heaven, forgiven people do." The Bible has told us that the *gospel* is the power of God that brings salvation to those who believe (Romans 1:16).

In your ministry to Muslim people, don't succumb to the temptation to let go of the absolute necessity of the *gospel* for them to enter the kingdom of God!

QUESTIONS TO PONDER

- Based on the warning above about the dangers of universalism, what will you do when your Muslim friend seems more spiritual (appears to pray and fast more and sin less) than you?
- Would you feel comfortable inviting a group of Muslims to your church to see what a Christian worship service is like and then to have a time of questions and answers (not debate) afterward? How do you think your pastor and people would respond to something like this?
- How could you promote such an event from a biblical perspective and

in a positive way? How could you prepare your church people to help Muslims feel at ease and welcome in your church worship service, and afterward as well?

- How much of the gospel would you feel free to share with Muslim visitors in your church building (knowing that they usually share what they believe when you do a scheduled visit at their mosque)?

"Do not neglect to show hospitality to strangers."
HEBREWS 13:2

CHAPTER 24

The Dearborn International Arab Festival: "Christians" Giving Christianity a Bad Name

They Called Themselves the "Bible Believers"

I t was not the organizers of the Arab Festival who gave Christianity a bad name.

Nor was it the thousands and thousands of Muslim people who attended the event.

Sadly, it was small groups of "Christian" protesters—mostly the group who called themselves by the name "Bible Believers."

Unlike Josh McDowell, whom we mentioned in chapter 20, these men certainly did little to "make Jesus Christ attractive to all," "to make Christ more accurately known," or to be "a credit to the Message of Christ" (Philippians 1:11, 20, 27, MSG).

This was the 16th annual Arab International Festival in Dearborn, and it attracted more than 325,000 visitors on June 17–19, 2011. Sadly, some of these "Christian" visitors just made trouble. Instead of sharing good news about Jesus, they used their signs and hateful voices to spread a lot of bad news.

When we went to the festival one Saturday, I could hardly contain myself as I watched their malicious behavior toward the Muslim people there! Miriam (my best friend and closest advisor) warned me against any unwise, rash actions against these men, but I just had to talk to them. They broke my heart and angered me immensely.

There was no kindness, no grace. There was no love in their words, their eyes, or the tones of their voices toward the Muslim people.

One of the Bible Believers' signs said,

"Ask me why you're going to hell."

What Muslim would want to follow their Jesus?

How sad for the gospel, for the reputation of Christianity, and for the Muslim people who did not get to see the Jesus they need through these men!

One of the Bible Believers was so hateful and mean to the Muslim teenagers he was talking to that I could take it no longer. Like Paul, "I had a face-to-face confrontation with him because he was clearly out of line" (Galatians 2:11, MSG). When I rebuked him for his lack of Jesus-like behavior, all he could do was berate me and call me names in a mean-spirited and arrogant manner. I was ashamed of him for conducting himself in such a despicable way, while at the same time associating himself with the matchless, holy name of Jesus. I told him exactly that. No one bearing the name Christian should ever, ever behave in such a horrible and hateful manner toward Muslim people (or anyone else).

Our Savior was assuredly harsh with Pharisees and other religious hypocrites (people I believe were much like the Bible Believers). Otherwise, His life was characterized by a perfect combination of "grace and truth" (John 1:14, one of Miriam's favorite verses). And we believe He would interact in just this way with Muslims today.

May our conduct toward Muslims be like that of Jesus!

The Lord has had us conduct outreach to Muslims in Dearborn, Michigan, many times. We can assure you that you can freely share the gospel there—particularly if you do it with gentleness and respect, as we are called to do (1 Peter 3:15)—not in the manner of the Bible Believers.

THE DEARBORN INTERNATIONAL ARAB FESTIVAL:
Lovers, Haters, and a Man Named John

The Bible Believers came to Dearborn for the second time in 2012 and really stirred things up. They entered the festival with a severed pig's head on a stick—a move clearly intended to offend and anger the Muslim attendees, since Muslims don't eat pork. These men also carried huge signs with provocative messages against Islam and Muhammad and shouted rudely at the Muslim teens who objected to their methods.

One such Bible Believer used his megaphone to shout at the Muslim teenagers,

> *"You're going to melt in the fires of hell, you dirtbags."*

Granted, the Muslim teens who threw eggs, water bottles, etc., at them should have been stopped by the police, though for some time they weren't. But the provocative signs and horrible behavior of the Bible Believers felt more like the actions of haters, not believers. To us, they just gave Christianity a bad name.

It seems to us that these outsiders came to Dearborn just to create an uproar and then to feel good about themselves when both epithets and eggs were thrown at them! Their satisfaction when this occurred demonstrated a false and twisted understanding of Jesus's words "Blessed are those who are persecuted for righteousness' sake, for theirs is the kingdom of heaven" (Matthew 5:10). These men might have stood in the "free speech zone" at the festival, but Jesus never gave them the freedom to point their fingers and speak the foul words that came from their mouths toward Muslim people.

In fact, their behavior begged the question,

> *"What Bible are the 'Bible Believers' believing?"*

Okay, enough about the "haters."

On a much more positive note, let's talk about some "lovers"—people who love and show kindness to others regardless of their religion, politics, country of origin, or the color of their skin.

There were some true believers at the Arab Festival who represented Jesus in a much more loving way. One such follower of Jesus there was a man named John. For many years John has gone to the festival with a huge orange container of ice water and hundreds of little plastic cups. I loved watching him give free cups of cold water to Muslims, Christians, and anyone else who passed by in the sweltering June heat and wanted a refreshing drink. It was my privilege to help John hand out water for a few hours. What a joy! It felt like the approach of Jesus: *being a lover, not a hater.*

Yes, John is a Christian—a genuine follower of Jesus. No doubt about it. He doesn't hide it. He can't hide it. It just comes out. He even had little pamphlets on top of the water container about the Jesus he loves. But he didn't push them, or his faith, in a way that demeaned the Muslim people he conversed with. He just . . . loved.

John didn't make the Channel 7 news for his hospitality that day. The *Detroit Free Press* didn't feature an article about his kindness. No one posted something on YouTube showing him smiling and blessing each person who took the little cups of water. No, that video would not have gone viral now, would it?

That's why we had to write something in this book about John. We had to write about lovers like John who are always at the Arab Festival but don't make noise or trouble or require riot police to enforce a free speech zone. They don't make the kind of sensationalistic news that so many seem to want to see.

But you know what?

Someone did see every act of John's kindness and love. Someone did keep a record of it. And someone delighted in it.

Yes, God Himself saw what John did, and will reward him for it. On two occasions the Bible records Jesus speaking about the beauty and value of simply giving someone a cup of cold water (Matthew 10:42; Mark 9:41).

Sometimes, only *God* sees what lovers quietly do for others. There is no press. No publicity. Just the Lord. In the end, that will be enough.

We think it already is . . . for a man named John.

QUESTIONS TO PONDER

- If you had occasion to speak to one of the haters mentioned in this chapter—one of the Bible Believers—what would you say to him?
- If you had occasion to speak to a Muslim person about one of the haters mentioned in this chapter, what would you say to them?

"We put no obstacle in anyone's way,
so that no fault may be found with our ministry."
2 CORINTHIANS 6:3

"Let your conversation be gracious and attractive
[Greek: "seasoned with salt"]
so that you will have the right response for everyone."
COLOSSIANS 4:6, NLT

CHAPTER 25

The Saudi International Student: *"That Day, I Was Praying to Meet a Kind American"*

How Many Others Are *Still Waiting?*

I t was such a hot, muggy day on the campus of the university that day in August of 2011.

I was passing out flyers for my friend, Frank, of ISI (International Students, Inc.)—an outstanding campus ministry all over America.

Frank was putting on his annual Labor Day weekend party at a nearby lake for international students, and I was helping by passing out flyers for it on the local university campus. Because my heart is so drawn to Muslims, I was specifically looking for them to be recipients of the flyers.

As I got down to my last ten or twenty flyers, I was hot, tired, and worried that I was going to get a parking ticket because I knew the meter had expired. But I was determined that I wasn't going to go back to the car until I had given away every last one of those flyers.

I prayed,

> *"Lord, please have me meet just the right students—*
> *especially Muslim students—*
> *for these remaining flyers that I have to pass out."*

I finally got down to my last flyer.

The . . . last . . . one.

A university bus pulled up a little distance from me at a bus stop. In the midst of the students who got off that bus, I could see an unusually tall Arab young man. I hurried over to him and greeted him with the words, *"Salaam alaykum!"* ("peace be upon you").

I think he was taken aback. I could imagine him saying to himself, "Who is this guy—this white guy with white hair—greeting me in the customary Arabic Muslim greeting?"

Nevertheless, this young man responded with the normal response, *"Alaykum salaam"* ("and to you be peace"), in a kind but surprised manner. And then we made some small talk: learning names, my finding out his country of origin and learning what he was studying, and my sharing a little bit about our years of traveling to the Middle East, followed by our exchanging of phone numbers.

It wasn't long before Khalil and I started going out together for dinner and memorable times of conversation. (I always wanted to go out with him to eat Middle Eastern food because Miriam and I can't get enough of it, and he always wanted to go to Red Robin because his Middle Eastern city has every American franchise restaurant except for that one!)

We just hung out.

We talked.

We did fun stuff.

We built a *relationship*.

Going to our local county fair was a big thing for him. He loved the demolition derby! He would take pictures of the cars smashing into each other and text them back to his family and friends in Saudi Arabia. Because he was a Muslim and not allowed to eat pork, he was fascinated by the pigs on display at the fair ("Do they taste good?" he inquired curiously).

Khalil was one of the most open Arab Muslims I have ever met. He was not necessarily open to becoming a follower of Jesus, but he was more open to different ways of thinking and looking at the world than is normal for a

Muslim from the Middle East. His father had gone to a university in Europe and had become a lover of various musical styles: from Bach to Jimmy Hendrix. He had passed along this kind of openness to his son. So, Khalil and I could talk family, music, movies, current events, US and world politics— even the very controversial politics of his own country. We grew closer and closer and really enjoyed our time together. I considered Khalil a real friend.

Khalil and I had spiritual conversations as well. He asked me once, "Is Jesus the only way?" "Yes," I said. I knew I had to speak the truth in love. Any other answer would not have been truth, nor would it have been love.

Khalil read the Gospels of Matthew and Mark from the Arabic-English Bible I gave him. He was intrigued by Jesus, and I excitedly asked him why (I had hoped he'd had a revelation from the Holy Spirit about Jesus's sacrificial death for us—or some other deep truth). His answer was not what I had been anticipating. He simply said,

"I loved how he outsmarted the Jews."

I should have expected that an Arab Muslim from Saudi Arabia would rejoice in that! But the Lord encouraged me: at least he had read two of the Gospels and looked at Jesus. I trusted that there was something there for the Holy Spirit to use later.

I was also blessed to plant seeds of the good news in other ways with Khalil: sharing many Scriptures with him, sharing contemporary Christian music CDs with him (he liked them), taking him to see the Christian movie *Courageous* (he enjoyed that!), talking to him about why Miriam and I travel to the Middle East to help with refugees, and doing what he liked the most—praying out loud for him. Regarding those simple times of prayer, I was pleasantly surprised when he said to me once,

"When you pray, I feel calmness."

After another prayer session for him, he said,

"I feel goosebumps. It is so genuine."

As was the case with other Muslim people, praying for Khalil—out loud, to the Father, in Jesus's name—was becoming more and more of an evangelistic strategy of the Holy Spirit in our ministry.

At some point early in our relationship, I told Khalil that I had prayed the day I had met him for just the right person to get my last flyer. In God's plan, it had been him. Two years after I met Khalil, we were eating together one night—probably at Red Robin—when he shocked me. He asked whether I remembered the hot August afternoon when we had met after he got off the university bus. I told him that I could never forget it and reminded him of my prayer that day. He said,

> *"While I was riding the bus that day,*
> *I prayed that*
> *I would meet a kind American."*

I can tell you that his statement moved me deeply. I'm sure that I got tears in my eyes.

QUESTIONS TO PONDER

- Did you find it interesting that God answered the prayer of a Muslim? Why or why not?
- How many other Muslims have come to America and have prayed the prayer that Khalil prayed that day: to meet a kind American? And how many are still waiting for a follower of Jesus to be the answer to that prayer?
- Unlike many other Muslims, Khalil did not have a negative image of Christianity. On one occasion, he said,

> *"Christianity is all about love."*

What are some practical ways you can help your Muslim "neighbor" say or sense the same?
- Two different men—leaders in their churches—told us that they would not go with us to visit a mosque or to eat at a Muslim owned and operated restaurant as part of our weekend Muslim outreach seminar. How would you have responded to them?

> *"While Jesus was having dinner at Matthew's house,*

many tax collectors and sinners came and ate with him and his disciples.
When the Pharisees saw this, they asked his disciples,
'Why does your teacher eat with tax collectors and sinners?'
On hearing this, Jesus said, 'It is not the healthy who need a doctor,
but the sick. But go and learn what this means: "I desire mercy, not sacrifice."
For I have not come to call the righteous, but sinners."
MATTHEW 9:10–13, NIV

CHAPTER 26

Muslim People Say to Us, *"You Love Muslims? Really? Why?"*

A Totally New—and Different—
"Operation Shock and Awe"

———

The late Rick Love, former international director of Frontiers (an impressive missions agency reaching out to Muslims), held a seminar in Phoenix in 2011 for Christians who wanted to learn about being peacemakers between Muslim and Christian people. It was a stretching time for me, and it turned out to be the genesis of a vision within me to start a new blog. I was resistant, but the Holy Spirit was persistent with this idea. The prompting continued and was strong. I knew it needed to include the words "I Love Muslims."

As I sat in that seminar, the Lord gave me the four goals for this blog:

1. building bridges of friendship between Muslims and Christians
2. tearing down walls of suspicion, fear, and anger
3. planting seeds of peace in a world of conflict

4.   inspiring dialogue on faith issues.

A local campus church we partner with and love, along with their pastor, Luke, helped us start the website. After that, the Lord soon gave me the idea to create a business card for it. The campus church lent their aid once again, this time in the design of a card with a church and a mosque on the front and the four goals of the blog on the back. Later on, Miriam suggested that I include the title in Arabic in addition to English, and this has been a brilliant, eye-catching detail that has really touched Muslim people.

———

How do Muslims react when we hand them our card? What do they say when they read the words "I Love Muslims" in English and also in Arabic? Here are some responses through the years:

"You love Muslims?"

"Really?"

"Why?"

"God bless you!"

"Look! I have goosebumps on my arms!"

"It's a good thing somebody does."

All of these responses tell us one thing: *Muslims are used to being marginalized in America. Sadly, they are accustomed to being rejected—even (and perhaps at times especially) by Christians.*

Why? Based on stereotyping, mostly by the media but also by preachers and churches. In our experience most Muslim people just can't believe it when a follower of Jesus tells them that they love them.

We want to be used by our Savior to see that change!

We want love to be the norm—the expected way in which Muslim people are viewed and treated by followers of Jesus!

Some of you may remember the 2003 US invasion of Iraq that our government called "Operation Shock and Awe." This has been defined as "the military usage of massive or overwhelming force to disarm or incapacitate an enemy." We don't wish to speak of bombs and bullets here, but we do have questions for you.

QUESTIONS TO PONDER

- Together, why don't we start a new kind of "operation shock and awe"?
- Why don't we make it our goal to humbly and kindly "shock" Muslim people with our love?
- And why don't we help them see the Jesus of the Bible and truly be in "awe" of Him?
- How might God use you and some like-minded friends to love like this where you live?

"Watch what God does, and then you do it,
like children who learn proper behavior from their parents.
Mostly what God does is love you. Keep company with him and learn a life of
love. Observe how Christ loved us. His love was not cautious but extravagant.
He didn't love in order to get something from us
but to give everything of himself to us.
Love like that."
EPHESIANS 5:1–2, MSG

CHAPTER 27

Our Muslim Good Samaritan #1— in Petra, Jordan

"Please Wait for Us!"

We had taken a bus to Petra from Amman, Jordan, which was over three hours away. Petra is an ancient city carved out of rock and is positively one of the most stunning places in all the Middle East. (Some believe that Petra is actually spoken about—but not by name—in the little biblical book of Obadiah.)

Seeing all the sights of Petra in the winter of 2012 was magical. We even went on donkeys up steep, scary cliffs to a magnificent place called "The Monastery." But we made a mistake: we did not do well in estimating our time to return to the bus for our trip back to Amman. When it was nearly time to be at the bus, we knew we were in trouble. We weren't going to make it. Nevertheless, we hurried as fast as we could.

When we neared the exit of Petra, I ran to catch our bus and saw a young man ahead of me who was running even faster. I recognized him as having been on the bus earlier and yelled to him to ask whether he would hold the bus for us. He signaled that he would do that, but when we got to the place where the bus was supposed to be to take us back, it was gone . . . and so was the young man!

We were totally out of breath from running and totally perplexed as to what to do to get back to Amman without paying a huge fee for a taxi—money we did not have with us.

After about five minutes, we heard the noise of a speeding vehicle in the distance, and soon it roared up beside us in the parking lot. It was a taxi, and in the passenger seat was none other than the young man himself—Ibrahim. He had caught a taxi to chase down the bus, but instead of doing that and getting on the bus himself (saving himself a lot of time, money, and hassle), he remembered us and came back for us. He had kept his promise! After a thirty-minute drive in the speeding taxi, we caught up with the bus and got back on, using our original tickets. This was a relief, but, to add to our embarrassment, we had spent the last of the money we had taken to Petra and could not pay the taxi driver. Ibrahim paid for us, too (and refused our offer to repay him later)!

Our Good Samaritan—by definition "a compassionate person who unselfishly helps others, especially strangers"—had rescued us!

On the entire three-hour ride back to Amman, Ibrahim, a devout Muslim, and I sat and talked about Islam and biblical Christianity while Miriam slept. This Good Samaritan young man had a lot of questions. I didn't have all the answers, that was for sure, but it was a pleasurable time of peacefully and graciously talking back and forth about faith issues.

Being with Ibrahim that day was beyond doubt a divine appointment—something we pray for regularly!

Sadly, some Christians can't believe a Muslim would do something to help a non-Muslim at their own inconvenience or cost.

We have joyfully learned that *they can and will.*

Like this young Muslim Good Samaritan, Ibrahim, *they do.*

This young Muslim practiced the "love your neighbor" teaching of Jesus from the story of the Good Samaritan in Luke 10:25–37. In that story, the last person the Jews expected to take care of the beaten man was a despised Samaritan.

Historically, the Samaritans had developed their own religion—a mix of idolatry and Judaism. They had built their own temple at Mt. Gerizim and had their own version of the Old Testament (which contained only the first five books).

"The Jews looked down on the Samaritans as
religious and racial half-breed heretics . . .
it was a sin to touch a utensil that a Samaritan had touched."
Ray Pritchard
(https://www.keepbelieving.com/sermon/the-woman-at-the-well-christ-
speaks-to-the-problem-of-a-guilty-past/)

"Some of the Pharisees prayed that no Samaritan
would be raised in the resurrection!
When His enemies wanted to call Jesus an insulting name,
they called Him a Samaritan (John 8:48)."
Warren Wiersbe
(https://www.biblegateway.com/resources/wiersbe-be-bible-study/samari-
tan-woman-4-1-30)

The hostility between Jews and Samaritans had a long history, much like
that of the Christian struggle with Muslims.

QUESTIONS TO PONDER

- Could it be that too many of us Christians in the 21st century are much
  like Jesus's Jewish listeners to the parable of the Good Samaritan in the
  1st century?
- Are we also filled with prejudice, too easily influenced by historical misconceptions, and afraid of or angry with Muslim people, in part because
  we think they are "not like us"?
- If so, how can we overcome these obstacles to loving our Muslim
  neighbor?

"Then Peter began to speak:
'I now realize how true it is that God does not show favoritism
but accepts from every nation
the one who fears him and does what is right.'"
ACTS 10:34–35, NIV

CHAPTER 28

† ☪

Our Muslim Good Samaritan #2— in Bethlehem, Israel/ Palestine

Lost, Alone, and Trying to Get Back to Miriam

———

I took a taxi from Jerusalem to Bethlehem for a conference sponsored by Bethlehem Bible College in the winter of 2012. After the conference ended, I wanted to save money on taxis, so I determined to walk from the hotel conference site to an Israeli checkpoint, hoping to pass through and catch a taxi on the other side. After getting verbal instructions, I began my twenty-five-minute walk.

As I approached the checkpoint on the sidewalk, I noticed a lot of cars backed up waiting to get through. Soon I noticed something else: soldiers walking toward me, yelling something in a language I did not know—and carrying guns! They definitely did not look happy, and they appeared to be most adamant about not letting me go through. It turned out that I was at a *car* checkpoint in Bethlehem, not a *walk-through* one.

I was completely out of my comfort zone: cold, hungry, lost, tired, and confused as to how to get back to Miriam at our guest house in Jerusalem.

After retreating from the car checkpoint and walking on some dark, cold streets in Bethlehem for over an hour, I finally found the walk-through checkpoint. I was excited because I made it through quickly; there was not a single person going through it except for me. But my excitement was to be short lived. I was expecting to find a taxi on the Israeli side to take me back to Jerusalem, but I had forgotten that it was Friday night—the Sabbath. The streets were deserted. No taxis. No people. *No one!*

I had absolutely no idea how to get back to Jerusalem to our guest house near the famed Damascus Gate. All I knew was that there was a huge-looking moon rising on my right—in the east—so I knew that I needed to go straight ahead—north, toward Jerusalem. I began to walk in that direction and did so for quite a while. Thank God, I was not really panicking. Somehow, I sensed that the Lord was with me on those dark streets. Nor was this the first time something like this had happened to me or to us. (For this very reason Miriam and I don't lead tours to the Middle East!)

I kept walking, and finally, in the distance, I could see a traffic light. I felt as though the Lord told me to go to that intersection and just wait—that He would bring a person there to take me back to Jerusalem but that I needed to be patient. I praised Him for His help and care for me and walked to the intersection. After what seemed like a long time (but probably wasn't), a taxi van pulled up driven by a Muslim man named Fadi. Fadi had been out with his family visiting friends. He was off duty and on his way home, but he kindly stopped to help me. He offered to drive me back to our guest house in Jerusalem for a very modest sum of money, not the normal fare.

After such a long time of my wandering around on deserted, dark, and possibly dangerous streets, this Muslim man rescued me and got me back safely to Miriam in Jerusalem.

I was exhausted, but so relieved—so thankful to the Lord—and to Fadi and his family. The Lord could have sent a Jew (even though it was the Sabbath) or a Christian, but He sent . . . a Muslim. When we left Israel to go home via Jordan, I knew whom to call to be our taxi driver to take us to the Jordanian border. It was a no-brainer. It had to be Fadi.

"Thank You, God, for Fadi.
Thank You for rescuing me through him
on that dark, lonely, winter night in Bethlehem.

Thank You for yet another . . . Muslim 'Good Samaritan'!"

We don't intentionally miss buses (as in the last chapter)—or get lost (as in this chapter)! But when we do find ourselves in those kinds of difficult positions, God sometimes leads us to ask for help from "Samaritans." Jesus is our example, as He asked for help from the Samaritan woman at the well.

Asking for the help of a Muslim person—as the Holy Spirit leads—can often open doors for the gospel, just as it did with the woman at the well and with our two Arab Muslim Good Samaritans. As Americans, we're not good at asking for help from people we don't understand or trust, but perhaps we can learn to see that being just a little bit vulnerable can create valuable opportunities to share seeds of the gospel and to love our Muslim neighbor.

This Good Samaritan was placed in my life by God to rescue me in a difficult but temporary time of *physical* lostness. We believe that God put us in his life to plant seeds to help him meet a Savior who wants to rescue him for eternity from *spiritual* lostness.

QUESTIONS TO PONDER

• Do you think you could feel comfortable asking for practical help from a Muslim person, as Jesus did from the Samaritan woman at the well? Why or why not?

> *"When a Samaritan woman came to draw water,*
> *Jesus said to her,*
> *'Will you give me a drink?'"*
> JOHN 4:7, NIV

CHAPTER 29

Helping Desperate Syrian Muslim Refugees

"Thank You for Listening to Our Pain!"

———

I had never met someone who had experienced such torture. Malek had been in a Syrian prison for a year and a half because he dared to stand in protest against the Syrian President Bashar al-Assad's atrocities. Eventually, the Syrian army threw his nearly dead body on a pile of trash, and, miraculously, he woke up in a nearby country (to this day he has no idea how he got there). From a hospital he had someone call his wife. Imagine her shock—she had thought he was dead!

Malek recovered to a large extent, but he could not use his hands because of damage sustained from all the torture. When our youngest son and I met him, he was very depressed. I shared the gospel with him, but he just wasn't ready for it yet. Still, we trusted that seeds had been planted.

A year later I saw Malek again in that country through a "chance" meeting on the street of a huge city. I wondered what it was about him that made his face look so different from before? An Arab Christian friend who was with me that day told me that Malek had been born again! This was Malek's explanation:

"I was sitting alone in my apartment. Smoking. Thinking.
A bright light came into the room. I could see a man, but not his face.
He said to me,
'Malek, I am the Savior of the world.
I am the way, the truth, and the life.
And I want to introduce Myself to you.'"

Malek didn't know John 14:6, but, of course, Jesus did, and He introduced Himself to Malek!

We see Malek every year when we travel to the Middle East, and he has become a cherished friend. Oh, how he loves Jesus! After several years his wife has also become a follower of Jesus (she told us she had *hated* Christian people before). Malek is so bold in his faith that he has been witnessing to fifty Muslim men in his area, at the potential risk of severe persecution.

Thus, something new was added to our ministry in 2012: helping refugees in the Middle East:

- Syrian Muslim refugees
- Palestinian Muslim refugees
- Yemeni Muslim refugees
- and Iraqi Muslim and Christian refugees.

These people would change our lives.

SHOES FOR PALESTINIAN REFUGEE CHILDREN

Before going to the Middle East in February of 2012, I read a thought-provoking book titled *Radical* by David Platt. Through this book I was convicted by God that we had not invested enough thought, time, or money into helping the desperate poor of this world. This conviction was about more than just giving help through a check in the mail to an organization; it was about giving help face-to-face.

While in a Middle Eastern country Miriam and I met a man who leads a magnificent relief organization that assists the poor. Yusef is a Palestinian Christian whose family originated in Israel. His family knows well what it means to lose a home and even a homeland. They had to leave Israel in 1948 and became refugees in another land. Because of this, Yusef loves refugees.

Whether they are Christian or Muslim, it makes no difference—he *loves* them, and he *helps* them. Refugees may be found in Lebanon, Jordan, and Turkey by the hundreds of thousands. His organization is overwhelmed by the needs of these people.

While visiting Yusef, we were blessed to gain an introduction to helping refugees. One day we found ourselves stopped on the side of a road looking down at a Palestinian refugee camp.

As we sat on a road in an SUV filled with children's shoes and sandals, our eyes were taking in the sight and our minds were trying to comprehend what it would be like to live in this camp under such trying circumstances. Soon a little boy in the camp noticed us and ran toward us, waving wildly and shouting to us with a big smile on his face. All of a sudden he turned abruptly and ran back to the camp, still shouting happily, but this time to gather more children for our arrival.

His work as a herald of good news was more than successful. As our driver, an extraordinary Jordanian Christian relief worker named Musa, took us into the camp, children emerged from everywhere!

The children knew the vehicle, . . . and they knew that we had gifts for them. This time it was shoes and sandals, something these refugee kids don't take for granted. It was really chilly in February, and many of them were barefooted.

BLANKETS AND RICE FOR POOR AND DESPERATE SYRIAN REFUGEES

What a privilege we had to take blankets and bags of rice to Syrian refugees! These people were unequivocally poor and desperate. One example was a Muslim woman who had escaped the tragedy and danger in Syria, only to come to a relatively safe but devastatingly poor living situation in the country we were visiting. This young woman had a "living room" in her apartment, which we entered.

Her living room had cold, bare cement walls that were covered with graffiti from previous occupants. No family pictures—or any pictures—hung on the walls. There was no furniture. There were no beds, only mats and a few cushions on the floor to sleep on at night. There were no windows to allow in sunlight, only a window from the living room to the bathroom. Yes, she had a "bathroom," but it was merely a hole in the floor.

She told us:

> "I am here with my four children. One is in the hospital here.
> I do not know what has happened to my husband in Syria.
> I cannot contact him.
> I do not know if he is dead or alive."

Like so many of the Syrian refugees we met, she was desperate for help; thanks be to God, the organization we were with was able to provide it.

"THANK YOU FOR LISTENING TO OUR PAIN"

In October of 2012, we were again in the Middle East visiting Syrian refugees. As we mentioned earlier, Miriam and I have been blessed to work with Christian Arabs who run a very special humanitarian relief organization. This organization is well thought of by the Muslim government of that country because of the stellar work they do on behalf of the poor.

During that trip we gave out three primary items: fifty-pound food bags (rice, flour, salt, cooking oil, cheese, pasta, soup, etc.), blankets for the coming winter, and small washing machines (the refugee women love these; it saves their hands a lot of hard work, considering their typically large families).

But the most satisfying part of our time with the Syrian refugees was simply being with them—sitting on the thin mats in their humble, sparsely furnished apartments; drinking tea with them; and, most of all, listening to their stories.

We want you to hear in their own words what they experienced in going from Syria to find safety in another Middle Eastern country:

- "We traveled from Homs to Idlib to Damascus and finally to this country."
- "We traveled at night to keep from being shot by the Syrian government soldiers."
- "Travel near the border took hours because we had to walk."
- "To keep our children quiet, we needed to give them a drug to help them sleep as we carried them."

- *"When we arrived in this country, the army helped us and put us in a refugee camp."*
- *"Now we are in this apartment, but we cannot find work."*
- *"Please pray for our children because of the memories they have of seeing dead bodies."*
- *"Pray that our government in Syria will change."*
- *"I was shot by a sniper in the leg. I was able to keep two of my grandchildren under me while they were shooting into my house"* (these are the words of an old woman whom we saw in a bed).
- *"Our family is scattered. Some fled to Turkey and some to other places."*
- *"We want desperately to go back to our homes in Syria, but they have been looted and burned or bombed. Still, we want to go back and rebuild."*

These stories touched our hearts. The four Christian Arab people—Yusef, Musa, David, and Yasmine (some of our best friends in the world)—who run the relief agency with which we work, see these families as so much more than numbers. They spend time with them, getting to know them and showing genuine interest. They do not just rush in, hand them a bag of food and a blanket, and rush on to the next needy person or family. Instead, they sincerely care, and these refugees know it because these Arab Christian friends come back and help these Muslim refugees again and again.

Helping a refugee is not a matter of which faith that refugee espouses. It is a matter of believers obeying the Word of God.

Receiving blankets for the coming winter was much appreciated by these refugees. One woman took her blanket out of the plastic bag, and she and her little girl ran their fingers over it the whole time we talked. This was a new priceless possession for them because they had virtually nothing else.

They appreciated the blankets, the food, and the washing machines. But listen to what they were most thankful for:

"Thank you for listening to our pain."

For us, there could have been no greater privilege.
A simple act of love—*listening*—can have a big impact.
Maybe even an eternal one.

Often these Muslim refugees ask our Christian aid worker friends *why* they help them. With finely tuned sensitivity, the workers share the good news of our Savior—little by little, step by step, visit by visit. The Holy Spirit does the rest, and over the years we have witnessed mind-boggling stories of redemption—like that of our treasured friend, Malek.

QUESTIONS TO PONDER

- Try to imagine yourself in the position of a refugee who has experienced war, poverty, prison, torture, and PTSD. What would be of the most help to you? What would you most long for?
- In this chapter we speak of the evangelistic strategies of servant evangelism and listening evangelism. How might you employ those loving strategies with those you know who have not yet decided to follow Jesus?

"What good is it, dear brothers and sisters,
if you say you have faith but don't show it by your actions?
Can that kind of faith save anyone?
Suppose you see a brother or sister who has no food or clothing,
and you say, 'Good-bye and have a good day; stay warm and eat well'—
but then you don't give that person any food or clothing.
What good does that do?
So you see, faith by itself isn't enough.
Unless it produces good deeds, it is dead and useless."
JAMES 2:14–17, NLT

"If anyone has material possessions and sees his brother in need
but has no pity on him, how can the love of God be in him?
Dear children, let us not love with words or tongue
but with actions and in truth."
1 JOHN 3:17–18, NIV

"Blessed is the one who considers the poor!"
PSALM 41:1, NLT

CHAPTER 30

Going to the Yemeni Mosque: *"You Have Insulted My Holy Qur'an!"*

And Then My Friend Said It Was Time to Go!

I n the summer of 2012, two Christian friends in my area wanted a tour of Dearborn, Michigan, where—as we have mentioned before—so many Arab Muslims live, work, and worship. I called a Christian man, John, who works full-time reaching out to Muslims in Dearborn, and he agreed to give us a tour—including visiting an old mosque (built in 1937) to observe a Muslim evening prayer time and enjoy the dinner that followed. (You read about John earlier in chapter 24.)

After dinner in the basement of the mosque, I approached some Muslim men—mostly from Yemen—to see where the Lord might take a conversation. The conversation was quite polite until one of the men asked me what I knew about Islam. I shared a few facts with him, and he seemed surprised that I knew as much as I did. An older man stepped in and asked very brusquely,

"Since you know so much about Islam, why haven't you said the shahada?"

(The *shahada* is the short statement of faith one says to convert to Islam: "There is no god but Allah, and Muhammad is His messenger.")

Then this man, Hakeem, began to preach at me, not allowing me to get a word in edgewise. He became louder and louder. It was creating a real scene. A crowd of young and old Muslim men increasingly gathered around Hakeem and me. My Christian friend, John, tried to get me to leave,

"Tim, I think it's time to go."

I don't know why, but I wanted to stay a little longer. I think—at least I hope—that it was not because of a personal desire to "win" this debate. Perhaps it was that I just didn't want to give in to fear and be viewed by the rest of the Muslim men there as some kind of defeated foe for the glory of Islam. And I wanted to reflect Jesus in a tense situation—His calmness and His kindness.

Hakeem's temperature kept rising, and at one point this old man from Yemen said,

"I challenge you to accept Islam and say the shahada!"

I had listened to him for quite a while by then—smiling, being respectful, and listening. I gently, quietly, but firmly responded,

"I challenge you to see that Jesus died for you on the cross and wants you to accept His sacrifice for you."

Hakeem was now hot—visibly angry—and shouted,

"You have insulted my holy Qur'an!"

At that point, even I knew it was time to go!

Hakeem followed me up the stairs, out the door, down the sidewalk, to the parking lot, and all the way to our car—talking all the way. As we walked, he even accused me of working for the FBI or CIA!

He finally declared with real irritation and frustration,

"You will be the first one in line on the Day of Judgment because you knew the truth and rejected it!"

I thanked him for the warning, spoke again of Jesus as the only Savior, and somehow was able to give him a hug (which he surprisingly received!).

———

After this story of my encounter with Hakeem, you might think it odd that we encourage you again (as we did in chapter 23) to visit a mosque if you haven't already done so.

In our years of Muslim ministry, we have been in mosques in Chicago, Illinois; Memphis, Tennessee; Aurora, Colorado; Anaheim, Fremont, and San Diego, California; Seattle, Washington; Atlanta and Clarkston, Georgia; Austin and San Antonio, Texas; Indianapolis and Kokomo, Indiana; Cleveland and Toledo, Ohio; Ann Arbor, Hamtramck, and Dearborn, Michigan; Columbia and St. Louis, Missouri; Green Bay, Wisconsin; Wichita, Kansas; Montgomery, Alabama; Baton Rouge, Louisiana; Cedar Rapids and Des Moines, Iowa; Lancaster, New York; Washington, DC; and many, many more cities.

We have also taken numerous Christians with us to mosques all over the US.

We can truthfully say that our reception by Muslims in almost all of these mosques—whether in a pre-arranged tour with a group or in an unscheduled visit just by us—has been very warm and kind (Hakeem notwithstanding!). Muslims will put their best foot forward when you go to the mosque.

Why?

Number one, they want to *convert* you! They want you to become a Muslim. If they sincerely believe Islam is the way to paradise, many of them compassionately want you to follow that way so you won't experience hell. Additionally, if you convert, it helps them get "points" (credit for good deeds)—and points are a key for *them* to obtain paradise.

Number two, *hospitality* is part of their culture, and they are not only obligated to practice it but are usually very good at it. We have usually been given bottles of water, tea, and even food when we've taken groups to visit mosques.

Finally, Muslims simply want you to see that they are like you—*normal people*. Not terrorists. Not people who want to take over America. Just . . .

people. They want to be good neighbors. They want to be accepted. Don't we want the same?

So please, don't be afraid to visit a mosque.

Why go there? You might build a new relationship, hear what Muslims believe in their own words, and be a light in a place that needs Jesus.

Before you visit a mosque:

- *Kindly and respectfully call for an appointment.* Mention that you and a few friends from your church would like to visit, hear a short presentation on Islam, and observe a prayer time. And say that you want to do this to be good neighbors to them as followers of Jesus.

- *Pray first.* Put on the armor of God for spiritual protection because Islam can be disguised as light (2 Corinthians 11:14). It can have a magnetic pull and be alluring (powerfully and mysteriously attractive and enticing). We believe that many Muslim people are sincere in their faith, but Islam—though it contains bits of truth—is *not* the way to heaven. It is, as Paul warned, *another gospel* (Galatians 1:8) because it is a religion of doing good works vs. receiving God's gift of grace (Ephesians 2:8–9).

- *Go with at least one other follower of Jesus—or preferably with a group.* Jesus sent his followers two-by-two for really important reasons—increased strength, confidence, prayer power, and the later ability to debrief in order to learn and grow. Please don't go alone. And don't go if you or others are new Christians. It is too easy to become confused or deceived by Islam if you are not rooted and grounded in the doctrines of the Bible.

- *Don't try to "win" an argument if one develops* (which it usually won't; the conversation we described above is very rare in our experience).

- *Don't go to a mosque with a big evangelistic agenda.* You don't have to march into a mosque and unload the gospel on any and all Muslims you meet there. Think about it: How would you like it if Muslims were to visit your church and preach at you within its confines? Wouldn't you prefer it if they were to contact you first and then come to simply learn what you believe as Christians? So, practice the golden rule in this regard. (This is not to say that you cannot verbally witness at the mosque, but be sensitive to the Holy

Spirit; sometimes He wants words, but sometimes He just wants you to smile and be kind, attentive, and loving.)

- *Speak to Muslims you meet at the mosque with humility.*
- *Be a good listener and a good learner.*
- *Relax and enjoy the kindness and hospitality* that you will often experience in visiting a mosque.
- *And be the light Jesus (re)made you to be*—with your smile, your demeanor, and your words (again, use a verbal witness if the Holy Spirit leads)!

QUESTIONS TO PONDER

- How would you feel about visiting a mosque with a group of believers?
- How might our verbal witness with Muslims be different at the mosque than at other places?

"Be wise as serpents and innocent as doves."
MATTHEW 10:16

CHAPTER 31

"Tim, I Just Want to Hit You Right Now!"

The Frustration of a Muslim Witness

I n August of 2012, I had just visited a mosque with my outreach partner, Gary, to observe the Friday afternoon time of prayer and listen to the sermon by the imam (the leader and preacher at the mosque). We went with two Palestinian Muslim friends, Amir and Yousef. Afterward, my outreach partner, Gary, and I went to see Amir and Yousef at Amir's place of business—an auto repair place we have visited many, many times over the years—to reach out to Amir with our love and with the good news.

We had quite a conversation that day.

Amir's friend, Yousef, weighed in heavily on the conversation. He wasn't happy. At all. He began to do what some—not most—Muslims do in a spiritual conversation. Like Hakeem in the last chapter, he preached Islam at us nonstop without giving us even a little break to respond.

It didn't work.

I just smiled at him and listened. I really didn't say much. (At times like this, it doesn't usually help to try to speak or counter the person; you just have to let the person get tired and run out of steam!)

At one point, Yousef was frustrated and flustered because he could see that he wasn't being successful in converting me to Islam. He was so exasperated that he finally said to me,

"Tim, I just want to hit you right now."

I had never met Yousef before that day, and so I didn't know what he was capable of. I can tell you for sure that I am not a brave person, but, somehow, I didn't really feel afraid. I just didn't know what to say. What came out of my mouth was,

"Well, alright, if it makes you feel any better, go ahead."

I think Yousef was stunned.
He actually started laughing, and the tension was diffused!
My friend Amir then said something very interesting to Yousef:

"Yousef, Tim knows that he will appear before God
in the Judgment someday.
He will have to answer for what he believes,
and if he told people."

Wow, thank the Lord. I didn't get hit, and . . . *my* Muslim friend helped me *witness* to *his* Muslim friend!
I have seen Yousef a few times since that memorable occasion—in a Muslim barber shop that I frequent and in a Muslim food market that I also visit often. On each occasion he has tried to preach at me and challenged me,

"Haven't you become a Muslim yet?"

One time I countered with a smile and asked,

"Haven't you become a follower of Jesus yet?"

———

We don't have all the answers for how to handle this kind of Muslim person who just preaches at you and doesn't really want to have an actual two-way conversation. We think the main thing is to keep loving them, while not allowing ourselves to be drawn into time- and energy-consuming interactions.

Consider following Jesus's example by answering a question with a question. You will generally never give a satisfactory answer anyway to someone who just wants to wear you down by preaching at you. That kind of person commonly does not want answers. They only want to "win." They want to prove to you that Islam is superior to your faith in Jesus.

Don't get sucked into a competition!

Consider smiling, and kindly answer them with questions such as:

"Have you ever asked Jesus to show you who He is?"
"Have you ever had a dream or a vision of Jesus?"
"Have you read the words of Jesus in the Injil [New Testament]?"
"Are you worried about the Day of Judgment?"
"Do you think Allah will allow you into paradise?"
"Is there anything I can pray for you about?"

If the Muslim person refuses to interact with these types of questions, ask the Lord to show you when to walk away from the conversation—or even the relationship.

You can't save anyone. You aren't the Messiah. There is only one of those. Let *Him* do what He does best.

QUESTIONS TO PONDER

• How have you diffused a potentially escalating situation when talking about religion with a Muslim (or someone else)?

"A gentle answer turns away wrath,
but a harsh word stirs up anger."
PROVERBS 15:1, NIV

"A hot-tempered person stirs up conflict,
but the one who is patient calms a quarrel."
PROVERBS 15:18, NIV

CHAPTER 32

Signs and Wonders Near Ramallah, Israel/Palestine

When Healing Opens the Heart of a Muslim Person

W hen you enter the West Bank areas of Israel, you will see bright red road signs (from the Israeli government) with words like this (quoted verbatim):

> *"This road leads to Area 'A'*
> *under the Palestinian Authority.*
> *The entrance for Israeli*
> *citizens is forbidden,*
> *dangerous to your lives*
> *and is against the Israeli law."*

Here is the specific sign that greeted us as we rode into a Palestinian area near the ancient city of Jericho:

> *"This road leads to*
> *Palestinian village.*

*The entrance for
Israeli citizens
is dangerous."*

These signs never bothered us or created fear in our hearts. Why? We were not Israelis; the Palestinian people (Christian and Muslim) treated us like kings; and, best of all, we knew the Lord Himself was taking us to these areas to be a light for Him.

While traveling in the West Bank of Israel in October of 2012, our friend Ted and I saw those signs when we stayed with Palestinians who were relatives of some of our Muslim friends in Michigan. They lived near the large Palestinian city of Ramallah, burial place of the infamous PLO leader Yasser Arafat.

One day during this visit, we went to see a man I had met in that area on a previous trip. His brother invited us to come to his home and pray for their mother, who had serious issues with her hips and knees. We prayed and asked her to try to walk. Honestly, we are not sure whether she experienced any healing, but another man in the room saw us praying for her and said,

"You must come to my house and pray for my mother."

We went to his home and found another older woman with severe issues in her joints, mostly in her knees. Ted prayed for her and asked her to walk—to carefully test out a possible healing. She brightened up and said,

"I am looking for pain, . . . and I can't find any!"

We learned that this woman—Fatima—had also been suffering from depression. I felt led to ask Ted to share his story of God's healing and deliverance with the seven or eight Muslim people gathered in the room. (Ted had found freedom nine years earlier from drugs, alcohol, anger, violence, and depression when men from our church had laid hands on him and prayed for healing. This had happened within a few minutes during a church service, and it is a story that verifies that nothing is impossible with God.)

After Ted told his story in this Muslim home, I sensed from the Lord that I should share Revelation 3:20 with all the Muslim people in the room: Jesus was knocking on the door of their hearts, and He wanted to come in (I knocked on their wooden coffee table for emphasis). Through an interpreter, I led Fatima in a prayer to invite Jesus into her heart, to ask Him for forgiveness for all her sins, and to be her Master. We think others in the room might have prayed as well (such as her son who had been so adamant that we come to pray for her).

It was so fulfilling to look at the expression on Fatima's face after she had received both physical and spiritual healing. She was beaming! What a difference in her face and spirit from when we had first entered her home!

As we were leaving, her son wanted to give us a gift. He took something from off the wall by the door—a decoration made of stalks of wheat. Ted and I thought this was a fitting symbol of this man's mother, as one of the people in the plentiful harvest Jesus asked his followers to look at (Matthew 9:38; Luke 10:2).

> *"I tell you, open your eyes*
> *and look at the fields!*
> *They are ripe for harvest."*
> JOHN 4:35, NIV

Healing can open the heart of a Muslim. It is a sign and a wonder pointing to Jesus and the kingdom of His Father. Just ask Fatima!

QUESTIONS TO PONDER

- Do any of your Muslim friends or acquaintances need physical healing?
- This situation might come up where you live now, or it could happen on a mission trip. We need to be led by the Holy Spirit. The question is whether you are willing to pray—in person, out loud, and in the name of Jesus—for a Muslim for any kind of healing they might need. How big a step of faith would that be for you?

> *"And he sent them out to*
> *proclaim the kingdom of God*
> *and to heal."*
> LUKE 9:2

> *"Heal the sick in it and say to them,*
> *'The kingdom of God has come near to you.'"*
> LUKE 10:9

CHAPTER 33

† ☾⋆

"Can We Both Be Right about What We Believe?"

In Jerusalem: Speaking the Truth . . . in Love

———

Ted and I were walking toward the Damascus Gate one night in the fall of 2012 during a ministry trip to Israel, Jordan, and Turkey.

The Damascus Gate is a prominent gate leading into the old walled city of Jerusalem. This gate also goes right into the Muslim Quarter, so you can see Muslims buying and selling on the huge area of steps leading down to the gate below. It is a busy, bustling area that is full of life, and Miriam and I love it.

Ted and I had been praying about ministry opportunities earlier that night as we approached the Damascus Gate. When we arrived, we noticed three young Muslim men in their early twenties who were sitting together on one of the steps.

A short greeting turned into a long, long conversation into the night about Jesus, Islam, and Christianity. The conversation was very respectful, and at one point one of the guys asked,

"Can we both be right about what we believe?"

I said,

> *"You asked me an honest question, and I must give you an honest answer.*
> *No, we can't both be right.*
> *Either Jesus died on the cross and rose again from the dead*
> [ironically, very near where we were sitting], *or He didn't.*
> *It can't be both ways."*

———

We think we have learned that we as followers of Jesus need to be *kind*, but also *unashamed*, in our conversations with Muslims.

Muslim people are often quite *bold* about what they believe. They don't apologize for it. Though we are to approach them with humble hearts and words, we shouldn't apologize, either.

We think that Muslims will actually respect us more if we are courteous and kind but also boldly honest and unashamed about our faith. *Grace and truth*. It is an important balance—a balance that Jesus exemplified for us.

ALL TRUTH, LITTLE OR NO GRACE

- *Some Christians let their "evangelism" get in the way of their kindness, friendship, and service to Muslims.*

They see Muslim people as projects or targets. They unnaturally force evangelism and do not serve Muslim people or build sincere relationships with them. Theirs is not a natural outflow of love for Jesus and for lost people. Let us ask God for His heart for Muslims and search for examples in the Gospels where Jesus displayed compassion for people.

ALL GRACE, LITTLE OR NO TRUTH

- *Other Christians let their kindness, friendship, and service to Muslims get in the way of their evangelism.*

They rightfully and humbly love and serve Muslim people, but they never get around to any kind of real or serious faith discussions for fear of losing the friendship. Your primary goal is not to get a Muslim person to like you—it is to see them bow their knee to Jesus as Lord and to follow Him. Let us ask God to assist us in being straightforward in letting Muslims know of our faith in Jesus in the very beginning of the relationship/friendship. (Generally speaking, the longer you wait to share your faith with a Muslim person, the harder it will be. Talk about Jesus early and often, but don't unnaturally force the topic. Ask the Holy Spirit to prompt and guide you.)

GRACE AND TRUTH

- *We need to offer relationship, respect, kindness, service, humility, and love in our outreach to Muslims—all of this balanced by sharing the truth claims of Jesus and inviting Muslim people into faith discussions and commitment to follow Him.*

Let us ask God to make us more like Jesus, the only perfectly balanced evangelist.

QUESTIONS TO PONDER

- Have you seen examples of Christians being too forceful in evangelism (all truth with little or no grace)? What were the results?
- Have you seen examples of Christians not being straightforward enough in evangelism (all grace with little or no truth)? What were the results?
- Which way do you normally tend to lean in your own evangelistic efforts: grace or truth?
- How can you move toward a more Jesus-like balance?
- What biblical stories are there of Jesus balancing grace with truth in his interactions with people?

"The Word became flesh and made his dwelling among us.
We have seen his glory, the glory of the one and only Son,

who came from the Father, full of grace and truth."
JOHN 1:14, NIV

"[Speak] the truth in love."
EPHESIANS 4:15

CHAPTER 34

Do You Look Different to Muslim People?

"Your Smile Entered My Heart . . .
The Grace of God Was Radiating through You"

"Hello Tim,

"I hope that you and Ted have reached the USA in safety and peace. Believe me, when I met you the first time, your smile entered my heart. In this time, it is difficult to find a man with such feeling in his heart, such as yours. I was amazed when you told me your age. You looked so much younger. Then you explained that Jesus is in your heart. He gives you life.

"I was also amazed by your website and to see and feel your love for Muslims. I hope one day to visit you in your country and to learn more and more about your feelings and faith. I am thankful for all the people like you that I meet through David. I hope also that one day you can come to my house and stay with me for a while. Even if you weren't able to be in our home, you are in our hearts.

"Your friend,
Bassam"

What a blessing and encouragement to receive this email in October of 2012.

Bassam is a Palestinian Muslim who lives in the West Bank of Israel/Palestine. Like all Muslims, he has been taught that Jesus did not really die on a cross and that there was no empty tomb.

He is a very kind man who has been befriended by an American Christian man named David. David unquestionably loves Muslims. He starts crying when he speaks of his feelings for them. David showed Bassam the love of Jesus every day while he lived for a few months in Bethlehem, and they have become close friends.

Bassam is seeking spiritually, and he and David have had in-depth spiritual discussions. When my friend Ted and I met Bassam in 2012, he told David in our presence,

"All the people you introduce me to
[the followers of Jesus who visit, as we did]
are like angels."

David replied humbly and sincerely,

"It is because of Jesus."

Ted and I were amazed at how many Muslims commented on that trip that we were *"different"*—and even that we *looked* different. All we could say is that the light of the world (John 8:12) was shining through us, His lesser lights (Matthew 5:13–16)!

Ted and I had the privilege in 2012 of meeting another Palestinian Muslim man, Akram, and of sitting and talking with him and his family in a refugee camp not far from one of the huge walls that the Israeli government has built. He too is a friend of David, who has constantly shown the love of Jesus to Akram in word and in deed.

Akram has had a dream of Jesus, and he doesn't know what to do with it. He faces the common dilemma of a Muslim on his/her journey toward giving their life to Jesus: he wants the new life—the peace, joy, and confidence of salvation that he sees in followers of Jesus—but he fears leaving Islam and the heavy pressure and hardships he would inevitably face. Like so many Muslims, he goes back and forth—struggling to make the final decision to gain Christ, while possibly losing everything else (his wife; children; job; place to live; reputation; and, potentially, his life).

Here is what Akram wrote to me after our time together on the West Bank in Palestine in February, 2020:

"Hi Tim,

"I really felt so blessed for meeting you, Miriam, and the rest of your group the other night. The Grace of God was radiating through you and onto us. Thank you for visiting and praying for us. Thanks so much for lifting my spirit. It was one of the most cherishable hours of our lives.

"My family enjoyed meeting you. Hoping to keep in touch so often. God bless you and all of your loved ones.

"Akram and family"

What will help these Palestinian Muslim men and their families to ultimately cross the line and say "yes" to becoming followers of Jesus?

Maybe meeting more Christians who will *love their Muslim neighbors* and *look different* to them.

NAVIGATING THROUGH THE ISRAELI/PALESTINIAN CONFLICT IN YOUR EVANGELISTIC EFFORTS WITH MUSLIM PEOPLE

One of Akram's real struggles in his life as a Palestinian is his view of the Israeli government. For him, the State of Israel is an enemy, and he feels deep resentment toward the Israelis. He has had armed Israeli soldiers knock on his door in the middle of the night, get all the children out of bed, and then harass the whole family at gunpoint. One of his daughters shakes whenever she sees Israeli soldiers. This is just one of his many, many grievances.

We mention this because the complex issue of the Israeli/Palestinian conflict will probably come up in your discussions with Muslim people at some point. They will want to know your position but will likely assume that you stand unreservedly for Israel because many—if not most—Western Christians do (this position is sometimes called Zionism). If you support Israel in this way and mention it, this can create a thick and high wall between you and your Muslim neighbor and impair further witness.

Here is our recommendation regarding how to answer the question Muslim people might bring up to you regarding your position on the Israeli/ Palestinian conflict:

> *"We are so sorry for all the suffering*
> *of the Palestinian people*
> *and we pray for them."*

Please notice that we took no position about Israel at all in our answer, either positive or negative. We didn't even mention Israel. We simply commented ever so briefly on the suffering of the Palestinian people. This answer has always satisfied our Muslim friends and acquaintances. They often respond—with some degree of surprise—by expressing a thankful, "God bless you." And the matter is usually closed.

(In Appendix 7, we list books you might read that speak to the issues of the Israeli/Palestinian conflict and the ever-present and intensely heated debate: "Whose land is it?" These books do not come from a Zionistic position but they are written by Christians. We list them because we believe it is good to be aware of another viewpoint and because there are many Arab Christians in the Middle East whom we know who long for Western Christians to learn about the injustice and pain they routinely experience.)

———

QUESTIONS TO PONDER

- Does your church take a position on the Israeli/Palestinian conflict? Have you heard your pastor or people in your church do so?
- If the Israeli/Palestinian conflict is brought up by your Muslim friend, will you be able to put your politics and church position aside during the conversation (for the sake of the gospel) and just listen?
- Will you be able to express compassion for the suffering of Palestinian

people in the conversation, regardless of your political or biblical opinions about the conflict?

• What can make us "look different" to Muslim people and pique their interest in the treasure—Jesus—that is in us as "clay jars"?

"You are the light of the world . . .
let your light shine before others,
so that they may see your good works
and give glory to your Father who is in heaven."
MATTHEW 5:13–16

"We now have this light shining in our hearts,
but we ourselves are like fragile clay jars containing this great treasure.
This makes it clear that our great power is from God, not from ourselves."
2 CORINTHIANS 4:7, NLT

CHAPTER 35

† ☪

"I Love You Too Much . . .
to Be Silent"

"Friendship Evangelism"
Should Mean Friendship *and* Evangelism

———

Some years ago we read about a Christian woman, Ruth, in a Middle East country who was meeting for coffee with several Muslim women friends as part of her outreach to them. Suddenly, a Muslim man—a relative of one of the women—burst angrily into the room of that house and began to preach Islam at Ruth as she sat there.

It was a very forceful, unfriendly, one-directional confrontation. This man told her in a very intimidating way that her doom in hell was certain unless she repented and took Islam for her religion. He also physically threatened her and her family.

We found her response to this harsh man to be very interesting—Spirit-led and out-of-the-box. Though she was completely terrified, after a few moments of anxious thought and prayer she simply replied to him with real honesty and sincerity,

"Hamza, thank you for telling me these things.

Your message to me must be because you care about me
and you don't want me to go to hell."

The Holy Spirit's strategic response had an immediate impact. Hamza was dumbstruck! His mouth was shut. He actually couldn't respond.

Ruth didn't back down from the proclamation of the gospel. She continued to reach out to Hamza's female relatives and to other Muslim women after that event. She did not let his intimidation stop her. Why? *She loved these Muslim women friends too much to be silent.*

(Later, amazingly, Hamza accepted a Bible from this woman as a gift, and the next time she saw him he was a different person; she believes he may now be a "secret believer"!)

"I love you too much . . . to be silent."

Those were the words I shared with a Palestinian Muslim friend in September of 2012. My friend Gary and I have reached out to him for several years. This Muslim man is one of the kindest, gentlest, most humble people I have ever met (including Christians). He loves God so much—as he understands Him, that is. We have had very warm faith conversations.

As I shared the gospel message of salvation by faith alone in Jesus's sacrificial death alone vs. a life of trying to do good works to earn salvation, my Muslim friend listened intently.

I finally told him,

"Since I believe God has provided only one bridge to heaven
through the death of Jesus, I have to tell you about it.
You are my friend and
I love you too much . . . to be silent."

Has he made the decision yet to follow Jesus? No, but my friend knows that *I love him* enough to share with him what I believe as it relates to where he will spend eternity. And I think he appreciates that. A lot.

Please hear the words of a friend of ours who has reached out to Muslim people for many years but is now seeking for the balance of Jesus in both friendship *and* evangelism:

"I have long embraced and believed in 'friendship evangelism.'
For two decades, I have taught and practiced it.
But now I see that my plan was incomplete.
I had no real or specific plan for sharing the cross
and the gospel with my Muslim friends.
Instead, I built relationships, dropped hints about Jesus,
and waited for them to ask me to spell out the gospel.
Because I had no plan to get to the gospel,
that's usually where I ended up—not getting to the gospel.
This is where God is challenging me, so now I am adding
a key additional step to my evangelistic approach to Muslim people:
have a plan from the outset to get to the gospel . . . and get to the gospel!"

Friendship evangelism should mean friendship *and* evangelism.
Let us *love our Muslim neighbor* too much . . . to be silent.

QUESTIONS TO PONDER

- From the first story above, how do you think you might have responded to Hamza in that tense situation? What is the best way to prepare for that kind of possible encounter?
- From the second story above, how effectively do you incorporate evangelism into your friendship with people who don't yet know Jesus? Do you have a mindset from the outset to get to the gospel with Muslim people? How can we resist the temptation to be silent about our faith?

"And the Lord said to Paul one night in a vision,
'Do not be afraid, but go on speaking and do not be silent,
for I am with you.'"
ACTS 18:9–10

"What is the greatest crime in the desert?"

Finding water . . . and keeping silent."
ARAB PROVERB

CHAPTER 36

✝ ☪

"You Are Sadder over a Lost Game than a Lost Soul!"

What Causes *You* to Be Sad?

———

Soccer—*futbol*—is without question the most popular spectator sport in the world.

It is always a fascinating experience to watch fans during the World Soccer Cup every four years—especially when their team wins. But when they lose, . . . oh, the sadness!

Real sadness and grief over the loss of a soccer match. Regardless of the country, these fans are:

disheartened
depressed
dismayed
dejected.

But they aren't the only ones. I have a little story about me.

On a cold winter afternoon in January of 2013, I was on my knees praying. I was really praying.

What about? Something deep? Something of eternal significance?

No, I'm embarrassed to say that it was about . . . a football game. An American NFL football game.

For years, when my favorite football team (at that time the Denver Broncos) would lose, I would really be down. Even, I confess, a little depressed. For days.

"Pitiful!" you exclaim. Yes, you're right.

After rooting for the Broncos for many years, I was blessed to speak at four or five chapel services for the Atlanta Falcons professional football team when they traveled to Michigan to play the Detroit Lions. Through conducting those chapels, our sons and I met many players and coaches, and I personally got really attached to them, especially coach Dan Reeves. I became an extremely devoted Falcons fan after having been a Broncos fan for so many years. (It didn't hurt that the Falcons always gave us free game tickets when I spoke at the chapels and often let our sons and me eat with the team the night before the games.)

On the day of my questionable spirituality (praying over the outcome of a football game), the Falcons were attempting to win a game through a last-second field goal. I felt close to those guys from all the chapels, and my response was just a reflex: I got on my knees . . . and prayed!

When I told a friend—a friend who has been recruiting global workers to the Muslim fields for many years—about my prayer, he rebuked me—in Jesus's name!

Why the strong reaction to my prayer?

He shared that, many years earlier, the Lord had lovingly reproved him when he was lamenting after his favorite pro football team had lost a game. In his despondency, he sensed the Lord saying to him,

"You are sadder over a lost game than a lost soul!"

He vowed that he would never again allow himself to be sad for more than five minutes after a loss by his favorite football team. He vowed to be moved, instead, by lost souls.

His words really hit home for me.

QUESTIONS TO PONDER

- "How much do we—and how much do you—*really care* about lost people"?

Like all of you, we have heard many sermons on the subject of the first Palm Sunday. It seems as though nearly all of them focus on the Triumphal Entry of King Jesus that day—the big parade and all the cheering for the long-awaited Messiah. But we don't remember anyone ever preaching on the "Tearful Entry" of King Jesus. Maybe everyone just wants to focus on the joyful, happy feelings of Palm Sunday, but Luke's Gospel says that Jesus was terribly grieved that day:

> *"And when he drew near and saw the city (Jerusalem),*
> *he wept over it."*
> LUKE 19:41

What a contrast on that first Palm Sunday: the people cheered, but Jesus wept.

Why?

First of all, it is important to see a little of the depth of Jesus's sadness. The word Luke used for "weep" (*klaio* in Greek) in Luke 19:41 means:

- to sob, weep aloud, express uncontainable, audible grief (*Strong's Concordance*)
- not merely that tears flow down the face, but suggestive rather of a heaving of the chest—the sob and the cry of a soul in agony (https://www.studylight.org/commentary/luke/19-41.html).

As many commentators rightly observe, Jesus saw what others could not see: the tragic siege and destruction of Jerusalem forty years in the future by the Roman armies under Titus. But we think there is so much more here! We believe that Jesus was not just seeing the temporary (though horrible) suffering that would happen in 70 A.D. We believe He was seeing eternal suffering.

May we be sad and weep with the Son of God—the perfect image of the Father—concerning the lostness of people. May we give our lives to reach them.

We can't all go to the Middle East or other parts of the Muslim world. We're not all called to do that. Not at all.

But we can all pray for Jesus's heart for lost people and the courage to reach out to them where we live in ways that are unique to our individual personalities and spiritual giftings.

In a worship song that we love—appropriately titled, "Hosanna"—there is a line that must not be sung glibly:

"Break my heart for what breaks Yours."

Have you ever prayed or sung those words?

If so, watch out. Your prayer just might be answered in a way in which your heart is broken—and your whole world changed.

Please let us ask you a few more questions to ponder—questions we are also asking ourselves:

- Are you in touch with the heart of our Father in heaven and of Jesus, His Son, when it comes to lost people?
- Are you in tune with what the Father and the Son see ahead regarding the horrible future for people who willfully reject the sacrifice of Jesus on the cross?
- When was the last time—if ever—that you were so saddened by the future of lost people that you wept aloud as Jesus did on that first Palm Sunday?
- When did you last find yourself in sorrow and grief like this for those who do not yet know Jesus, including Muslim people?

"With Christ as my witness, I speak with utter truthfulness.
My conscience and the Holy Spirit confirm it.
My heart is filled with bitter sorrow and unending grief
for my people, my Jewish brothers and sisters.
I would be willing to be forever cursed—
cut off from Christ—if that would save them."
ROMANS 9:1–3, NLT

May we never hear our Father in heaven say,
"You are sadder over
a lost _____ (you fill in the blank)
than a lost soul."

CHAPTER 37

✝ ☾

Many Muslims Are Secretly Seeking

"Excuse Me, Sir, . . .
Could I Have Five Minutes of Your Time?"

———

hen coming back from the Middle East in March of 2013, I was wearing a T-shirt that a young Christian boy from Mexico had made for me as a gift. This special young man and his family were part of the international English-speaking church we worked with for years in the Middle East. The words on the shirt are based on something he had heard me preach there—the delighted (paraphrased) statement of God the Father about His Son, Jesus, at His baptism (words all sons and daughters need to hear from their fathers):

"I love you.
I'm proud of you.
You're Mine."

On the back of the shirt were the words to John 3:16. I don't normally put on witness wear like this in the Middle East. We prefer much more discretion! But this was our last day with this family before we flew home, and I wanted to honor this young man by wearing it with him as his family took us to a favorite mouthwatering restaurant and then on to the airport. Besides this, I just felt led of the Lord to keep the shirt on instead of changing.

I got a lot of looks wearing that T-shirt—both in the airport and on the plane! One Muslim man with a long beard stopped me on the plane that night while I was returning to my seat from the restroom. He said,

"Excuse me, sir. I saw your shirt.
Could I have five minutes of your time?"

I first went back to my seat and asked MJ to pray. I had no idea what this man was going to say to me. Was he deeply offended by my shirt as a devout fundamentalist Muslim (long beards are often worn by such men, and he was wearing one)? Was he some kind of religious leader who was going to reprimand me for wearing these words on my clothing in his land before we left for another country? My imagination was running wild. As it turned out, this courteous and reserved man, Bilal, shared his interest in learning more about following Jesus!

He had been reading various Christian books and wanted to ask me some questions. We had a meaningful conversation, shared email addresses, and I gave him a book to read that I had brought on the trip: Tim Keller's classic *The Prodigal God.* Believe it or not, Bilal had read another of Keller's books (and could name it).

———

We met a man from a Muslim background who had lived most of his life in Baghdad, Iraq. Sami and his family were now refugees in another Middle Eastern country awaiting approval to immigrate to Canada. He had become a follower of Jesus, and his face was filled with joy. We excitedly asked about his spiritual journey. Sami shared his story, and we were struck by all of it, but one point stood out: his secret search for Jesus. He had heard his spiritual leader in the mosque—an imam in Baghdad—speak favorably about Isa (the name for Jesus in the Qur'an). He then read about Jesus in the Qur'an and was intrigued. He wanted more. He was thirsty. As a further step, he was able to obtain a New Testament and secretly read it to learn as much as he could about this Messiah. Sami chose to become a follower of the One and

Only. We wish you could have witnessed the love for Jesus that filled his soul with such childlike wonder it was hard for him to contain it!

———

A number of Muslim people around the world—like Bilal and Sami—are searching for more than what they currently possess spiritually. Most of them are likely doing so secretly. Asking questions. Struggling with doubts. Ask God to bring these seekers across your path as divine appointments—as with Bilal on the plane. Ask Him to connect you with people who are open to the gospel. Then be ready to listen, love, and . . . share His truth.

———

QUESTIONS TO PONDER

- Have you met a Muslim who expressed doubts about their faith? How did you respond?
- Do you think you listened well to that person—compassionately and patiently—without trying to immediately give them pat Christian answers or an overwhelming dose of biblical truth all at once?
- Where would you point a Muslim secret seeker (like the Jewish men Nicodemus and Joseph of Arimathea in the Gospel of John)? Which Bible verses, books, websites, or phone apps would you recommend to them? (After you answer this question, please see our recommendations for resources in Appendix 7.)

"Now there was a man of the Pharisees named Nicodemus, a ruler of the Jews. This man came to Jesus by night."
JOHN 3:1–2

"After these things Joseph of Arimathea, who was a disciple of Jesus, but secretly for fear of the Jews, asked Pilate that he might take away the body of Jesus, and Pilate gave him permission. So he came and took away his body. Nicodemus also, who earlier had come to Jesus by night, came bringing a mixture of myrrh and aloes, about seventy-five pounds in weight."
JOHN 19:38–39

CHAPTER 38

✝ ☪

When a Terrorist Attack Happens, How Do You Respond to the News?

What Is a Jesus-Like Response?

———

ife in this world can be so hard—so tragic.

There are natural disasters and disasters caused by humans as well.

In 2013 an English soldier was savagely murdered by Muslim extremists in London. The world was shocked and angry. Talk about horrific. How could this happen in broad daylight . . . on a city street . . . in a Western city? After all, this was not in Iraq or Iran or Afghanistan or Somalia. This atrocity happened after the terrible bombings by Muslim extremists in Boston a short time earlier. Both of these events stunned us all.

How are we to respond as Jesus-followers to terrorist attacks by jihadists?

Some time ago we heard a very godly man teaching on reaching out to Muslims with the gospel. A Christian woman in that workshop angrily related a story of a time when she had been in the home of American Muslims during the first Gulf War. The TV was on in that home, and a reporter was telling how many Americans had died that day in the fighting. The woman in the workshop shared with us that she was shocked and outraged when members of this Muslim family openly celebrated when they heard how many Americans had been killed. After the Christian woman told that story in the workshop, she asked the speaker—with obvious anger—what he thought about "those people." She was literally demanding an answer. His response was unforgettable to us. He looked down, got emotional, and softly said,

"It just goes to show how much they need Jesus."

———

QUESTIONS TO PONDER:
Why Do Muslims Hate Us, . . . or
Are There Better Questions to Ask?

In April of 2013, the terrorist bombings at the Boston Marathon by two young Chechen Muslim extremists made big news all over the world. We are sure that many of you asked yourselves this question then and after subsequent terrorist attacks:

"Why do Muslims hate us?"

We certainly don't have an insight into the psyche of radicals, although we know that in the minds of such people their hatred is justified because of perceived injustices (invasion and occupation of their lands), the undeniable immorality coming from the West that covers the globe (portrayed openly in Hollywood movies and television), and many other things. When you add this to the older complaints of the exploitation of colonialism and the atrocities of the Crusades and then mix in the teachings of jihadist clerics, you see a perfect recipe for the development of a terrorist mindset.

We think it is important for you to know that, unlike these two brothers who committed this atrocity, the vast majority of Muslims we know *don't* hate America; more specifically, they do not hate Americans as people. You might be surprised to hear that what they do hate is terrorism! Events like the bombing in Boston are very painful to them on two fronts:

1. like us, they grieve the loss of innocent human lives;
2. unlike us, they know they will be lumped together with every ter-

rorist and every act of terrorism, with the resulting fallout of prejudice or possible mistreatment directed against them.

While we can all speculate about why Muslim extremists hate us, maybe it is time—or past time—to ask a better and more biblical question:

"Why don't we—as Christians—love Muslims more?"

And maybe we need to ask *this* question about the Boston bombers who came to the US as refugees from Chechnya:

"Were there any Christians who reached out in genuine,
Jesus-like kindness to Tamerlan Tsarnaev and his brother?"

Tamerlan Tsarnaev famously said in 2010:

"I don't have a single American friend.
I don't understand them."

Isn't that tragic? How many other Muslim refugees in our country feel the same way?

Brother Andrew, famous for his book *God's Smuggler* about his work smuggling Bibles into the former Soviet Union, is one of our heroes. After his ministry shifted to the Muslim world, he wrote these words:

"What is your first thought when someone offends you?
Anger? Indignation?

"Perhaps, if we're honest, our hearts even want to see
some kind of retaliation or revenge.

"But you know, Jesus is clear: revenge is not the answer. Love is.
Especially when it comes to the Muslim world.

"That's why, instead of retaliating when we read of a bomb attack . . .
I suggest our response should be repentance!
Repentance that we have not prayed, have not cared,

have not gone to the Muslim world to proclaim
the true life and freedom we have in Jesus!

"Let's keep asking God to truly change hearts—
that we might love, serve, and pray more fervently . . .
for the advancement of His Kingdom and the glory of His name
in the Muslim world, and beyond!"

Perhaps we could allow Brother Andrew's words to lead us in taking some time to pray every time we learn of a terrorist act by radical Muslims—for the victims, of course, but also for the perpetrators and those Muslims who wrongly support them by celebrating their terrible deeds.

The kind teacher we heard in the workshop that day wants us to remember that each terrorist attack, "just goes to show how much they need Jesus."

"I tell you, love your enemies and pray for those who persecute you,
that you may be children of your Father in heaven.
He causes his sun to rise on the evil and the good,
and sends rain on the righteous and the unrighteous."
MATTHEW 5:44–45, NIV

† ☾

CHAPTER 39

"They Wanted to 'Arrested' Me... for Fasting"

Look for Opportunities—Not Excuses—to Be a Witness

———

U ncle Bud was quite a witness for Jesus. He loved to get into spiritual conversations with people and see if they might want to receive Jesus and commit their lives to following him. He shared with us his perspective that, when it comes to "witnessing," many Christians look for *excuses*, not *opportunities*.

———

We were on our way to have frozen yogurt with coworkers in Knoxville, Tennessee, in June of 2014 when God gave us an opportunity to be His witnesses. It turned out to be a humorous—and also a kind of a sad—experience with two young Muslim international students.

God has given me a kind of radar to spot Muslims in crowds. Since he has put them on my heart so much, I often run toward the opportunity to meet them, excitedly seeing whether I can start a conversation with them and then observing what God will do (it is such a joy to work together with Him!).

As we approached the yogurt place that night, I spotted two young men

I assumed must be Arab Muslims. After a few years of doing our ministry, I could tell that they most likely were from Saudi Arabia or Yemen.

Miriam and the others had gone into the yogurt place for dessert, but I chose to follow these young men for a minute as I contemplated yelling out to them. I finally did just that:

"Salaam alaykum!"
(*"Peace be upon you!"* in Arabic).

These young Saudi men turned around in pleasant surprise to hear their language—and their common greeting. (It means the world to Muslims for you to greet them in this way. It takes so little effort to learn these two words, and it often creates openings for the gospel. By the way, proper pronunciation of the words is not nearly as important as your sincere effort to say them!)

I invited them to join us for yogurt, and Miriam and I engaged in a pleasant conversation with them—including some talk about faith matters—for about forty minutes. One of the young men, Saad, told us how strange it had been for him to come to the States. He told us of an experience he'd had in Texas the previous year when he was new to the US. He said in his broken English,

"They wanted to 'arrested' me for fasting!"

I responded incredulously,

"What?!
Was it during Ramadan
[the traditional time of fasting]?

Miriam was way ahead of me in understanding what Saad was trying to say. With a little more time and effort from Miriam and Saad, I finally grasped his intended meaning. The police in Texas had wanted to arrest him because he was *speeding*—a word he had yet to learn. When Miriam inquired as to how fast he was "fasting," he replied, "120 miles per hour." Saad told us that no one in Saudi Arabia had explained that there were speed limits on highways in America! It was an endearing and humorous conversation with these two Arab Muslim young men.

The other young Saudi man, Fares, sent this memorable text to me later that evening in his broken English:

"Hello Tim! This is Fares.

"Sorry if did bother you this evening. Just wanna say that it was really an honor for me to meet a man like you who is trying to endure (understand) the difficulties that we encounter throughout this life (as people from another country).

"To be honest with you, I have lived in this country for 2 years and I have never had this kind of spirituals [spiritual conversations] *with the American.*

"You did not treat me as an alien like most people do and I was amazed by that!

"Eventually, I would like to thank you for that frozen yoghurt, and I hope to meet you guys again one day."

———————

I said earlier that our experience that night in Knoxville with these two young Saudi men was both humorous—and sad. Why? In two years, not one American Christian had taken the time or the effort to speak to Fares about Jesus. Not one!

Many Muslim international students come to our country *expecting* Christians to talk about faith matters with them. Like Fares, they are surprised when we don't.

How sad also that Fares felt as though most people in the US had treated him like "an alien." Like so many other Muslim international students, he felt marginalized and rejected, even by Christians.

There is nothing exceptional about Miriam and me except the Jesus inside us. Just like most of you, we are unlikely candidates for Muslim ministry. The question for all of us is whether we want to "make the most of every opportunity" to extend kindness to our Muslim neighbors. Are we willing to make that personal contact that Muslim people so often need in order to find Jesus?

We pray that you, too, will look for opportunities, not excuses, when it comes to being witnesses for Jesus to people like Saad and like Fares.

With kind young men like them, it really is not difficult to *love your Muslim neighbor.*

A WORD OF WARNING TO CHRISTIAN WOMEN
ABOUT DATING AND MARRYING MUSLIM MEN

(Note: In Islam, it is permissible for a Muslim man to marry a Christian woman, but not for a Muslim woman to marry a Christian man. That is why our warning is to Christian women here.)

We hope it is abundantly clear by now how much we love Muslim people! But at the same time we feel it is important for us to warn Christian women about Muslim men who come to the US, mostly as international students. We have seen Christian women on university campuses swept off their feet by these intriguing, handsome Muslim men. They often have a charming mystique about them and treat Christian women so well in the dating stage (better than some Christian men).

But please, ladies, you have no idea what kind of extremely painful difficulties you will most likely encounter if you date and then marry a Muslim man, especially if he moves you back to his home country. This is because of the way of life required by Islam.

What if your Muslim husband pressures or even requires you to become a Muslim after you marry? If he lets you remain a Christian, how will you raise your children? In which faith? Do you know what the Qur'an says about a husband striking his wife? Do you know what it says about divorce? (Please see this website to get an accurate picture/warning of what marriage to a Muslim man might entail: *Loving A Muslim—A Support Group for Christian Women Dating or Married to Muslims* http://www.domini.org/lam/home.html.)

In Christian witness to Muslims, we strongly recommend male to male and female to female interaction, unless it is in a group. This will prevent the possibility of extremely painful situations down the road, should an unwise marriage (a Christian woman to a Muslim man) take place.

Again, we have a deep and profound love for Muslim people, but please heed our advice about the dangers of marriage within Islam and the proven wisdom of Scripture in this matter.

QUESTIONS TO PONDER

- Why do you think Muslim international students who come to our country expect Christians to talk to them about faith matters?
- What do you think would make a Muslim international student feel loved while in our country?

"Be wise in the way you act toward outsiders;
make the most of every opportunity."
COLOSSIANS 4:5, NIV

"Do not be bound together with unbelievers."
2 CORINTHIANS 6:14, NASB

"Can two people walk together without agreeing on the direction?"
AMOS 3:3, NLT

CHAPTER 40

✝ ☪

"Can You Believe It? God Loves the World!"

How One Iraqi Muslim Friend Grew to Love John 3:16— and Died with It on His Lips

I n December of 2014, a close friend of ours died—a former Muslim. Ali was an Iraqi from a Shia Muslim background. We continue to miss him, but we believe he is enjoying being with Jesus now.

We can still hear his voice joyfully quoting John 3:16. When he first heard it, he asked with childlike wonder,

> *"Tim, can you believe it?*
> *God loves the world!"*

Like us, you might take that glorious truth for granted, but Ali didn't. He was somehow under the impression that the Bible says that God loves only Christians and Jews—not Arabs, and certainly not Muslims. To him this was a new and delightful revelation. He called the verse *"unbelievable."*

But let us back up and share how God brought Ali into our lives.

Our outreach partner, Gary, met Ali when he was working at the meat and seafood counter in a local grocery store. Gary always has something about Jesus in his cargo pants' pockets or in his backpack to give away to seekers. It doesn't matter what language the person speaks, Gary seems to have a DVD, a tract, or a New Testament for anyone in just about any language! The day they met, Ali went to that store to purchase some fish—but got something infinitely better. You see, Gary is a "fisher of men," and he gave Ali a gospel tract in Arabic. A short time later Gary introduced me to Ali, and, slowly, an enjoyable friendship began to form among the three of us.

Gary, Miriam, and I—and others in a small group—reached out to Ali for over four years. For the first year or so of our relationship, whenever Gary and I spoke about Jesus, Ali would change the subject. It was so frustrating! Once it seemed as though he were turning a corner; he seemed very close to becoming a follower of Jesus. His back had been miraculously healed after a young lady in our small group had prayed for him following a serious injury that had left him bedridden, and his heart was touched. But then he would vacillate. A few months later, Ali proclaimed,

"I am a Christian and a Muslim."

He was betwixt and between—"in an intermediate, indecisive, or middle position."

As we said in chapter 9, such can be the nature of evangelism with Muslims! But we never gave up on Ali.

"So let's not get tired of doing what is good.
At just the right time we will reap
a harvest of blessing if we don't give up."
GALATIANS 6:9, NLT

Though often frustrated, Gary and I just kept on loving Ali and meeting with him every Thursday. Miriam went to his home and spent time with his wife and daughters, enjoying their hospitality. She also blessed them by sending cards and making food for them.

We all concentrated on meeting his needs—taking him to his primary doctor, the eye doctor, the pharmacy, grocery stores, the library, and the Iraqi consulate.

We took him out to eat. We took walks. Ali became a treasured friend.

He turned a corner spiritually when Gary and I invited him to watch some of the *Al Massira* DVDs with us in the fall of 2014. These exceptionally well done biblical messages in Arabic, filmed in the Middle East and North Africa, touched Ali's heart profoundly. I remember that, when we were sitting in a restaurant watching them on Gary's laptop, Ali exclaimed,

"Though I am in pain, they have all my attention."

We were to learn more about that pain later on.

As we mentioned before, Ali grew to love and even to memorize John 3:16—going so far as to leave it on my cell phone as a message when he could not reach me. (I have kept some of his messages on my phone and play them for churches when we speak on Sundays or do our weekend seminars; it is still so moving to hear his voice quoting that verse.)

To watch Ali's heart being opened by God to the gospel was a marvelous thing. It was like watching a flower open. I told Miriam and Gary,

"I feel like we are watching a person slowly being born again."

In November of 2014 Ali informed us that he had to go back to Iraq for something related to a pension from his time of teaching in a university there. We begged him not to go. By that time his kidneys were extremely damaged, but he refused to go on dialysis, though he was often in pain and his doctor (and we) strongly encouraged him not to do it. I told him firmly that I would not take him to the airport. I would not contribute to his death. We pled with him because we feared he would die in Iraq, and he did . . . one month later.

The last day I saw Ali—the day I took him to the airport to go to Iraq (the Lord told me to do it and to put him in His hands)—I quoted this Scripture to him at his home before we left,

"If you declare with your mouth, 'Jesus is Lord,'
And believe in your heart that God raised him from the dead,
you will be saved."
Romans 10:9, NIV

He said with a quiet but resolute voice,

"I believe."

When you pour your life into Muslim people, you long to hear a statement of faith like that, because for most of us in this ministry this doesn't happen every day.

That was one of the happiest days of my life.

But very soon—because of his impending death—the day became bittersweet. This was to be the last day I would ever see Ali on this earth.

I was blessed to speak with him two or three times before he died. He would call from his hospital bed in Iraq.

Each time he called, Ali would begin by saying the same thing. Can you guess what it was? If you guessed Jesus's words in John 3:16, you guessed correctly. He would be in the hospital in Iraq, getting blood transfusions and quoting that beautiful verse to me.

Gary and I were blessed to speak on the phone with Ali just two days before he died. It was a Thursday, our habitual outreach day together. We were visiting Ali's wife and children when he called from the hospital in Iraq. Ali's health was declining, but he was determined to get back to the States if they could get him well enough to travel on Sunday—just three days later. He would have a layover in another Middle Eastern country on the way home.

I felt I had the perfect idea. I knew people in that country, a country that offered excellent medical care. I contacted my friends there, and we set up a plan for them to pick up Ali at their airport and get him into a quality hospital to provide better treatment. It seemed as though this was all from the Lord, and I was excited about how He was putting everything together.

But Ali never made it.

He was to fly to that country on Sunday, but he died on Saturday.

(We believe that Ali ultimately must have bled to death. We found out from his family in Iraq that he had been taking large dosages of pain killers for his kidneys for quite some time, and he must have developed ulcers and then suffered a considerable amount of internal bleeding. Finally, after numerous blood transfusions, they couldn't save him.)

When Ali died, I was devastated . . . and very, very angry at God.

I'd had plans for Ali. I believed he was to be the cornerstone of a new Arabic speaking church in our area—the first of other Muslim people who would through his inspiration eventually count the cost and make the choice to follow Jesus. I prayed with pain and exasperation,

"God, how could You do this?
He only needed to live another day and

he would have gotten the medical care he needed.
Why, God, why?

"We poured four years of our lives into this man, and finally . . . finally,
he embraces You and Your Son, Jesus, and You let him die?

"Why, God, why?
What are You thinking?
This is not a good plan."

In his wisdom and sovereignty, though, God had other plans. Better plans than mine—plans with eternal purposes. He is, after all, God, and we are not. And Jesus should be the only cornerstone of any church (Acts 4:10–12; Ephesians 2:19–20; 1 Peter 2:7).

God was so gracious to me, inviting me to keep talking with Him about my anger and to work through it with Him. Because of His gracious love for me, I was able to be brutally honest with Him and share my displeasure, disappointment, and deep sadness— and then, after a time, to let it all go. To surrender. To let God be God.

"He is the Rock, his works are perfect, and all his ways are just.
A faithful God who does no wrong, upright and just is he."
Deuteronomy 32:4, NIV

Slowly but surely, this brought the healing I needed to move forward, still grieving, but not as one with no hope (1 Thessalonians 4:13).

Gary and I began to concentrate on serving Ali's widow, Farida, and their children—mowing their grass, cleaning out their gutters, scooping their snow, helping with important paperwork.

"Pure and genuine religion in the sight of God the Father means
caring for orphans and widows in their distress."
James 1:27, NLT

Incredibly, Farida began more and more to open up to Gary and me. She began to refer to us as her "brothers." We think a lot of that was because we simply served Farida—with no strings attached.

"So we cared for you. Because we loved you so much,
we were delighted to share with you
not only the gospel of God but our lives as well."
1 THESSALONIANS 2:8, NIV

At the invitation of another couple, Jim and Paula, Farida actually began to attend Bible studies with Miriam, me, and others. These times of oral Bible storytelling and discussion were in English but were interpreted in Arabic by a Lebanese brother in Christ.

Before Ali's death, Farida had shown no interest in Jesus. Zero. Sometimes we had to leave their house because she didn't like us talking about Jesus. We think she is the one who had put our gospel tracts out in their garage!

But after Ali died, Farida's heart began to open little by little. Step by step.

God continues to use the death of her husband to move in Farida's heart. We wish you could hear her repeat the Bible stories and ask probing questions as we study the Bible together. She remains a Muslim, but she has come so far in her understanding and appreciation of Jesus in her journey toward the kingdom of God.

QUESTIONS TO PONDER

- What lessons can you glean from this story about reaching out and connecting with Muslim people through friendship and service evangelism?
- Why do you think God would take a BMB home so soon after he had entered the kingdom of God?
- How do you think you would react if you had poured your life into a Muslim friend, they had chosen to follow Jesus, . . . and then shortly after that had died?

"I tell you the truth, unless a kernel of wheat
is planted in the soil and dies, it remains alone.
But its death will produce many new kernels—
a plentiful harvest of new lives."
JOHN 12:24, NLT

CHAPTER 41

† ☾

"If You Go to Iraq, You Will Never See Your Grandchildren Again"

Three Voices Telling Me Not to Go

I felt sick. I was so afraid I thought I might vomit.

It was March 24, 2015, in a city in the Middle East, and I was to fly to Iraq very early the next morning.

It was a night of paralyzing fear.

The fear had started long before that horrible night. For many years I had experienced a nagging fear of being kidnapped by jihadists, held hostage, and ultimately . . . *beheaded.*

When I decided to go on this trip to Iraq, I had three strong and distinct voices tell me not to go.

VOICE #1 IN ARIZONA:

"If you go to Iraq, you will never see your grandchildren again."

A month after Ali died in Iraq, we were with our middle son and his family in Colorado. During a time of worship in a church service with them, I had a sudden desire to go to Iraq and visit Ali's family. I prayed during the praise songs:

"Lord, I want to go to Iraq.
I want to go tell them that I am so sorry for their loss.
And I want to tell them about Jesus."

I began to talk to Miriam about this idea. She is a fabulous wife who supports me in some pretty unusual leadings of the Lord, and she did not discourage me from making this trip, either. Her response was just like always—to simply "trust and obey," as in the original confirmation of our calling.

The next week we were visiting our oldest son and his family in Arizona when I heard the first voice telling me not to go to Iraq. It was not audible, but it was very, very real:

"If you go to Iraq, you will never see your grandchildren again."

The strange thing was that this "voice" was not evil sounding or scary at all. It was just very matter of fact. It was more like if you go, then this will happen.

I knew Miriam would be okay if something bad were to happen to me. She is so emotionally tough, but I felt profound sadness that our sons might not have me for much longer. Since I had grown up without a dad, this was very painful to me. I was also grieved that our grandkids might grow up without me.

Beyond the sadness and grief, I was totally bewildered. I just didn't know what to do with what I had heard. Was this God—telling me to count the cost? Was it the devil—trying to keep me from going to Iraq? I finally told Miriam about the voice, and we prayed. At first, we didn't know the source. We couldn't discern it. But after a little time we came to believe that it was a scare tactic from the evil one, who can "roar" in various ways—sometimes loudly and sometimes matter-of-factly. The result is the same: a fear that can paralyze the prey.

> *"Stay alert! Watch out for your great enemy, the devil.*
> *He prowls around like a roaring lion, looking for someone to devour."*
> 1 PETER 5:8, NLT

We got past the first "voice" and moved on to start the visa process for Iraq, only to discover that I had let my passport expire. What an embarrassment for someone who wants to reach the nations and had already gone on a number of trips to the Middle East!

I felt as though I needed to go on this journey to Iraq very soon, and so I called the passport office. There weren't any available appointments for many weeks, and they said I could not go to the office to get a passport without one. But . . . I went anyway. When I got to the office in downtown Detroit, there was a sign that said something like "By Appointment Only." I shuddered but got in line. When it was my turn, I explained to the woman what my situation was. She took my information and had me sit down to wait. There was no rebuke at all for coming in without an appointment. In twenty minutes they called my name and told me to come back the next day to get a new passport! Others who came in before me were still waiting as I walked out the door.

How I rejoiced! God was really paving the way, but there was another hurdle: getting a visa to enter Iraq—I would need to go to the Iraqi consulate for that.

VOICE #2 IN THE IRAQI CONSULATE:
"What are you thinking? They'll kill you!
They have to kill you! It's in their book!"

Miriam and I and Ali's widow, Farida, went to the Iraqi consulate together. I came prepared with a typed statement explaining why I wanted to go to Iraq (to offer condolences), including a picture of Ali and me together. We settled in for what we thought would surely be a very long wait.

As we sat there, I saw a Middle Eastern man come into the consulate wearing a clerical collar. He went up to the glass window and very briefly said something to one of the workers there. I had met him before and remembered him as being an Iraqi pastor of a church in the area. I approached him, and he came over and joined us, inquiring what I was doing there (Miriam and I stood out as the only non-Arabs in the room). I shared with him about my desires to go to Iraq to bring condolences and the love of Jesus to Ali's family.

He almost exploded,

> *"What are you thinking? They'll kill you!*
> *They have to kill you! It's in their book!"*

He kept going,

"I wouldn't go back to Iraq for one night if you paid me six million dollars!"

On the way to the consulate, Miriam was feeling fear creep in for the first time about my going to Iraq. Now she was really feeling it! Farida kept reassuring Miriam that her family would take care of me.

After about ten minutes of trying to get me to abandon my crazy idea to go to Iraq, the pastor simply got up and walked out. He didn't go back to the counter to do any business. He just walked out!

Again, we were bewildered. Was this a warning from God? Or was it a tactic of the devil to bring us more fear? How was it that we just "happened" to be in the Iraqi consulate the same day and time as this Iraqi pastor? And why had he not conducted any business there (at least none that we could see)?

This second "voice" required even more prayer and discernment. And it took some time. After all, I knew this man had a reputation as a godly pastor, and he certainly knew his home country far better than we ever would. Also, we trust in God's sovereign timing. It was no accident that he had come into that building when we were there.

Here is what we believe we received from the Lord: this event at the consulate was something like one of the occasions when Jesus told his disciples about his impending suffering, death, and resurrection. We can almost hear Peter exploding (like the Iraqi pastor).

"But Peter took him aside and began to reprimand him for saying such things.
'Heaven forbid, Lord,' he said. 'This will never happen to you!'
Jesus turned to Peter and said, 'Get away from me, Satan!
You are a dangerous trap to me.
You are seeing things merely from a human point of view,

not from God's.'"
MATTHEW 16:22–23, NLT

Peter no doubt loved Jesus, but his was a human love. He didn't understand God's purposes and calling for Jesus at that particular time. Jesus had to go to Jerusalem and the cross. But Peter was looking at Jesus's situation "from a human point of view, not from God's." And, sadly, he was being used by Satan to try to keep Jesus from fulfilling His divine mandate to go to the cross. It was a trap—a setup meant by Satan to stop Jesus—through one of His closest disciples.

We came to believe that Satan was using a similar tactic with me that day in the Iraqi consulate.

This pastor had a love for me, but it was a human love. He didn't understand God's purposes and calling for me at that particular time. He, too, was looking at my situation "from a human point of view, not from God's." And sadly, he was being used by Satan to try to keep me from fulfilling my divine mandate to go to Iraq. It was a trap—a setup meant by Satan to stop me—through a godly, well-meaning pastor.

We didn't blame him. Without prayer, our first reaction to someone like me would have probably been similar.

(By the way, incredibly, in just two hours that day, I had a visa to go to Iraq. This never happens—it can take weeks!)

So, once again, Miriam and I continued on toward what we believed God had called me to do.

There was just one more "voice" yet to come . . . and to overcome.

VOICE #3 IN THE MIDDLE EAST:

"Why are you going to Iraq? To our city? They tried to kidnap her there. That's why we left!"

After navigating through the difficulties of discerning the first two "voices," I traveled to the Middle East to do some ministry with Syrian and Iraqi refugees with a team from the States. The plan was to do that for a week, go to Iraq for five days to see Ali's family, and then come back to the first country for a few more days of ministry with the team.

Two days before I was to leave for Iraq, our team in the Middle East made a visit to see a large family from Iraq. As in all of our visits to refugees, we gave them bags of much needed food, sat together, and then listened to their story of hardship and heartache. But one thing stood out with this family: unlike the vast majority of Iraqi refugees we had visited through the years, this family was from the same city where I was going to visit Ali's family!

The spokesperson for the family was a young lady in her twenties. Why had they left Iraq? One day as she was walking to her university, a car had pulled up next to her. The radical Muslim occupants got out and tried to drag her into the car. A shop owner—probably a moderate Muslim man—came out and stopped it. As the would-be kidnappers drove away, they shouted,

"We know who you are. We know where you live.
You Christians are ruining Iraq."

You could tell that this had been a traumatic experience for this young woman.

When she finished her story, I mentioned to the family that I was flying to their former city very soon. They were incredulous and said,

"Why are you going to Iraq? To our city?
They tried to kidnap her there. That's why we left!"

Fear began to creep in yet again. Terrible fear. Thoughts once again of being beheaded by extremists.

Was this third voice a final warning? I had found discernment and peace after the other two voices, but this one hit me really hard. Of all the hundreds of thousands of refugees in that country, why had our team gone to visit a family from the exact city in Iraq where I was going? This was no accident. We don't believe in accidents.

Two nights later I called Miriam from my hotel. The flight to Iraq was very early the next morning. I felt sick, afraid for my very life. I was so afraid that I felt like vomiting.

I still don't remember what Miriam said when she prayed for me, but the terrible fear lifted! It was remarkable. How I thank God for her! I still had some nervousness after she prayed, but it was manageable.

Before I went to bed for a few short hours of sleep that night, I read Proverbs 4:25–27 (NLT) from my One Year Bible, a Christmas gift years earlier from Miriam,

"Look straight ahead,
and fix your eyes on what lies before you.
Mark out a straight path for your feet . . .
Don't get sidetracked."

It was clear that I just needed to get on that plane the next morning. I felt God saying through those verses,

"Don't look around. Don't think about other things.
Just get on that plane."

I did.

By the grace of God, I did.

I did not know what would happen to me in Iraq. Doubts about the rightness of this trip still troubled me some, but I was going. I wasn't turning back.

As I sat on the plane waiting to take off and watched the sun come up outside my little window, I listened to music on my iPod and worshiped to Michael W. Smith's song, "Draw Me Close."

Real peace settled in.

So, what happened in Iraq?

Through an experienced Christian interpreter, I was able to talk to many family members of our cherished friend Ali, who had passed away (and to his wife's family as well). I was able to share the good news with many of them. My interpreter encouraged me not to hold back, since these Iraqi Muslim people had seen pictures of me and heard stories about me from Ali. I was even able to give Arabic-English New Testaments to many family members. I told Ali's two grieving sisters that I had given their brother a book. I can still hear their answer through my interpreter:

"We know. Give us that book!"

I did.

Before I left, Ali's father-in-law, a Muslim leader of his tribe in his mid-seventies, graciously told me,

"You have family now in Iraq."

One of his sons kindly said,

"You are my brother forever."

I plead with our Father in heaven that these things will become true in a spiritual sense. How I burn in my soul for their salvation! That is one of the two reasons I went there. May Ali's death be the seed going into the ground that bears much fruit (John 12:24)—both in his family and in his wife's family.

As I was waiting to board my plane to leave Iraq, a big, muscular former soldier from England asked me what I had been doing in Iraq. He was a bodyguard for oil executives. I told him my story, and he asked whether I'd had a bodyguard while I was in that city. When I told him I hadn't, he was shocked, replying,

"What were you thinking?
Didn't you know that you are the kind of people
they [extremist kidnappers] *are looking for?"*

Jesus had been my bodyguard.

God did beautiful things in Iraq, but it had all started years earlier when Gary, Miriam, our small group, and I began to demonstrate God's love to Ali—*our Muslim neighbor.*

QUESTIONS TO PONDER

- God has said repeatedly in His Word that we should not fear. What is the accompanying promise that He gives?
- What kinds of fears or anxieties have you experienced related to going on a mission trip?
- What is the main thing you are afraid of when it comes to sharing the gospel?
- What lessons has God taught you about Himself through times of deep fear?

"The one who formed you says,
'Do not be afraid, for I have ransomed you.

I have called you by name; you are mine.'"
ISAIAH 43:1, NLT

"Don't be afraid, for I am with you.
Don't be discouraged, for I am your God.
I will strengthen you and help you.
I will hold you up with my victorious right hand."
ISAIAH 43:10, NLT

"Oh, magnify the LORD *with me,*
and let us exalt his name together!
I sought the LORD, *and he answered me*
and delivered me from all my fears . . .
This poor man cried, and the LORD *heard him*
and saved him out of all his troubles."
PSALM 34:3–6

CHAPTER 42

Washing the Dirty Little Feet of Jesus

Learning about the Power of
Servant Evangelism in Ethiopia

I n March of 2016 we had the great joy and privilege of going together to Ethiopia on a team to visit and work with an effective Christian ministry there.

What we saw in Ethiopia exceeded our expectations. We continue to be astounded!

In the early 1990s an Ethiopian couple who follow Jesus (now in their late eighties) was asked by the elders of a 95% Muslim area to come and build a school and a medical clinic.

They built schools—and continue to do so.

They built more than a clinic. They built a fine hospital, complete with the capability of performing surgeries. We met the surgeon there—a dedicated follower of Jesus.

They paved roads. They put in electricity. They changed the way cattle breeding was done to vastly improve milk production. They changed the way farming was done to vastly improve crop production.

Finally, this godly couple put in water wells—twenty of them—that now serve 30,000 people.

We should also mention that they taught the Muslim people how to do all these things vs. doing these things for them. This Ethiopian Christian couple brought in workers skilled in all these areas to train the local people so they could grow in self-sufficiency. They wisely did not want to be guilty of the kind of deficient—and all too prevalent—missions practice that is described as "when helping hurts."

The way God has used this elderly Ethiopian couple to serve and love the Muslim people toward faith in Jesus is positively inspirational. As they said to us,

> "We did not come to this Muslim community
> with Bibles under our arms.
> We couldn't.
> We came to serve."

And serve they did!

But all that service, all that effort to make life better for those Muslim people, was used by the Lord to cause these people to ask about the Savior whom this couple follows. And of course, they told them!

Now churches have been planted.

Now several thousand Muslim people in the region have come to Christ!

232 FEET . . . OF JESUS

While we were in Ethiopia with this highly regarded couple and their co-workers, we had the privilege of doing just a little bit of the kind of servant evangelism this couple and their ministry have been faithfully practicing for over thirty years.

We had the honor of what we called "washing the dirty little feet of Jesus."

Though not on the scale of building schools, or hospitals, or roads, or drilling wells, this was a simple act of serving. Of loving.

The first full day we were there with our team, we had the privilege of helping 116 (mostly) Muslim kindergarten children, ages five through nine, get new TOMS brand shoes. But first, we had to wash the feet of each child. Some of these tiny feet were the dirtiest you could imagine.

So many had black toenails from so much bruising and damage.

Others had ugly black spots on their feet indicating the need for the work of the three nurses on our team:

- cutting open those spots,
- squeezing out the white worm eggs,
- and applying healing medicine.

But it was not hard. It was a joy because each little Muslim child was so valuable.

So beautiful.

Most of all, to us, each child represented *Jesus.*

———

As we said above, this area in Ethiopia had been 95% Muslim when this ministry started there in the early nineties. And as we also said earlier, since then several thousand of those Muslims have become followers of Jesus.

Why? How?

Of course, people become followers of Jesus and enter the kingdom of God because the Holy Spirit works in their hearts. But the Holy Spirit uses His people. And because this ministry—amongst doing so many other things that we mentioned—*washes feet.*

Literally.

What we saw in Ethiopia—serving Muslim people in Jesus's name—will always be in our hearts and minds.

Someday we trust that those little Muslim children will grow up and ask the people at this ministry about the hope that is within them (1 Peter 3:15) because they were served and loved so well.

We pray that they—like several thousand before them—will become followers of Jesus.

———

QUESTIONS TO PONDER

- Why do you think such menial service might be used of the Holy Spirit to open up the heart of a person to hear the good news of Jesus?

- In what specific ways could servant evangelism be used where you live to love your Muslim neighbor?

"The King will reply,
'Truly I tell you, whatever you did
for one of the least of these brothers and sisters of mine,
you did for me.'"
MATTHEW 25:40, NIV

CHAPTER 43

† ☾

The Holy Spirit Said, *"Be Quiet!"*

Trying Too Hard and Talking Too Much

———

It was dark as we drove along the hills of a Middle Eastern country.

(It was 2016, just after our memorable time in Ethiopia. Miriam returned to the US, and I traveled on to the Middle East on Saudi Arabian Airlines, sleeping for a night in the airport in Jeddah, Saudi Arabia.)

As my Arab Muslim friend drove, I was trying so hard to come up with the right words to share more of the good news with him. We have known each other for years, and I desperately want him to know Jesus and enter the kingdom of God.

Ahmed is a brilliant man, educated in the US. Though he heads up a department in a university in his home country, Ahmed is a very humble person. You get the impression after talking with him for just a few minutes that this soft-spoken Muslim is also very gentle and peaceful.

As we drove, I kept thinking of what I might say to win Ahmed over to Jesus, to help him see the Jesus of the New Testament. Finally, I guess the Holy Spirit had had enough of my human effort, and the impression came to me pretty strongly,

"Be quiet!"

Maybe He said, *"Shut up!"* I can't remember!

Though hard for a big talker, I obeyed. I stopped talking. Do you know what happened?

All of a sudden—almost simultaneously with the time I quit talking (and trying so hard)—Ahmed began to ask me serious, probing, vital questions about the heart of the gospel! After that the door was open, and I was blessed to share so much that the Lord then put on my heart.

Sometimes in reaching out to Muslim people—or in evangelism with anyone—*we try too hard.* In trying to find just the right words to convince our friend to follow Jesus, *we can talk too much.*

May we give you an encouraging word that someone gave us?

"Let the Holy Spirit do the heavy lifting."

Of course, we are not saying that you should not talk at all—that you are not to share your personal faith journey or the words of Jesus from the Bible. Of course not. But sometimes, as a song puts it,

"You say it best . . . when you say nothing at all."

Sometimes that's when the Holy Spirit does *His* best talking.

QUESTIONS TO PONDER

- When you are in a conversation with an unbelieving friend or acquaintance, can you ever sense the Holy Spirit telling you when to talk and when to listen? What to say, and what not to say?
- How can we develop this kind of sensitivity to the Holy Spirit, both in general and, specifically, in our evangelistic efforts?

"[There is] a time to keep silence, and a time to speak."
ECCLESIASTES 3:7

"Not by might, nor by power, but by my Spirit, says the Lord.*"*
ZECHARIAH 4:6

"I did not speak on my own,
but the Father who sent me commanded me
to say all that I have spoken."
JOHN 12:49, NIV

CHAPTER 44

† ☾

"God Would Never Allow His Prophet to Be Killed! It Doesn't Make Sense!"

He's Right, You Know . . .
That Kind of Love *Doesn't* Make Sense

A nwar is a Palestinian Muslim who longs to make it to paradise. Anwar, Gary, and I often have long conversations about faith. The best thing about our conversations with Anwar is that we can be honest with each other about what we believe but also remain good friends. When we part ways, we shake hands, hug each other, and part as friends who disagree but still really care about each other. A two-hour conversation in 2017 was no different.

During that long chat, Anwar confessed that he is constantly afraid of the Day of Judgment—of whether he has done enough good works and whether his good works are good enough. He prays the Islamic prayers and also fasts two days each week.

When we tried to share about Jesus's death for all of us—since none of us can ever do enough good works to earn our own salvation—he said something that he says often,

"God would never send one of his prophets and then allow them to be killed."

But this time, he added forcefully and passionately,

"It doesn't make sense!"

Anwar explained that if he were to send someone to another country as his representative, he would always protect them and not let anything happen to them. How much more, by this reasoning, would God protect Jesus as His "messenger."

"It doesn't make sense!"

Those words keep ringing in my ears for days after that conversation.
And you know what? Anwar is right. It doesn't make sense . . . *at all.*
How could God love us so much that He would send Jesus—His One and only—to *die* for our sins?
How could Jesus love us so much that He would give Himself up for us in such a terrible, shameful, and painful death?
It doesn't make sense.
Or, more precisely, it doesn't make *human* sense. *Common* sense.
Maybe it makes sense in a different way. Maybe it makes sense . . . *to* God.
I think we need to help our Muslim friends to be careful when they talk about God and His actions that don't seem to make sense to human, finite minds.
God is *King*. He cannot be limited.
God can do *anything* . . . anything He wants that is consistent with His perfectly holy character.
And if He wants to do something so astonishing; so loving; and yes, something that doesn't makes sense to us—like sending Jesus to die for us—who are we to say,

"It doesn't make sense!"?

It *does* makes sense.
It makes infinite sense . . . *to God.*

QUESTIONS TO PONDER

- What do you think is the best approach with Muslim people: approaching them with low pressure over a prolonged period of time (low pressure, long range), or sharing the gospel but then moving on if they don't show interest?
- If you didn't grow up in the church, when you first heard the good news—the gospel—did it make sense to you? If not, how long did it take?
- We heard years ago that it takes the average believer from a Muslim background seven years from the time they first hear the gospel until they put their faith in Jesus and follow Him. That statistic may or may not be accurate. But if it is, why do you think it takes so long?

> "*For my thoughts are not your thoughts,*
> *neither are your ways my ways,*
> *declares the* LORD.
> *'As the heavens are higher than the earth,*
> *so are my ways higher than your ways*
> *and my thoughts than your thoughts.*"
> ISAIAH 55:8–9, NIV

> "*For the message of the cross is foolishness to those who are perishing,*
> *but to us who are being saved it is the power of God.*"
> 1 CORINTHIANS 1:18, NIV

> "*The god of this age has blinded the minds of unbelievers,*
> *so that they cannot see the light of the gospel*
> *that displays the glory of Christ, who is the image of God.*"
> 2 CORINTHIANS 4:4

CHAPTER 45

✝ ☪

Islam and Christianity: Is There Just a Thin Line between Us?

"The Difference between Us and You
Is No Thicker than This Line."

———

I n the summer of 2018, I visited a mosque in Michigan that was predominately made up of Muslim people from Bangladesh. I very much enjoyed meeting the imam (again, the leader of a mosque), his wife, his son, and his daughters. They were so kind and hospitable to me and to the Christian group I was with. We had a pleasant conversation outside the mosque before the prayer time about the significant work this man and his congregation are doing to improve their community, including the large adjoining community garden.

After our conversation, our group went inside the small mosque and observed the prayer time. The imam then sat down with us and shared about the five pillars of Islam and other Muslim beliefs and practices. We were listening to his presentation when his adult daughter, Jamila, spoke up and said something we've heard so many times from Muslims in many places where we have traveled:

> *"There really isn't much difference at all between*
> *what Muslims believe and what Christians believe."*

I really liked this imam and his daughter a lot. As I said before, they were both so kind. As this young lady spoke, she had such a gentle, sweet look on her face. I debated briefly in my mind,

> *"Do I contradict her in her place of worship?*
> *Or do I let it go?"*

I chose to do the former.

I said to Jamila—and to the rest of the Muslims who were present, including her father, the imam,

> *"We can say that there is really just a little difference*
> *between what Muslims and Christians believe,*
> *but would that really be honest of us?*
> *Would that really be truthful?"*

I went on to say,

> *"If we build a strong bridge of friendship,*
> *we can be honest enough to talk about not just the similarities in our religions*
> *(and we most definitely have them) but also the differences.*
> *We have real . . . significant . . . differences.*
>
> *"We have differences in who Isa—Jesus—is:*
> *Is he a great prophet or is he the spiritual Son of God?*
>
> *"We have differences in the way we view Jesus and the cross:*
> *Did Allah take Jesus to paradise and put someone else looking*
> *like him on the cross, or did Jesus really die on the cross for all our sins?*
>
> *"We have differences in how we expect to get to paradise:*

Do we get there by our good deeds outweighing our bad deeds,
or is paradise a free gift received by faith alone?

"Let's not deny these differences.
Let's talk about them!
With respect.
With love."

———————

HOW THIN IS THE LINE BETWEEN ISLAM AND CHRISTIANITY?

Moustapha Akkad's 1977 Islamic movie *The Message* tells of an early event in the history of Islam—known as the First Hegira (migration). In this migration, Muslims fled from Arabia to Abyssinia (modern day Ethiopia and Eritrea) to find refuge.

Muhammad's followers sought protection in eastern Africa because of persecution against him and his followers in Mecca from the ruling Quraysh tribe of Mecca. These early Muslims were reportedly boycotted, and several of them were restrained in their homes. Some were stoned. Because of this, Muhammad ordered Ja'far ibn Abi Talib to take some of his followers—perhaps about eighty people, not counting small children—and emigrate to Abyssinia in A.D. 615.

When the persecutors—the Quraysh—got wind of this group's plans, they sent a search party to forcibly bring this group back to Arabia. The group evaded them and made their way to Abyssinia. The Quraysh then sent an envoy to the king of Abyssinia to convince him not to give refuge to the fleeing Muslims.

When the envoy requested that the "rebels" be returned, the king is said to have replied,

"I cannot put souls into chains without first hearing them."

They were then taken before the king—supposedly a Christian—and his religious leaders to see whether he would allow them to stay in peace or give them up to be taken back to Mecca. The Muslims were called before the king, and this is one report of their defense before him through Ja'far.

The king to Ja'far:

> *"Speak to me of Christ!"*

Ja'far:

> *"We say of Christ what our prophet has taught us.*
> *That God cast his holy spirit into the womb of a virgin named Mary.*
> *And that she conceived Christ, the apostle of God . . .*

> *"Mary withdrew from her family to a place in the east.*
> *We sent to her our angel Gabriel who said,*
> *'I am a messenger from your God to announce the birth of a Holy Son to you.'*

> *"She said, 'How can I have a son when no man has touched me?'*
> *And Gabriel replied, 'For your lord says it will happen.*
> *We appoint him as a sign unto man. And a mercy from us.*
> *It is a thing ordained.'"*

The king drew a thin line in the sand with his staff and said to Ja'far and the Muslims seeking protection,

> *"The difference between us and you,*
> *is no thicker than this line.*

> *"Not for a mountain of gold will I give you up.*
> *You may live in Abyssinia in peace for as long as you wish.*
> *And may God's blessings be upon you on your return."*

———

Is there just a "thin line" of demarcation between Muslims and followers of Jesus in what we believe and how we practice our respective religions?

Are the theological differences between us *insignificant*, as some believe?

Are the differences simply a matter of *semantics?*

Should we focus only on our *similarities*—what we have in common— as some people like to say?

Or, . . . if we honestly value friendship and a deeper level/depth of relationship, can followers of Jesus and Muslim people talk honestly and respectfully about our *differences?*

We submit to you that, while we have many things in common in what we believe as Muslims and Christians, we also have some huge, significant differences.

Let's talk about those differences.

Let's not sweep them under the rug.

Let's listen to each other.

This is part of *loving our Muslim neighbor.*

THE HONEST MUSLIM PANELIST

I was having lunch in a terrific Middle Eastern restaurant in 2018 with a new pastor in our area. We began to talk about Christianity and Islam and our mutual love for the Middle East and the Muslim people there. We also talked about the efforts of some churches and well-meaning Christians to have interfaith meetings that virtually ignore the differences between our faiths in an effort to practice tolerance; political correctness; inclusivity; and, by their definition, "love."

My pastor friend related a different perspective in the story below, which we hope you will find informative and thought provoking regarding the supposedly "thin line" between Islam and Christianity.

"Several years ago my wife and I were attending an interfaith panel at _____ University. _____ is known as a politically, culturally, and socially progressive/liberal university community and almost all of the panelists reflected that basic mentality. There was a humanist chaplain from an Ivy League school, an Episcopalian bishop, a Reformed Jewish thinker, and several others who generally believed that the purpose of interfaith dialogue was for different faith traditions to see that we are basically all the same, save for a few small insignificant differences.

"However, one panelist came from a completely different perspective. He was a Muslim thinker from Chicago who was part of an interfaith group in that metro city. At one point in the panel discussion, he said,

'*My best friend is a Southern Baptist pastor who tells me I am going to hell. But he's my best friend because I know he loves me.*

'"*He loves me enough to tell me what he really believes and not to pretend that actually our differences don't really matter. In fact, to pretend that we do not have real differences diminishes the integrity of both of our faiths.*

'"*So he is a committed Christian and that means that he thinks I am wrong. And I am a committed Muslim and that means that I think he is wrong.*

'"*But we still love each other, and acknowledging those differences is one of the ways that we show our respect for one another and our respective faiths.*

'"*And that's what gives us the ability to have real substantive discussions.*'

"*The whole place was just frozen in silence. It was a like an earthquake just happened in their heavy-handed culture of tolerance and 'everyone has their own truth' and 'we're all right because we're all basically the same.' And actually, it captured in such a profound way that pretending we're all basically the same is actually not tolerant at all because it does violence to the distinctiveness of all traditions and insists they all be like each other. It says Muslims aren't allowed to be distinctively Muslim and Christians aren't allowed to be distinctively Christian. But actually, true tolerance, true respect, true love is honestly acknowledging the differences and loving one another in the midst of those differences.*"

We would love to meet this Muslim panelist.
We love his *honesty*.

QUESTIONS TO PONDER

- Have you shared honestly and compassionately with a Muslim friend about the real and significant differences in your faith traditions? How did he or she respond?
- Have you heard a Muslim say that there are just a few minor differences

between what Muslims and Christians believe? How did (or would) you respond?

• Have you heard a so-called Christian distort the Word of God and say, "We all believe basically the same thing"? How did (or would) you respond?

> *"Wounds from a sincere friend are better*
> *than many kisses from an enemy."*
> PROVERBS 27:6, NLT

> *"We do not try to trick people into believing—*
> *we are not interested in fooling anyone.*
> *We never try to get anyone to believe that*
> *the Bible teaches what it doesn't.*
> *All such shameful methods we forego.*
> *We stand in the presence of God as we speak*
> *and so we tell the truth, as all who know us will agree."*
> 2 CORINTHIANS 4:2, TLB

> *"Rather, we have renounced secret and shameful ways;*
> *we do not use deception, nor do we distort the word of God.*
> *On the contrary, by setting forth the truth plainly*
> *we commend ourselves to everyone's conscience in the sight of God."*
> 2 CORINTHIANS 4:2, NIV

CHAPTER 46

✝ ☾

The Holy Spirit and the Moroccan Rug Salesman

Is There a "Silver Bullet" in Outreach to Muslim People?

———

Morocco.

It was a wedding anniversary to remember!

In the summer of 2018, we experienced a fabulous ministry trip to Greece for a gathering of global workers. We decided to add on a vacation for our fortieth wedding anniversary and stay in Spain for a week, since friends had graciously provided free housing there.

One day, the proximity of Morocco to Spain was more than we could resist. We jumped on a fast ferry to make the twenty-mile journey across the stunning Mediterranean Sea to an exotic land that had always intrigued us.

As in most Arab Muslim countries, the people of Morocco were very welcoming—from the port of Tangier to the delightful restaurant we went to with our guide to the huge market with its many varieties of olives to a carpet place where they "rolled out the red carpet" for us!

Actually, they unrolled carpet after carpet (rugs) for us in this "carpet showroom" in the market in Tangier. The manager, Salah, served us cold drinks and tried diligently to persuade us to purchase gorgeous rugs made by—as he said—"poor Berber women."

After his persistent efforts, he finally left us alone to "talk it over" and make our decision.

We were not interested in the rugs, but we were interested in sharing the gospel with this Muslim man, Salah.

The Holy Spirit put a creative response in Miriam's heart for me to explain to Salah when he returned:

> "We don't want to buy a rug,
> even though they are so beautiful.
> We would rather give you money
> for the poor Berber women who made them."

He was so surprised and pleased as we handed him a prayerfully agreed upon sum of money for him to give to those women!

Miriam's idea from the Holy Spirit created open doors for us to begin a spiritual conversation with Salah.

He declared that,

> "There really isn't that much difference between Islam and Christianity."

(After the last chapter, does this sound familiar?)
I was so proud of Miriam's kind but firm response,

> "Well, there is that thing about Jesus dying on the cross."

Led by the Holy Spirit, we began to share some of the gospel with him. He was really listening as we spoke of Jesus's sacrificial death for him on the cross.

We asked Salah if we could pray for him for anything. He had a physical heart issue, and we prayed out loud for him in Jesus's name.

This Muslim man was so happy after our prayer and discussion that he asked us to go with him and pray for his Muslim family members who were working downstairs. We prayed for them and gave them all our "I Love Muslims" cards before we left for the rest of our tour of Tangier. They, too, were so happy!

We left with no rugs under our arms but with full hearts.

Seeds had been planted in Morocco.

━━━

Muslims everywhere—from Michigan to Morocco—just want to be loved by followers of Jesus, and if you *serve* them in some way (like the gift for the poor women) it can open their hearts to listen to what you have to say about the good news of Jesus and to pray for them.

In all our experiences with Muslim people in thirteen years and in nine Islamic countries, we have found that there is no "silver bullet" (a simple and seemingly magical solution to a complicated problem) in reaching them for Christ. Every Muslim is different. Every situation when you meet a Muslim person is different.

We believe in and use different strategies in our outreach (see Appendix 9), but we don't depend on any of them—even our oft repeated encouragement to build relationships with Muslims. All of us need to depend upon the Holy Spirit! He knows the heart and mind and background of every Muslim person. We want to be led by Him, as Miriam was in this story.

Undoubtedly, this time with Salah and his workers was a divine appointment. an open door (Revelation 3:8) for the gospel—something we pray for often. It seems to be a delight to the Lord when His children pray for open doors because He seems to answer that prayer so often and so readily!

━━━

QUESTIONS TO PONDER

- In reaching out to Muslim people, how much better it is to be led by the Holy Spirit than to rely on human strategies, no matter how good they may seem! How have you seen the Holy Spirit give you words or thoughts in your witness that you know came from Him—just for that moment?
- The next time you travel somewhere, ask the Lord to give you a "divine appointment" with a man or woman who is *open* to the gospel (such as Lydia in Acts 16). Consider writing down what you experience and then sharing it with other believers. Wouldn't this build your faith—and theirs as well?

"So, setting sail from Troas, we made a direct voyage to Samothrace,

and the following day to Neapolis, and from there to Philippi,
which is a leading city of the district of Macedonia and a Roman colony.
We remained in this city some days.
And on the Sabbath day we went outside the gate to the riverside,
where we supposed there was a place of prayer,
and we sat down and spoke to the women who had come together.
One who heard us was a woman named Lydia, from the city of Thyatira,
a seller of purple goods, who was a worshiper of God.
The Lord opened her heart to pay attention to what was said by Paul . . .
she was baptized, and her household as well."

ACTS 16:11–14

CHAPTER 47

† ☾

"I Fear for Your Soul on the Day of Judgment!"

The Bold and Loving Words
of a Muslim Man to Me

———

I n the fall of 2018, I was at a mosque in Nevada scouting it out for a visit for a church group the next day. After observing the Friday prayers and sermon, I spoke to various Muslim men, and then to the president of the mosque. As has been the case at nearly every mosque we have been to in our years of ministry to Muslim people, these men received me with hospitality and kindness.

When I left the prayer room to retrieve my shoes from the shoe shelf near the front door (shoes are not allowed in the prayer room—the sanctuary of a mosque), there was only one man left putting on his shoes. He was Samir from Palestine. This was to be another of many divine appointments that God had provided in our ministry to Muslim people. I immediately felt drawn to this man, who was so warm and inviting with his huge smile and joyful demeanor.

After sitting and talking with Samir for a half hour or so, he asked me if I was hungry. I responded that I surely was and that I had planned on

239

going to a Muslim owned and operated restaurant nearby for some Middle Eastern food (Miriam and I cannot get enough of it!). But Samir, a Middle Eastern man, had other ideas. He wanted to go to El Pollo Loco (The Crazy Chicken)! What could I say? If I wanted to be with this gregarious Palestinian Muslim man, I would have to go eat some "crazy chicken"!

Actually, Samir and I ate a lot of chicken that day. He ordered the family dinner for us and then proceeded to add other menu items to it. I hate to admit it, but the two of us ate the whole thing!

While we ate, we spoke about our wives and kids and backgrounds. Just normal life kind of stuff. But then we went deeper and engaged in conversation about following Muhammad or following Jesus. We spoke about our individual faiths with real candor.

At that table after we had eaten a lot of chicken, Samir made a shocking and bold statement to me:

> *"I fear for your soul on the Day of Judgment."*

This Muslim had boldness!
I responded to Samir,

> *"You must really care about me to say such a thing.*
> *You believe Islam is the way to paradise and you want me there.*
> *You don't want me to go to hell.*
> *Thank you, my friend!"*

———

As we stated in the last two chapters, so many Muslims say to us

> *"There is really not much difference between our faiths—only just a little bit.*
> *Only just a few things.*
> *We need to focus on what we agree on.*
> *We basically believe pretty much the same way."*

But not Samir. This was not his approach! No, he spoke about truth (as he understands it, that is). He knows and admits that the Qur'an and the Bible have distinctively different paths to paradise and that they can't both be the truth. Samir spoke with real heart. Real feeling.

Can we learn something from Samir—a Muslim—about *boldness* in evangelism?

Is it possible for us to care about our lost family members, friends, co-workers, classmates, and neighbors enough to say something like he did? Might we, like Paul, ask the Lord to open our mouths to boldly proclaim the mystery of the gospel (Ephesians 6:19)? Can we ask our Father for the courage to speak the truth in love (Ephesians 4:15)?

There can be no doubt that we are all different. We each have different personalities, gifts, and approaches in sharing our faith. But it seems to us that boldness for Jesus and His gospel is something that all of us need as standard equipment. We hope it goes without saying that we are not suggesting being rude or needlessly aggressive in our witness. We are not talking about being disrespectful. No, none of that. That is not the way of Jesus.

But we all need courage. We need *boldness*.

We need a love for people in which *fear for their soul* on the Day of Judgment means more to us than *fear of their response* to our witness in the here and now.

Let us pray as the early church prayed:

> *"'And now, Lord . . . grant to your servants*
> *to continue to speak your word with all boldness,*
> *while you stretch out your hand to heal,*
> *and signs and wonders are performed*
> *through the name of your holy servant Jesus.'*
>
> *"And when they had prayed, the place in which they were gathered together*
> *was shaken, and they were all filled with the Holy Spirit*
> *and continued to speak the word of God with* boldness."
> (ACTS 4:29–31)

No matter who we are or what our personality traits, God can give each of us this filling of the Holy Spirit and boldness. Let us ask Him for it, just as the early church did in Acts 4.

It will be invaluable as we go about *loving our Muslim neighbor.*

QUESTIONS TO PONDER

- Does it surprise you that a Muslim expressed genuine concern for the soul of a non-Muslim? Why or why not?
- Is boldness a personality trait, or is it something that each of us can receive from the Lord and grow in?
- How might additional boldness from the Holy Spirit impact your outreach to Muslim people?

> *"[Pray] for me, that words may be given to me*
> *in opening my mouth* boldly
> *to proclaim the mystery of the gospel."*
> (EPHESIANS 6:19)

CHAPTER 48

✝ ☪

"Are You Having 'Success' in Your Ministry to Muslims?"

Johnny Appleseed, Muslims, and a Different Metric: "One Step Closer"

When I was a boy, I was fascinated by a small book about Johnny Appleseed Chapman (1774–1845). His passion was to plant apple seeds all over the then American frontier (Pennsylvania, Kentucky, Ohio, Illinois, and Indiana), with a vision that these seeds would one day become fruit-bearing trees and bless people.

Ministry to Muslims is much like the vision of Johnny Appleseed in that we are planting "seeds" of the good news in the hearts of Muslim friends and acquaintances to bless them for eternity.

It is very important for all of us to understand that *reaching Muslim people often (but not always) involves various Jesus followers sharing the good news with a Muslim person many times over many years.*

Some will plant, some will water, and some will harvest (John 4:35–38; 1 Corinthians 3:6–7). May God give all of us a vision for the seeds of God's love growing in the hearts of Muslim people into trees that will bear much fruit to the glory of God (John 15:8).

QUESTION: *"HOW DO YOU MEASURE 'SUCCESS' IN MINISTRY TO MUSLIMS?"*
Our Answer: *"One Step Closer!"*

When we were in college together in Oklahoma in the mid 1970s, we both learned something interesting in our freshman English class,

"Meanings are not in words; meanings are in people."

So, when people ask whether we are having "success" in evangelizing Muslims, we have to respond,

"What do you mean by 'success'?"

What we are endeavoring to avoid in our concept of evangelism—and what we are trying to get you to avoid in yours—is the idea that successful evangelism means that someone always responds to our evangelistic efforts by immediately asking, "What must I do to be saved?" That would be fantastic, and we have no doubt that it can and does happen, even for Muslim people (you can read in Appendix 9 about the "Any 3" ministry strategy of first-time conversations leading to immediate conversions). But we believe that more often—for most of us—evangelizing Muslim people is a *process*. And it can be a *long* process.

The following list (adapted and modified from the Engel scale by James F. Engel) shows some of the steps a person might take as God brings them to Himself. Of course, there is no real sequential order—nothing so neat or predictable. Everyone's spiritual journey is *unique*.

POSSIBLE STEPS IN ENTERING THE KINGDOM OF GOD AND GROWING IN NEW LIFE

1. Going one's own way: spiritually dead, blind, enslaved, rebellious, lost
2. Personal problem/crisis/emptiness/searching for more
3. Awareness of a Jesus follower
4. Relationship with and awareness of difference in a Jesus follower
5. Positive attitude toward a Jesus follower

6. Initial awareness of the basic truths of the gospel
7. Grasp eternal implications of the gospel
8. Positive attitude toward the gospel
9. Conviction of sin and the need of a Savior

10. NEW BIRTH providing repentance and faith in Christ alone!

11. Evangelistic fervor, telling others what God has done
12. Hunger for the Bible, fellowship, baptism
13. Simple faith, obedience, love, worship
14. Incorporation into a caring community
15. Conceptual and behavioral growth
16. Growing in Christ-like character
17. Discipling others; multiplication

As you think about this list of possible steps, please hear the words of Paul Hazelden:

> *"If you understand something of the journey a person*
> *must take in order to discover God,*
> *then you know that helping someone take one more step*
> *towards God is successful evangelism*
> *just as much as helping them over the final line."*
> (http://www.hazelden.org.uk)

Isn't that quote by Hazelden brilliant?

Doesn't it bring a new freedom and encouragement?

You don't have to do *everything* in seeing someone become a follower of Jesus, but God can use you to do and say *something* to bring them one step closer.

We have talked in this book about different means of evangelism, but here are some suggestions for *verbal witness* that we have discovered:

- Ask your Muslim friend or acquaintance about their *spiritual journey* and then share about what God has done in your life in bringing you to Himself
- Talk about how God has so faithfully answered your *prayers*

- Share *Scripture verses* that have helped you through a tough time or tragedy
- Tell *"Jesus stories"* (stories about what Jesus did or stories He told in the Gospel accounts), with this as one example,

> *"What we are talking about reminds me of a story that Jesus told about how much God loves sinful, lost people so much. There once was a man who had two sons . . ."*

  This might be called story evangelism, and we have found that Muslim people will almost always listen to a Bible story without interruption. Who doesn't like a good story?
- Appendix 3 has many good *spiritual conversation starters* you can discuss with a Muslim person, including questions such as,
    - » Do people talk about religion in your country, or is it more of a private thing?
    - » Why do you think people were created?
    - » What do you think paradise is like?
    - » How do you get to paradise in Islam?
    - » Would you like to hear what the Bible says a true follower of Jesus is?
    - » Would you like to hear the key points of the Bible?
- Finally, you can ask your Muslim friend how you might *pray for them* and, if the Lord leads, do it right on the spot—out loud, in Jesus's name. Few will turn you down (we have found this to be reliably true of Muslims: only one has turned us down in thirteen years!). We believe that prayer evangelism can be one of the most effective tools in your evangelistic toolbox.

As we end this chapter, we want to emphasize that sharing Jesus with a Muslim friend might possibly be a long and hard struggle. He or she might come one step closer to following Jesus but then take two (or more) steps back.

Ultimately, God knows their hearts, and we rest in what His Word declares about His passionate love for lost people (Luke 19:10; 1 Timothy 2:4; 2 Peter 3:9) and His divine calling (Romans 8:29–30).

The bottom line is this: God delights in using you in the process of sharing the good news with Muslim people—of bringing a Muslim person just *one step closer* to Himself. And who knows, you might just be the one who helps them over the line in a commitment to follow Jesus. Don't be afraid to ask!

It all starts with *loving your Muslim neighbor.*

QUESTIONS TO PONDER

- What are the hurdles and obstacles a Muslim person will have to overcome as they move step-by-step closer to entering the kingdom of God?
- What is your reaction to the definition of "success" in evangelism as used in this chapter?
- How has God used you to move someone *one step closer* to following Jesus?

"Look around you!
Vast fields of human souls are ripening all around us,
and are ready now for reaping.
The reapers will be paid good wages and will be
gathering eternal souls into the granaries of heaven!
What joys await the sower and the reaper, both together!
For it is true that one sows and someone else reaps."
JOHN 4:35–37, TLB

CHAPTER 49

†☪

What Happened to Our Muslim Friends? They *"Disappeared"!*

Islam Does Not Let Go of Its People Easily

———

Though it can be a joyful time of year for many followers of Jesus, Christmas reminds us of the painful fact that we have many Muslim friends who do not understand or believe in something we take so for granted: the Incarnation of Jesus—the Divine putting on human flesh to save us from our sins and restore relationship to the Father.

Just before Christmas of 2018, three of our Muslim friends "disappeared."

"MANSOUR" FROM SYRIA

It was incredible watching this gentle older Muslim man grasp the gospel! The Holy Spirit was giving him splendid insights into the stories of Jesus in the Gospels. We felt as though we were watching him slowly being born again! I once told him exactly that and showed him Jesus's words about being born again in John 3. I also explained that for some people this happens very quickly but that for others it can be a long process. He joyfully and loudly proclaimed in his deep, husky voice,

> "For me, the process is slow.
> But it is strong!"

On another occasion I was meeting with Mansour and asked him if he had come to believe that Jesus died on the cross—obviously something the Qur'an denies. I will never forget his unexpected response:

> "If Jesus didn't die on the cross,
> then who was the man that came out of the tomb?"

Mansour was grasping the historicity of Jesus's identity and the essentials of His gospel!

But then, Mansour just . . . *disappeared.* All of a sudden, there was no more contact. He would not return phone calls, texts, WhatsApp messages, Facebook messages—nothing. When I went to visit him at his house, his family would tell me he was "asleep" or "gone" or something else. I knew this was not always true. Different grandkids at his house would even give me different answers about where he was or what he was doing.

What happened to Mansour? In the visible realm, we believe that his family or his mosque probably found out about our many gospel conversations and pressured him not to meet with us. In the invisible realm, we believe that spiritual forces likely pressured him with fear of what he could lose if he continued to pursue a relationship with Jesus.

One thing we knew: our battle was *not* against Mansour's family or the leaders and people of his mosque. It was against unseen spiritual forces.

"ASIF" FROM IRAQ

My outreach partner, Gary, and I had several very positive meetings with a young man from Baghdad, Iraq, by the name of Asif. Asif enjoyed Starbucks, and we would always meet there. He seemed to warmly receive our interest in learning about his personal life: his background in Iraq, his family, his desire to become more proficient in English, his educational goals, etc. And he would also listen attentively as we shared Bible verses with him, prompting us to give him the gift of an Arabic-English New Testament.

But then, like Mansour from Syria, Asif simply . . . *vanished*. And would not return any messages.

What happened? Probably the same thing that had happened to Mansour: pressure from people and pressure from unseen powers. *A spiritual battle for his soul.*

"KARAM" FROM SYRIA

Like Mansour from Syria, Karam seemed to love stories of Jesus and began to comprehend His message. He loved being with believers and listening to the stories of the Bible.

But, once again, even though he was steadily progressing in grasping the good news, suddenly he too just . . . *dropped out of sight.*

Thankfully, unlike the other two men, Karam did not cut off communication. He just stayed away from our Bible study times with other followers of Jesus and Muslim seekers.

When we contacted him, he confirmed what we suspected about our other two Muslim friends: he was pressured by Muslims from the mosque to stop studying the Bible with us.

Dear readers, you need to know that if your Muslim friend begins to believe in Jesus's death and resurrection and commits to give his or her heart to Him, they will likely experience heavy pressure—pressure such as few of us have ever known:

- *Well-meaning Muslim family and friends will sincerely fear for their souls.* As we have said previously, Muslims have no assurance of gaining paradise, but there is an assurance of hell if they become followers of Jesus and see Him as the Son of God. This is called *shirk* (ascribing a partner—an equal—to God) and is idolatrous, blasphemous, and unforgivable. Family and friends of your Muslim friend will, quite understandably, want to save their loved one from this fate and will find ways to pressure them to stay in Islam to save their eternal souls!

- *Leaving Islam brings tremendous shame to one's family, tribe, village, mosque, etc.* Muslims are part of an "honor-shame" culture. Westerners generally have little knowledge of this way of life, but we need just accept that, in such a culture, there is nothing greater than possessing honor and nothing worse than bringing shame upon oneself and one's family—such as that of leaving Islam and following Jesus.

We once heard a BMB say, "I did not give up Islam easily," as she described the hard decision to follow Jesus. Believe us when we say that Islam does not easily give up its people, either.

But know this: our battle is *not* against *Muslim people.*

Our fight is against unseen spiritual forces that want to hold on to Muslim people and not allow them to explore new ways of looking at the person and work of Jesus. These forces do not allow any expressions of doubt or any questioning of Islam. They oppress the Muslim person and want to keep them from the freedom that comes in knowing the truth about our glorious Savior and all that He has for them (John 8:32, 36).

So, let us *love our Muslim neighbors* and fight for them on our knees in prayer.

God is with us—and *He loves Muslim people!*

QUESTIONS TO PONDER

- If your Muslim friend is pressured to stay in Islam by family, friends, or the mosque but decides to leave their faith, will you be there for them? How? They may well lose their family and community because of the shame such a decision will bring. What can you and other followers of Jesus do to fill that huge void in their lives?
- As you are nearing the end of this book, what do you see as the primary difficulties in reaching out to Muslim people with the good news of Jesus? What do you see as the primary joys and fulfillment that come from this kind of outreach?
- How can you gain spiritual strength for the battle spoken about in this chapter? What resources might you utilize to help you reach out to Muslim people with the good news of Jesus?

"God is strong, and he wants you strong . . .
stand up to everything the Devil throws your way.
This is no afternoon athletic contest that we'll walk away
from and forget about in a couple of hours.
This is for keeps, a life-or-death fight to the finish
against the Devil and all his angels.
"Be prepared.
You're up against far more than
you can handle on your own.
Take all the help you can get."
EPHESIANS 6:10–13, MSG

CHAPTER 50

✝ ☾

Links in the Beautiful Chain of One Muslim's Salvation

Even Someone Picking up Trash for the Glory of God!

When we met him in 2018, Hassan was an outstanding young man but without a real faith.

Hassan had left Islam before he came to America from the Middle East, so he was basically without a religion when he came here. Some would still have called him a Muslim, but he probably would not have self-identified that way—at least not in his heart. As with so many other young people from his country, he was fed up with Islam. What he saw in the religious and political leaders of his Islamic country had become repulsive to him.

God was using that dissatisfaction with his old faith to bring him to a new one.

It is interesting to follow the links in the beautiful chain of God's redemption of Hassan. As for all of us, God uses various means to call people to Himself—each as a link in His chain. For Muslims, this may be:

- a *conversation* or *relationship* with a follower of Jesus

- a blog or article on a *Christian website*
- a program on *a Christian TV station,* such as SAT-7 (for Arabic speakers) or SAT-7 PARS (for Persian speakers)
- hearing a *Bible* verse or actually obtaining a Bible in their language
- a *dream* or a *vision* of Jesus
- a *healing* or other *answered prayer* after being prayed for by a Christian.

Hassan was first introduced to Christianity when he was in the military in his country in 2012. This was through some Armenian Christians in the army who became friends and talked to him—just a little—about Christianity. These men were the first links in the chain of his salvation that he can remember.

The next link in God's redemption of Hassan was when he came to the Midwestern US in 2016. He was invited to study the Bible with other international students through a campus ministry. That was the first time in his life that Hassan had ever heard a verse from the Bible! God sovereignly brought several Christ followers into his life in those months. The Good Shepherd was pursuing Hassan, His lost sheep!

Sometime later, in the fall of 2017, Hassan met our good friend Gary on a public bus, when Gary was—of all things—picking up trash on the bus. Hassan was amazed (Who does that, anyway?). Gary is a humble man who will do anything for the glory of God (1 Corinthians 10:31). Gary saw Hassan sitting alone, sat down next to him, and talked to him a bit about the Lord Jesus. Before the two parted ways, he also gave Hassan a small booklet on the history of redemption in the Bible. They providentially saw each other in a mall a short time later and began to connect. Gary conducted short Bible studies with Hassan, usually at McDonald's, to see whether there was a sincere interest in Hassan's heart to know more about the Savior. (Since he does not own a car, Gary is a link in the lives of so many people, including Muslim people from all over the world, through his international bus ministry.)

I, too, became a link in the chain when Gary introduced me to Hassan in early 2018. We started studying the Bible together as a threesome, almost always at McDonald's. I was able to give Hassan a New Testament in his own language, and he loved it! Gary and I felt that Hassan needed to be able to quickly access any verse of the Bible, so we helped him install the Bible App

YouVersion on his phone. This enabled us to text him Bible verses in his language. The New Testament and the Bible app were indeed links God used in Hassan's chain of salvation.

During one of our early sessions together, I shared with Hassan my positive experiences in Europe with former Muslims from his country who had become followers of Jesus. I explained how they went out onto the streets with backpacks full of New Testaments and gave them to Muslim people whom they met, along with a card with the address of a church where they could go for more information. Hassan was intrigued by this.

One night as I was teaching Hassan about the core teachings of the Bible, I showed him the website (another link) of a ministry to Muslims in the Middle East, including a picture of former Muslims being baptized. He said that he would like to be baptized someday! I told him that Gary and I wanted to help him gain more knowledge of Jesus before he made that weighty decision but that we would be glad to help him do that as he gained more knowledge and counted the cost (Luke 14:28) of following Jesus. Even in the beginning of our relationship, we wanted him to know that becoming a follower of Jesus could mean severe persecution—even death—if he went back to his home country. We did not want him to make this decision lightly.

Hassan began to plug in to a local church (another link). He was learning about Jesus—about the primary teachings of the Bible and what it means to follow Jesus—before he made the commitment to surrender his life to Him. And he was making more and more Christian friends.

Gary and I began to watch a Christian DVD series—*Al Massira*—with Hassan at McDonald's on Friday mornings. He loved watching each session and hearing it in his language. He was very attentive and spiritually hungry. These DVDs were a significant link in his progress toward salvation. As happens with many Muslims who follow Jesus, we were discipling Hassan into relationship with Him.

In December of 2018, Miriam and I took Hassan to a living nativity Christmas program. He loved seeing the live animals. Our friend Syd shared the gospel with Hassan there using an Evangelism Cube, and a former Muslim woman from the Middle East shared with him her story of being found by Jesus. Hassan was, again, intrigued and listened intently to both of them. These were still more links—more steps toward a commitment to following Jesus.

As with our friend Ali, we had the privilege of watching Hassan being slowly born again through the Spirit of God. It was wondrous!

After some months Hassan again expressed a desire for baptism, but this time it was very strong. He was firmly determined to take this step. He called his parents in his Islamic home country and told them of this desire, and they said it was his choice. He responded,

"I choose freedom [to follow Christ]*."*

His devout Muslim mother warned him to keep this decision off social media. She feared for his safety.

Hassan and I met with two pastors in our home church who support our ministry to Muslims and have been with us on trips to help refugees in the Middle East. I wanted these pastors and deeply respected friends to hear Hassan's testimony and desire for baptism. They were significantly moved by his story and approved his request.

Hassan knew at that time that there could be severe persecution back home if his baptism was discovered. His response is recorded here in his text messages that I have saved:

"He died for us. For our sins. This is the greatest gift.
He paved the way for us.
Following him is greater than the cost [persecution because of baptism]*."*

"So many people are lonely.
But I am not lonely because I have Jesus in my life."

"Baptism is a new chapter in my life. A new Hassan.
Jesus has helped me, and I want to respond to him."

"Baptism would be the greatest experience for me."

"I am so excited."

I had a text interchange with Hassan the day after we met with the pastors regarding his desire to be baptized. I wanted to warn him about the doubts that might come into his mind from Satan if he followed through with this momentous step.

He responded:

"Hi Tim my dear friend. No I don't have any doubt about my decision.
It is very hard for me to explain my feeling.

"Last night I didn't feel good and I had nightmares that I got in an accident.
After I was baptized, I went back to my country
and people were waiting for me.
They were very angry.
I tried to get away from them in my car.
I drove away and went off the road.
Only word came out of my mouth was 'Jesus help me.'
Right now I feel him in my life."

Hassan was baptized on Easter Sunday, April 21, 2019. Gary and I were privileged to do this in front of the congregation, and Miriam was there acting as Hassan's "spiritual mother." Before we baptized him, Hassan gave public profession to his new faith in Jesus Christ and of his desire to follow Him. We cannot describe to you what remarkable joy all of us had—especially Hassan!

I told Hassan that he did not need to immediately tell other Muslims of his baptism unless he felt that Jesus wanted him to do this. I wanted him to learn to hear the Shepherd's voice and obey Him vs. depending entirely on us for guidance. And I wanted him to have more time to grow in his faith— to grow deep roots that would withstand the winds of persecution that would surely beat against his soul—before he told too many other Muslims.

After the baptism that Easter Sunday, Gary and his wife and Miriam and I wanted to take Hassan to a nice restaurant of his choice to celebrate his new beginning in the kingdom of God. He chose McDonald's because that was the place where we had done all of our Bible studies together! During that Easter dinner at McDonald's, he did a FaceTime call with his father, mother, and brother at their home in the Middle East. He was so excited and told us that he just *had* to tell his family of this huge step in his life! His excitement and joy far outweighed any fear of this news getting out to other people in his Islamic home country.

Since his baptism, Hassan has continued to grow in his faith. He has soaked up all the Bible verses we have shared with him about living as Jesus's follower. Gary and I have met with him many, many times to disciple him. We text him regularly to share with him encouraging things from the Bible, as well as Christian worship songs in English and also in his own language.

We regularly engage in phone conversations in which we pray together. Hassan prays out loud as well in those calls—without being asked.

But life has not been easy since Hassan made the decision to become a follower of Jesus:

- His Muslim employer became angry and threatened him on account of his baptism, so Hassan decided to leave that job.
- Without income, he became more and more in debt from student loans, etc.
- Without income, he had to move out of his apartment (thankfully, a Jesus follower took him in).
- Hassan began to read more and more about persecution in his home country of Muslims who had converted to Christianity. This put real fear in his heart and mind—sometimes a terrible, debilitating fear—not just for his own wellbeing but mostly a concern for his mother's potential grief. (He cried when he told us of his apprehension about her sorrow if something happened to him.)
- Besides fear, Hassan has battled loneliness. He has no wife. Attempts to date have painfully fallen through.
- Besides loneliness, he has fought through depression and hopelessness. Every one of the hundreds of jobs he has applied for has been met with rejection.
- Without income, Hassan finally took a full-time job at Walmart selling cell phones—work far below what he had dreamed of after coming to the US and getting his MBA.

No, life has not been easy or comfortable or safe for this former Muslim young man who has given his heart to Jesus.

But Hassan won't give up. He refuses to quit. He keeps applying for jobs in his field, and he keeps growing in his faith.

Below are more of Hassan's text messages to Miriam and me in broken—but endearing to us—English. They reveal his perseverance in the faith.

"You taught me so many things, my relationship with you is miracle in my life.
How Gary by God's hand come across my life.
How Miriam with her heart is supporting me.
Dear Lord helped me in these storms of my life . . . to feel Joy."

"I love you like my baba, my dad.
Thanks for your support in all aspects my life.
Thank Lord that put friend like you on my way."
"My relationship with you is the most valuable gift from Lord.
I am so blessed that I get baptized by you."

"Thanks for both of you. My spiritual dad and mother.
I am thankful Lord that have you in my life.
Jesus loves me so much that put you in my way.
Love you both."

"I really appreciate your help in all aspects of my life
specially in growing my faith and loving Jesus . . . I won't give up."

"Thanks God. Thanks in all circumstances for this is
the will of God in Christ Jesus for me."

"I love Jesus so much!"

Dear readers, there is nothing like being a link in the chain of a Muslim person's salvation, especially if you have the privilege of being the final link of watching them enter the kingdom of God! We pray for you to experience that time of rejoicing and joyful celebration!

"'Rejoice with me . . .'
there will be more joy in heaven over one sinner who repents
than over ninety-nine righteous persons who need no repentance."
LUKE 15:6–7

"'Rejoice with me . . .'
there is joy before the angels of God
over one sinner who repents."
LUKE 15:9–10

"'Let us . . . celebrate.
For this my son was dead, and is alive again;
he was lost, and is found.'

And they began to celebrate."
LUKE 15:23–24

"This is a wonderful time, and we had to celebrate.
This brother of yours was dead, and he's alive!
He was lost, and he's found!"
LUKE 15:31–32, MSG

It all starts by simply *loving your Muslim neighbor.*

———

QUESTIONS TO PONDER

- Hassan grew in dissatisfaction with Islam before he embraced Jesus. Is that kind of dissatisfaction something we should pray about for our Muslim neighbors—and for Muslims around the world?
- After Hassan was baptized, many things in his world fell apart. Are you willing to help your former Muslim friend if this happens in their life? What might your help look like?
- As you read about the chronological links in the story of Hassan's salvation, how many of those involved personal contact with followers of Jesus?

"Who do you think Paul is, anyway? Or Apollos, for that matter?
Servants, both of us—servants who waited on you
as you gradually learned to entrust your lives to our mutual Master.
We each carried out our servant assignment.
I planted the seed, Apollos watered the plants, but God made you grow.
It's not the one who plants or the one who waters who is
at the center of this process but God, who makes things grow."
1 CORINTHIANS 3:5–7, MSG

CONCLUSION

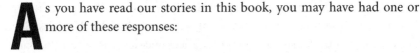

"Throw Us Out, Lord, Throw Us Out!"

May God *Throw Some People Out of The Church* . . . and into the Harvest Fields!

A s you have read our stories in this book, you may have had one or more of these responses:

1. *"I'm not like you."*
2. *"I'm not an extrovert."*
3. *"I'm not an evangelist."*
4. *"I'm not a courageous person."*
5. *"I don't have warm feelings toward Muslims like you do."*

We understand, we really do.

But please let us try to answer each of these responses in order:

#1 - We don't want you to be like either one of us. Be who you are in Jesus as you evangelize. Be who He made *you* to be in all your uniqueness. That is where you will experience His smile so that you may shine for Him in this dark world.

#2—Miriam is more introverted than I am. I, Timothy, am an extrovert. God uses *both* kinds of personalities equally and beautifully for His glory. And God uses *both* kinds of personalities equally and beautifully for sharing His gospel. The approach just looks different.

#3—Neither of us has a strong gift of evangelism. Miriam has gifts of service, helping, and hospitality. I have gifts of pastoring, teaching, and encouragement. You don't have to have a gift of giving to give money to a person in need. You don't have to have a gift of mercy to show compassion for someone. In the same way, you don't have to have a gift of evangelism to *do* evangelism. You simply need God's heart for lost people, obedience to His Great Commission, some helpful tools, and the filling and leading of the Holy Spirit.

#4—Believe us, we are not courageous people! We don't think anyone would refer to us as being particularly bold. But, like you, we can ask for boldness and courage as the early Church did in Acts 4. God will surely answer that humble, dependent prayer.

#5—In 2006, God gave me, Timothy, a supernatural love for Muslim people over the course of one weekend. (My heart burns for them to be in heaven.) At that same conference in Dearborn Michigan, Miriam did not gain any kind of new "warm fuzzies"—feelings of sentimentality—for Muslims. She determined to love Muslim people out of sheer obedience to Jesus, who said, "Love your neighbor." (And if you think Muslims are your enemies, He has an additional command for you—and you already know what that is!) More of you are like Miriam than like me when it comes to Muslim people. Please follow her example and be obedient to Jesus out of love for Him. We believe that this posture brings pleasure to God's heart more than doing something because you have warm and sentimental feelings about it! Jesus declared,

"If you love me, you will keep my commandments."
JOHN 14:15

We hope you can see that Miriam and I are *not* extraordinary people. We are not especially spiritual, or talented, or gifted, or intelligent, or bold.

We are both simple people from small towns in which we did not grow up with, or even see, Muslim people.

We are merely an unlikely couple whom God has called to go from the Midwest to the Middle East to let Muslim people know how much He loves them and has proven it by what Jesus did for them on the cross (Romans 5:8).

In our own different ways, we love Jesus and are trying to follow where He leads us in our ongoing journey to *love our Muslim neighbor.*

So, back to you and our final questions to ponder:

- What are you willing to do—and where are you willing to go—to help Muslim people come *one step closer* to following Jesus and entering the kingdom of God?

One thing is clear: if you hear the call of God to love your Muslim neighbor, your life will most definitely *change.*

Pastor Ray Pritchard speaks about this kind of change:

> *"A very wise friend summed up the truth this way:*
> *'Everyone wants progress. No one wants change.'*
> *That one statement summarizes the problem*
> *facing almost every church in America . . .*
>
> *"We all say we want to make progress in reaching the world,*
> *but no one wants things to change.*
>
> *"Change propels us out of our comfort zone . . . forces us out of our ruts . . .*
> *challenges our priorities . . . disrupts our plans . . .*
> *introduces us to a whole new set of problems . . .*
> *stretches us in ways we don't want to be stretched . . .*
> *upsets the apple cart . . .*
>
> *"We are to pray that God will light a fire inside the church*
> *that will ignite a movement inside many hearts that will result in people*
> *being 'thrust out' of the church into the harvest fields . . .*
>
> *"We need to pray that God will throw some people out of the church."*
> (https://www.keepbelieving.com/sermon/2007-02-25-Ballistic-Christianity/)

No wonder Jesus said to His disciples,

> *"The harvest is plentiful, but the laborers are few;*
> *therefore pray earnestly to the Lord of the harvest*
> *to send out laborers into his harvest."*
> MATTHEW 9:37–38

("Send out" here in Greek is *ekballo*: to cast out, drive out, compel, expel; it is where we get our English word *ballistic*.)

Amen, Lord, amen!

Throw us out into Your harvest fields—where we live or across the ocean—so we can joyfully follow You in *loving our Muslim neighbors!*

———

> *"I tell you, open your eyes and look at the fields!*
> *They are ripe for harvest."*
> JOHN 4:35, NIV

> *"And the master said to the servant,*
> *'Go out to the highways and hedges and compel people to come in,*
> *that my house may be filled.'"*
> LUKE 14:23

> *"While I was . . . focused on myself, there was a whole world*
> *with literally billions of people who had no idea who God is,*
> *how amazing He is, and the wonders He has done for us.*
> *They are the ones who are really suffering.*
> *They don't know His hope, His peace,*
> *and His love that transcends all understanding.*
> *They don't know the message of the gospel.*
> *How could I consider myself a follower of Jesus*
> *if I was not willing to give hope to the hopeless?"*
> (The late Dr. Nabeel Qureshi, a BMB, who died of cancer in 2017 at age 34,
> in his classic book *Seeking Allah, Finding Jesus*, p. 283)

> *"'Everyone who calls on the name of the LORD will be saved.'*
> *But how can they call on him to save them unless they believe in him?*
> *And how can they believe in him if they have never heard about him?*

And how can they hear about him unless someone tells them?
And how will anyone go and tell them without being sent?
That is why the Scriptures say,
'How beautiful are the feet of messengers
who bring good news!'"
ROMANS 10:13–15, NLT

APPENDIX 1

A GLOSSARY OF TERMS COMMONLY USED BY MUSLIM PEOPLE

---

abaya—a long and loose-fitting robe-like dress, or cloak, worn by some Muslim women. It differs from a *burqa,* which covers the whole body from head to feet with only a mesh screen for the eyes, allowing the wearer to see in front of her.

Al-ham-du-li-llah—"Praise be to God!" in Arabic. It has basically the same meaning as *"Hallelujah!"*

Allah—the Arabic word for *"God."* It was used by Christians long before the time of Muhammad. Arabic speaking Christians still use *"Allah"* today in referring to God, though there are some inherent and significant differences in the definition of who Allah is.

Allah-u-Akbar—"Allah is greater" in Arabic. It means that Allah is greater than anything or anyone. This phrase is recited by Muslims in many differ-ent situations: when very happy, expressing approval, to prevent one from becoming prideful by reminding them that Allah is their source of success, or as a battle cry. The phrase is not found in the Qur'an.

Eid al Adha—a commemoration of Abraham's willingness to sacrifice his son (the Qur'an does not specify who, but Muslims believe it was Ishmael, not Isaac).

Eid al Fitr—the celebration that marks the end of the month of fasting (Ramadan).

Hadith—an account of things said or done by Muhammad recorded by his followers and taught as a part of Islamic theology. These were put together 200 years after the death of Muhammad.

hajj—the religious pilgrimage to Mecca, Saudi Arabia, that is expected of all adult Muslims if finances and health allow it.

halal—something that is lawful and permissible for a Muslim to do (usually in reference to food, but halal also applies to almost every aspect of life and conduct).

haram—something that is not lawful or permissible for a Muslim to do.

hijab—the headscarf worn by many, but not all, Muslim women.

imam—literally, *"leader."* It is a common term for the leader of a mosque and one who leads prayers there.

Injil (or Injeel)—a holy book given to Isa (Jesus) by Allah that Muslim scholars claim is the "true" Gospel whereas the Gospels of the New Testament are generally considered by them to be corrupted. Nevertheless, some Muslims will call our four Gospels—or even the entire New Testament—the Injil.

Inshallah—a very common term used by Muslims that means, *"If Allah wills."* It is a term of acceptance or resignation.

Isa al Masih—the name in Islam for *"Jesus the Messiah."*

Islam—the religion of Muslims. The word means "submission" or "surrender" (to Allah).

jannah—literally, *"paradise, garden."* The final abode of those Allah allows into paradise in Islam.

jihad—means *"struggle."* This is struggling or striving for Allah's cause in one of two ways: the great jihad is the internal, nonviolent, spiritual struggle against temptation to sin; the lesser jihad is the external, militaristic struggle to protect the interests of Islam.

jinn—invisible, supernatural beings made out of smokeless flames of fire. They can be good or bad. Evil jinn are feared by Muslims and thought to be menacing creatures that can harm humans through sickness, accidents, deception, mental illness, etc. They can hide in places such as the drain of a sink, in the bathroom, or in any filthy place. Some Muslims wear designated amulets and chant specific prayers for protection from evil jinn.

Kaaba—the word means *"cube"* in Arabic. It is the *"House of Allah,"* a square building in Mecca draped in a silk and cotton veil. Muslims pray toward it wherever they live in the world. It is the holiest shrine in Islam.

kafir—from the word *kafara*, *"to hide."* Refers to those whom Muslims believe deliberately hide the truth: non-Muslims in non-Islamic countries or states, unbelievers, truth-concealers. It is also a common derogatory term used by different Islamic factions such as Sunni and Shias to denounce each other as non-Muslims.

Mecca—Muhammad's birthplace in Saudi Arabia; the holiest city in Islam; the location of the hajj. Muslims are expected to face Mecca when praying.

Medina—a city in Saudi Arabia where Muhammad fled after he and his followers experienced persecution in Mecca. It is the burial place of Muhammad.

minaret—a tower built beside or onto a mosque. The call to prayer is made from the top of a minaret by a live person or by a recording—both through a *loud* loudspeaker!

Muhammad (or Mohammed)—literally, "one who is praised"; the founder of Islam and the last—or *"seal"*—of the prophets in Islam.

mosque—the place of worship for Muslims; literally a place of prostration for prayer (*masjid* is the Arabic term for mosque).

Muslim—follower of Islam; one submitted to Allah.

niqab—a face veil worn by some Muslim women that leaves only the eyes uncovered. It is most often seen in Yemen, Saudi Arabia, Oman, and the UAE.

Qur'an (or Koran)—literally, "recitation"; the primary holy book for Muslim people; it is about the length of the New Testament.

Ramadan—the ninth month of the Islamic calendar and the obligatory month of fasting. It is thought to be the time when Muhammad received the Qur'an from a spirit-being he believed to be the angel Jabril (Gabriel).

"Salaam (or salam) alaykum"—a common greeting meaning, *"Peace be upon you,"* in Arabic. (Spellings and pronunciations differ.)

salat (or salah)—the obligatory Muslim prayers performed five times each day by Muslims pointing in/facing the direction of Mecca.

sawm—an Arabic word meaning "fasting" and usually associated with not eating or drinking during the daylight hours during Ramadan.

shahada—the creed/declaration of faith and first of the five "pillars" of Islamic beliefs: *"There is no god but Allah, and Muhammad is His messenger."* We have seen different forms that replace "god" with "deity" and replace "messenger" with "prophet." There is also the longer version, which adds, "I bear witness" two times: *"I bear witness that there is no deity but God, and I bear witness that Muhammad is the messenger of God."*

Sharia—the laws of Islam derived from the Qur'an and from the teachings and example of Muhammad (hadiths) that regulate the actions of Muslims.

sheikh—a title or a nickname for an elderly person or one who is knowledgeable in Islam. This title is also given to a leader or a wise person.

Shia—the second largest sect of Islam after Sunni Islam. Shia (or **Shi'ite**) Muslims believe that the rightful successor (caliph) to Muhammad after his death should have been his cousin and son-in-law, Ali. They comprise about ten percent of Muslims globally.

shirk—the blasphemous act of regarding anything else as equal with Allah. This includes idolatry, polytheism, or attributing divinity to a person such as Jesus.

Sufism—a mystical branch of Islam that emphasizes self-denial as a means of communion with Allah. Sufis strive to draw close to Allah and experience his divine presence.

Sunni—the largest branch of Islam (perhaps eighty-five percent of Muslims in the world today). Sunni Muslims believe that the first four successors to Muhammad after his death were the rightful leaders, and not his son-in-law Ali, as Shi'ites believe.

surah—one of the sections—or chapters—of the Qur'an, which are traditionally arranged in order of decreasing length. The Qur'an contains 114 surahs.

Tawrat—In Islam, the Tawrat (also Tawrah or Taurat) refers to the Torah, which Muslims believe to be a holy book given by God to Musa (Moses).

umma—Arabic word meaning *"community."* The global community of all Muslim believers.

wudu—the washing the hands, mouth, nostrils, arms, head and feet with water before prayer. This is an important part of ritual purity in Islam and is typically done in preparation for formal prayers and before handling and reading the Qur'an.

Zabur—the holy book of the Psalms given to King Dawud (David).

zakat—a form of almsgiving which is regarded as a religious obligation or tax in Islam.

APPENDIX 2

ISLAM'S ORIGIN, PRACTICES, AND BELIEFS—A SIMPLE OVERVIEW

I. ISLAM: THE *ORIGIN*

Note: many scholars say the early history of Islam cannot be known with absolute certainty because of the lack of documents about this period outside of Muslim sources.

A. THE PROPHET MUHAMMAD/THE QUR'AN—Muhammad was born in A.D. 570 into a family believed to be descended from Abraham's son Ishmael. His father died before his birth; his mother died when he was six. As a forty-year-old adult, Muhammad was appalled at the idol worship of his day. In a time of meditation in a cave outside Mecca in about A.D. 610, Muslims believe that he was visited by the angel Jabril (Gabriel) and that from then until the end of his life in 632 he received "revelations" from Jabril which were later compiled by his followers into the Qur'an. The Qur'an is 114 chapters (suras) in length and is considered by Muslims to be the last infallible witness of Allah — an exact, word-for-word copy of God's final revelation.

B. MUHAMMAD'S REACTIONS TO THE "REVELATIONS" AND SUBSEQUENT VISIT WITH A "CHRISTIAN"—When Muhammad received revelations from the "angel," he is reported to have had numerous negative reactions: panic, terror; sweating profusely; ringing in the ears; foaming at

275

the mouth; trembling; snorting like a camel; loss of consciousness or faint-
ing; bewilderment—fear that he was possessed by a demon or going mad;
suicidal depression.

Because of the confusion and terrifying intensity of these revelations,
some believe that Muhammad's first wife, Khadija, took him to a "Christian" relative of hers— Waraqah bin Nawfal (he was probably part of a sect
outside of true, biblical Christianity). Sadly, this man apparently believed
Muhammad's calling as a prophet to be authentic and affirmed it.

Note: Waraqah may have been at least partly invented by Muslims more
than a century after the life of Muhammad. Maybe the tradition is accurate,
but some scholars are dubious concerning this story about Waraqah and
his relationship to Muhammad. But if the story is historically correct, let us
consider what might have happened had Waraqah known and cited Galatians 1:8—if even an angel preaches another gospel, let him be accursed—
and 2 Corinthians 11:14—Satan disguises himself as an angel of light—to
Muhammad and Khadija. How might history have been changed if Muhammad had understood—and heeded—those biblical warnings?

C. MUHAMMAD'S PREACHING, FLIGHT, FIGHT—It is believed that
in the beginning Muhammad publicly preached a message of one God, a
stop to the polytheistic idol worship in Mecca, and a coming day of God's
judgment (in Mecca, he was a "warner"). During twelve years of this preaching, most did not listen. Muhammad's message evidently threatened not
only the popular polytheism of his day, but also the political and economic
powers. Muhammad and his followers were forced to flee 200 miles north
from Mecca to Medina in A.D. 622 to escape the persecution they were experiencing. During his time in Medina, Muhammad became a strong political
and military leader, winning numerous military battles (in Medina, he was
a "warrior"). It appears that in Medina, Islam began to become not just a
religion but also a political power. Muhammad later returned to Mecca and
took control of it. Two years after his death, all of Arabia was under Islam.

**D. AFTER MUHAMMAD'S DEATH (C. A.D. 632), THE SUNNI SHIA DI-
VIDE**—A difference arose over who would lead Islam. Most believed the caliph (successor) should be Abu-Bakr, the father-in-law (through his famous
young daughter, Aisha) of Muhammad and one of the first converts to Islam.
Others believed that Ali, Muhammad's son-in-law and cousin, should be the
successor. Two camps formed. Ali's followers became known as Shiites, and

Abu-Bakr's followers became known as Sunnis (perhaps ninety percent of Muslims in the world today). Abu-Bakr became the first caliph, followed by Umar, Uthman, and then Ali. Islam advanced far and wide during the reigns of those leaders. Thirty years after Muhammad's death, Islam had expanded to include parts of North Africa, the Middle East, the Caucasus, and most of modern-day Turkey.

II. ISLAM: *PRACTICES & BELIEFS*

A. THE *"FIVE PILLARS"* OF ISLAM (we have seen these listed in different sequences)

1. **Shahadah (the profession of faith)**—*"There is no god but Allah, and Muhammad is His messenger."* This is the most frequently repeated sentence in the life of a Muslim. It is the first thing spoken into the ear of a newborn baby. It is spoken daily in prayers; at weddings; and if possible, is the last thing heard and spoken at death.

2. **Salat or Salah (prayer)**—prescribed prayers said five times a day facing Mecca. These and other prayers are said on Fridays in the mosque. The call to prayer can be heard from minarets, TV, and radio and is always in Arabic. Before prayer, Muslims must ritually cleanse certain parts of their bodies with water (this is called "wudu").

3. **Zakat (almsgiving)**—middle- and upper-class Sunni Muslims are expected to give 2.5% of their possessions and wealth in charitable donations.

4. **Sawm (fasting)**—during the month of Ramadan, no food or drink is allowed from dawn until dusk. Some devout Muslims will attempt to not swallow their saliva to fulfill this obligation.

5. **Hajj (pilgrimage)**—if physically or financially possible, a pilgrimage to Mecca is expected at least once in one's lifetime.

B. THE QUR'AN IS COMPLETELY OPPOSED TO THE BIBLICAL CONCEPTS OF GOD AS FATHER, THE TRINITY, AND THE DEITY OF JESUS

Note: it may be helpful to understand that Muhammad was battling polytheism and the worship of idols in his day. As a result, the idea of God's absolute oneness developed. Muslims saw the concepts of God's Fatherhood and Jesus as the "Son of God" as blasphemous violations of God's oneness and otherness. This is why Islam has become so opposed to the Trinity and the Sonship of Jesus and is so adamantly monotheistic. Also, Muslims consider it blasphemous to call God "Father" because it implies to them that He had sexual relations. They do not have our biblical understanding that the Father and the Son have a *spiritual* relationship, not a *physical* one. Like Peter, a Muslim can believe in Jesus's Sonship only through a divine revelation of God (Matthew 16:16–17)!

- **The Qur'an: Jesus Is Revered but Still Only a Prophet**—"O People of the Book! Commit no excesses in your religion: Nor say of Allah aught but the truth. Christ Jesus the son of Mary was (no more than) a messenger of Allah, and His Word, which He bestowed on Mary, and a spirit proceeding from Him. So believe in Allah and His messengers. Say not 'Trinity;' desist. It will be better for you for Allah is one Allah. Glory be to Him, (far exalted is He) above having a son." (The Qur'an 4:171, Yusuf Ali translation.) The Bible says: 1 John 4:15.
- **The Qur'an: Jesus Is Not the Son of God**—"The Christians call Christ the son of Allah. That is a saying from their mouth; (in this) they but imitate what the unbelievers of old used to say. Allah's curse be on them. How they are deluded away from the Truth!" (The Qur'an 9:30, Yusuf Ali translation). The Bible says: 1 John 5:11–12.
- **The Qur'an: The Trinity Is Blasphemous**—-"They do blaspheme who say: 'Allah is Christ the son of Mary.' But said Christ: 'O Children of Israel! worship Allah, my Lord and your Lord.' Whoever joins other gods with Allah, Allah will forbid him the garden, and the Fire will be his abode. There will for the wrong-doers be no one to help. They do blaspheme who say: Allah is one of three in a Trinity for there is no god except One Allah. If they desist not from their word (of blasphemy), verily a grievous penalty will befall the blasphemers among them." (The Qur'an 5:72–73, Yusuf Ali translation). The Bible says: John 1:1; 14:9.
- **The Qur'an: Jesus Did Not Die on the Cross**—"And because

of their saying (in boast), "We killed Messiah 'Isa (Jesus), son of Maryam (Mary), the Messenger of Allah,"—but they killed him not, nor crucified him, but the resemblance of 'Isa (Jesus) was put over another man (and they killed that man), and those who differ therein are full of doubts. They have no (certain) knowledge, they follow nothing but conjecture. For surely; they killed him not [i.e. 'Isa (Jesus), son of Maryam (Mary)]." (The Qur'an 4:157, Mohsin Khan translation). The Bible says: John 20:24–31.

C. BELIEFS ABOUT OBTAINING SALVATION IN ISLAM

- **The Qur'an: Islam is the True Religion**—"If anyone desires a religion other than Islam (submission to Allah), never will it be accepted of him; and in the Hereafter He will be in the ranks of those who have lost (all spiritual good)." (The Qur'an 3:85, Yusuf Ali translation). The Bible says: John 3:16; John 14:6; Acts 4:12; 1 John 4:1.
- **The Qur'an: Angels Record Good and Bad Deeds**—"(Remember!) that the two receivers (recording angels) receive (each human being after he or she has attained the age of puberty), one sitting on the right and one on the left (to note his or her actions). Not a word does he (or she) utter, but there is a watcher by him ready (to record it)." (The Qur'an 50:17–18, Mohsin Khan translation; cf. 82:10–12). The Bible says: Revelation 20:12–15.
- **The Qur'an: Scales Weigh Good and Bad Deeds**—On the Day of Judgment, Allah will place one's good and evil works on the divine scale: "Then those whose balance (of good deeds) is heavy, they will attain salvation. But those whose balance is light, will be those who have lost their souls, in Hell will they abide." (The Qur'an 23:102–103, Yusuf Ali translation). The Bible says: Ephesians 2:8–9; Titus 3:4–7.
- **The Hadith: Uncertainty of Salvation for a Muslim, Even Muhammad**—There is *no guarantee* of paradise for Muslims. They can never be sure of their destiny. Good works can only give one *hope* for heaven. A devout Muslim would not rely on good works alone because doing so would presume upon the sovereignty of Allah. Muhammad himself questioned his own salvation: "By Allah, though I am the Apostle of Allah, yet *I do not know what*

Allah will do to me" (Sahih Al-Bukhari, Hadith 5.266)! Muslims can only say, *"Inshallah . . ."* ("If God wills . . ."). The Bible says: 1 John 5:13.

D. THERE ARE SIMILARITIES BETWEEN JESUS IN THE BIBLE AND "ISA AL MASIH" IN THE QUR'AN—PRAYERFULLY CONSIDER USING THEM FOR BRIDGE-BUILDING CONVERSATIONS WITH MUSLIM PEOPLE (WITHOUT EXALTING THE QUR'AN OR ISLAM)

Note: In looking at the following verses from the Qur'an that contain truths (or partial truths) about Jesus, perhaps we can see an application of Acts 14:17 regarding God's concern for lost people:

"Yet he did not leave himself without witness . . ."

Though the Qur'an is certainly *not* inspired by the Holy Spirit, there are some "streams" (truth) in the "desert" (The Qur'an) that God has graciously allowed there for the thirsty Muslim soul to lead them on to the complete, saving truth of the Bible:

- **The Qur'an: "Isa" Had a Virgin Birth**—"Behold! the angels said: 'O Mary! God hath chosen thee and purified thee; chosen thee above the women of all nations . . . O Mary! God giveth thee glad tidings of a Word from Him: his name will be Christ Jesus the son of Mary held in honor in this world and the Hereafter and of (the company of) those nearest to God. He shall speak to the people in childhood and in maturity and he shall be (of the company) of the righteous.' She said: 'O my Lord! how shall I have a son when no man hath touched me?' He said: 'Even so: God createth what He willeth; when He hath decreed a plan He but saith to it `Be' and it is! And God will teach him the Book and Wisdom the Law and the Gospel.'" (The Qur'an 3:42, 45–48, Yusuf Ali translation; cf. 19:16–22)
- **The Qur'an: "Isa" Performed Healings and Raised the Dead**—"And will make him ['Isa (Jesus)] a Messenger to the Children of Israel (saying): 'I have come to you with a sign from your Lord, that . . . I heal him who was born blind, and the leper, and I bring

the dead to life by Allah's Leave.'" (The Qur'an 3:49, Mohsin Khan translation)

- **The Qur'an: "Isa" Lived a Sinless Life**—"(The angel) said: 'I am only a Messenger from your Lord, (to announce) to you the gift of a righteous son.'" (The Qur'an 19:19, Mohsin Khan translation) "He said: 'Nay, I am only a messenger from thy Lord, (to announce) to thee the gift of a holy son.'" (The Qur'an 19:19, Yusuf Ali translation)

- **The Qur'an: "Isa" Will Come Again**—"And he ['Isa (Jesus), son of Maryam (Mary)] shall be a known sign for (the coming of) the Hour (Day of Resurrection) [i.e., 'Isa's (Jesus's) descent on the earth]. Therefore have no doubt concerning it (i.e., the Day of Resurrection). And follow Me (Allah) (i.e., be obedient to Allah and do what He orders you to do, O mankind)! This is the Straight Path (of Islamic Monotheism, leading to Allah and to His Paradise)." (The Qur'an 43:61, Mohsin Khan translation)

APPENDIX 3

FINDING MUSLIM PEOPLE WHERE YOU LIVE + HELPFUL CONVERSATION STARTERS

"HOW DO I FIND MUSLIM PEOPLE IN MY AREA?
IF I FIND THEM, HOW DO I TALK TO THEM?"

Finding Muslim People Where You Live:

- Do an internet search on:
    - » Muslims in _____ (your town or city)
    - » Muslims at _____ (local university/community college)
    - » mosques in _____ (your town or city)
    - » Middle Eastern food in _____ (your town or city)
    - » "halal" food in _____ (your town or city)
    - » "halal" market in _____ (your town or city)
    - » refugees in _____ (your town or city)

Conversation Starters with a Muslim Person:

1. *Salaam alaykum!* (*"Peace be upon you"* in Arabic.) Your pronunciation of this common greeting to a Muslim person is not nearly as important as your effort to say it! They usually love that you tried!

If you struggle too much with this greeting, go with a normal English greeting like the one immediately below.

2. Hello! How are you? What is your name? My name is . . .
3. I really enjoy your accent. Would you mind telling me where your family is from?
4. How long have you lived here, or were you born here?
5. What do you miss the most about your country?
6. What do you like the most about this country?
7. I am sorry for the suffering your country (perhaps Syria, Iraq, Yemen, or Palestine) is experiencing. I will pray for your country.
8. What is your favorite *futball* (soccer) team? Who is your favorite player?
9. This is a great sale, isn't it? Do you shop here often?
10. Your kids are beautiful. Thank God." (Without fail, you *must* include giving thanks to God, or a Muslim parent will fear that demon-like creatures might attack their kids—or any other object that is complimented.)
11. We are glad you have come to America (or Canada, etc.). (Don't feel you have to say this; say it only if you mean it.)
12. What can Christians do to make Muslims feel more loved at this time in America (or Canada)?
13. Is there anything I can pray about for you or your family? (Then— if it is appropriate—ask them if you can pray there, on the spot; if they agree, pray aloud to the Father and in the name of Jesus—be humble, but be confident!)
14. I would like to see you again! Would you like to get together some time for coffee?
15. Could we exchange phone numbers or email?

Conversation Topics to Get to Know Your Muslim Friend a Little More:

Muslim people come in all shapes and sizes. As chapter 10 emphasized, they are not *"one size fits all."* Each individual Muslim must be known on his or her own terms. We hope these questions will help you in your quest to learn about and build relationship with your Muslim friend.

1. How do you greet people in your culture? What is an appropriate

way for me to greet you and a culturally appropriate way to say goodbye?

2. I would really like to learn about what life was like for you as you grew up. What can you tell me about your family? Your house? Town/city? School?

3. What would be good for me to know about your country? Could you share with me something about its history?

4. What are some traditional foods that you miss from home? Is there any food here that you've really liked or not liked?

5. Do you mostly drink coffee or tea in your country? What kind? What is your favorite beverage?

6. How do you celebrate birthdays in your country? How do you normally celebrate holidays? What holidays do you celebrate? What are your favorite holidays?

7. How are weddings celebrated in your culture? How long have you been married (if applicable)? Do you have any pictures of your wedding that you can show me next time we get together? Do you have pictures of your family? Would you like to see my wedding pictures (if applicable)?

8. How is studying at a university here different from at one back home? (Question for an international student)

9. Do you have a favorite sport? Do you like going to sporting events?

10. Are there hobbies or sports you played back home that you have been able to keep doing here? Ones that you haven't?

11. Are there any animals here that you don't see in your country? Are there any animals that you are uncomfortable being around? Dogs? Cats?

12. Is music important in your culture? Do you play an instrument? Is music used in any traditions or celebrations? Do you listen to music? What is your favorite type of music?

13. Did you learn any of our country's history before coming here? Are you interested in learning some of our history? What would you like to learn about or see?

14. Is there any place you would really like to go in our area that I can show you?

15. What things did you think would be true about Western culture that are not true? What are some good surprises you have dis-

covered about our culture? Does anything in the Western culture perplex or confuse you?

16. What is something that your culture values that is not a common value here (or vice versa)?

17. What has been the hardest thing about living here?

18. What is one thing you've learned about yourself and your culture while living here?

Spiritual Conversation Starters with a Muslim Person:

1. Do people talk about religion in your country? Or is it more of a private thing?

2. Would you say that people are more or less religious here than in your home country?

3. What have you noticed about religion here? What questions do you have about it?

4. When did you first hear the name *Allah*? What did you learn about Him in your growing up years?

5. What are the religious traditions of your family?

6. How is your practice of Islam the same as in your family? How might it be different?

7. What does prayer look like in Islam?

8. May I ask, how often do you pray? Do you pray before meals?

9. Why do you think people were created?

10. Does your culture have any traditions or stories of how the earth and people were created?

11. What do you think is the purpose of life? What does your culture say it is?

12. When bad things happen, how do you view them? Do you have peace? Do you have hope?

13. Do you believe Allah cares about human beings? Why or why not?

14. Do you believe that Allah is a God of love? Do you believe that Allah loves you?

15. Is forgiveness something that is practiced in your culture? Do you believe Allah forgives us when we do something wrong?

16. If you could ask Allah any question, what would you ask Him?

17. What do you believe happens after we die?

18. What do you think paradise is like?

19. How do you get to paradise in Islam?

20. What does the Qur'an say about paradise? About hell?
21. When you hear the word "Christian," what do you think of? How would you describe what a Christian is? Their beliefs?
22. What do Muslims think about Christians and Christianity in your country?
23. Do you think everyone in Western countries is a Christian?
24. How do you think people in Western countries look at Islam and Muslims?
25. How have people treated you here as a Muslim?
26. Do you know why people celebrate Christmas here? Or Easter?
27. Have you read any part of the Bible?
28. Would you like to hear what the Bible says a true follower of Jesus is?
29. Would you like to hear the key points of the Bible?
30. Would you like to read the Bible together?
31. Have you ever been to a church here?
32. Would you like to go with me?

APPENDIX 4

CULTURAL DO'S AND DON'TS IN REACHING OUT TO MUSLIM PEOPLE

I. PRACTICE CULTURAL AWARENESS WITH MUSLIM PEOPLE
(adapted with permission from Dr. Ed Hoskins' excellent book, *A Muslim's Heart*)

- *Relationships/Hospitality* - people are more important than events.
- *Generosity* - be careful what you admire—it might be given to you!
- *Family* - emphasis on the extended family/tribe vs. the nuclear, immediate family.
- *Aging* - valued, respected; aged given decision-making priority in Muslim culture.
- *Status* - in the West, it is usually earned; in Muslim society, it is usually inherited.
- *Rights* - society is more important than the individual; very much group oriented.
- *Change* - of little value and often shunned.
- *Time Orientation* - the past and traditions are valued over the future.
- *Education* - rote memory vs. integration and application of facts.
- *Time Usage* - punctuality not as important in the East as in the West.
- *Honor and Shame* - all-important! "Honor is the ship that floats all of Muslim culture. It is more important than logic, truth, and even

life itself. This may seem odd to us in the West, but honor is an actual commodity to Muslims; it can be bought and sold, added to, and subtracted from . . . Anything that subtracts, namely shame, is to be avoided at all costs; female sexual immorality and changing religion top the list" (Hoskins).

- *Sin* - "Sin is not taken as seriously in the East as it is in the West. Although it is considered wrong for a Muslim to sin, it is not nearly as bad as the shame of committing sin and then getting caught. Sin is relative and largely external ('What if someone sees what I did and tells others?'), as opposed to the Western view of sin, which is more internal ('What do I do about the guilt I feel because of my moral failure?')" (Hoskins).
- *Confrontation* – remember that preserving honor, pride, dignity—"saving face"—is a top priority! Blame is avoided or transferred. Confrontation is often done through a third party, or through a story vs. a direct approach.

II. PRACTICE CULTURAL COURTESIES WITH MUSLIM PEOPLE
(some of these points are also adapted with permission from Ed Hoskins' book, *A Muslim's Heart*)

- *Greetings* - shaking hands is a polite greeting, but never use your left hand. With the opposite gender, never extend your hand first. If they want to shake your hand, they will reach theirs out to you first. "Peace be upon you" (*salaam alaykum*) is a standard greeting, and "And upon you be peace" is the standard response.
- *Refreshments* - every Muslim host, no matter how poor, wants to be known as hospitable. A lack of hospitality subtracts from family honor, which is to be avoided at all costs. If you visit, you will usually be given something to drink (tea, juice, soft drink) and often something to eat (nuts or sweets). If you are visited, be sure to set out nice dishes and offer similar refreshments to your Muslim visitors. Be prepared for a long visit—perhaps several hours—and don't be the first to suggest that the visit is over!
- *Food and Drink* - Muslims believe that God has forbidden them to eat pork or drink alcohol. Serving almost any other kind of meat to them is a safe choice, especially chicken or lamb. If the meat can be "halal," all the better. Look up halal markets near you to pur-

chase these meats, which are like the Jewish concept of "kosher." Unclean foods: avoid anything made with lard such as cookies and cakes. Use vegetable fat (oil) and check labels!

- *Dogs* - Usually considered dirty animals. If you host Muslims at your home, keep dogs restrained and out of sight for the sake of your Muslim guests.
- *Repetition* - If a Muslim makes an invitation to you once, it may not be intended to be fulfilled. It may just be being polite. If an offer is genuine, it will be repeated two or even three times. Pay attention.
- *Gifts* - When visiting a Muslim's home for the first time, take a gift such as flowers or candy. The closer the relationship, the more expensive the gift should be, but try to keep the gifts even in value (Muslims will do almost anything to not be in your debt).
- *Clothing* - Muslims are repelled by the way Westerners dress. In building friendship with a Muslim person, modesty is vital for both men and women. True story: a man was afraid to become a Christian because he thought his wife and daughters would then dress immodestly and become immoral. (As we said in this book, a famous female singer sometimes wears a cross on stage, but little else. What message does this send to a Muslim person?)
- *Avoid Loaded Topics Guaranteed to Start an Argument* - Israel, Palestine, the Gulf Wars, the Crusades, oil, our presidents, and politics in general. Don't be sucked in. Don't let your nationalistic pride or politics get in the way of your disciple making. Evangelism is more important for eternity than patriotism!
- *Avoid Win-Lose Debates* - Discussions are for friends; debates are for opponents. Be resolute but respectful and loving (smile!) regarding your faith. Keep the focus on *Jesus* when possible—His miracles, His stories, His character—*Him!*

APPENDIX 5

SUGGESTED GUIDELINES FOR INTERACTING WITH YOUR MUSLIM FRIEND

---

1. We Are Ambassadors for Christ—Represent Him Well!

- We are to represent the Jesus we know, love, and worship more than anything or anyone else. More than our church, more than our ministry, more than our politics. It's all about *Jesus* (2 Corinthians 5:20)!

2. Relax—Enjoy Yourself!

- Give your stereotypes to God. Seek His help with any fear, anger, or suspicion related to Muslim people.
- It's normal to be nervous as you engage with a Muslim, but this is a perfect opportunity to trust God and venture out in new places with Him as your Guide.
- You don't need to be an "expert" in Islam, or even Christianity and the Bible. You don't have to have all the answers.
- It's always okay to say, "I don't know, but I will do my best to find out."
- Don't walk on eggshells worrying about making mistakes. Just smile a lot and do your best!
- This is serious business. Eternity is at stake for your Muslim

friends. But there are times when you need to have "holy fun" with Muslims. You will generally find them to be wonderful people.

3. Engage in *Discussions* and *Dialogues*, Not *Debates!*

- This is not a competition—it is not the Christians vs. the Muslims - so, you don't have to feel the pressure to "score points" or "win."
- Don't argue or get defensive. If it feels like an argument is beginning, remember that "a gentle answer turns away wrath" and prayerfully consider moving on to another subject (Proverbs 15:1; cf. James 1:19).
- Ask questions but never give the impression that you are fascinated with Islam and want to become a Muslim.
- If you use apologetics, do it in a confident but kind manner. And remember, most Muslims are not influenced to Christ by apologetics as much as by the loving friendship evangelism of real Christians.
- You can also discuss biblical principles for daily living by sharing Bible verses on worry, fear, anger, moral purity, work, finances, singleness, marriage, raising kids, etc.
- Show respect and honor. Listen carefully to the Muslim's points of view. Where they agree with the Bible, you might say something like, "We have some common ground there. Let's talk more." Or "The Bible says something very similar. Please let me show you." This is not compromise. It is building bridges. Be patient, courteous, and polite (1 Peter 2:17a) without showing approval of Islam or the Qur'an.

4. *Don't Unnecessarily Put Down* Islam, Muhammad, or the Qur'an!

- This just builds huge walls—or strengthens the ones that are already there. There may be Holy Spirit led times to challenge and confront the tenets of Islam with your Muslim friend to help awaken them to biblical truth. But *your role is not as much to persuade a Muslim about the wrongness of Islam as it is to show them the rightness of the biblical Jesus.* Muslims are like a person holding a candle. They have a little bit of light. You can either try to blow out their light or you can show them the sun—Jesus, the Light of the World. If they truly accept Him, sooner or later, they will let go of their candle and bask in the sun!

- If you are asked why you do not believe in Islam, Muhammad, or the Qur'an, be humble but unwavering in your response: "The Bible says that we cannot do enough good works to get to paradise on the Day of Judgment. God loved us so much that He made a bridge —one bridge—to paradise. That bridge is the person and sacrifice of Jesus to remove our sin and shame. I pray with all my heart that someday you will join me on that bridge and know that love."

5. *Lift Up Jesus,* Your Savior!

- *He* is the One Muslims need. He is the One we all need! Speak of His teachings, His actions, His sinlessness—His incomparable beauty (2 Corinthians 4:5).
- Muslims will often say to you, "We love Jesus. He is one of our prophets. We cannot be Muslims without loving Jesus." Respectfully challenge them by asking them what they love about Him. Listen carefully and then share why you love Jesus. Be specific— both from the Bible and from your relationship with Him.

6. Use and Show Respect for Your *Bible!*

- Use it as your primary source/guide for belief and behavior (2 Timothy 3:16).
- Never put your Bible on the floor (or even on your chair if you can help it) when with a Muslim. To the Muslim, this shows a lack of respect. Hold it above your waist or keep it on a table. And never keep a Bible (or a devotional guide with scripture in it) in your bathroom where a Muslim visitor to your home might see it! A bathroom is a spiritually unclean place for Muslims.
- Let the Bible speak for itself. Trust it. There is power in God's Word (Hebrews 4:12)!
- As much as you can, use Scriptures from the Gospels and focus on stories that Jesus told or stories about Jesus. You can use any verses from the Bible, but the sayings and stories of Jesus Himself are sometimes better received by Muslims than verses from other biblical writers such as Paul (some Muslims erroneously believe Paul changed/corrupted the original New Testament).

- Muslims often view our many English translations as a sign of weakness (though they actually have many of the Qur'an as well). If this comes up, simply share that every credible Bible translation from the earliest manuscripts until now contains the same essential message: God's loving plan to save/rescue lost sinners through the person and sacrifice of Jesus. John 3:16 has never been changed from John's pen in the first century to the present time!

- Muslims believe our Bible is "corrupted" in places. The Qur'an says that Jesus is not the Son of God and did not die on the cross. Don't argue about it. Just give them a New Testament or Gospel of John in their language as a gift. Let them read it for themselves. Let God work. (You might ask them *where* the Bible has been corrupted, *who* corrupted it, and *when* it was corrupted—but do this respectfully.)

7. *Share Stories* of *God Working in Your Life*— Including Your "Testimony"!

- There is nothing like a personal sharing of how God initially saved you (Acts 26) or later did something in answer to prayer. It shows that you have connection with Him.

- Share your examples (with enthusiasm) about how you see Jesus as being so incredible, so loving, so utterly amazing. He is the Key. He is the One and Only (John 14:6; Acts 4:29).

8. Build *Relationships!*

- When you meet a Muslim, think about exchanging emails or cell phone numbers, getting together for coffee, lunch, etc. Be friendly, and be a friend.

- Build a relationship, don't just communicate information (1 Thessalonians 2:8).

- Focus on the heart—kindly probe how the Muslim perceives his or her relationship with God in daily living. Don't just share doctrine or theology; share your heart.

9. Practice *Righteous* and *Wise* Male-Female Interaction

- Do not touch someone of the opposite gender. If they offer you their hand to shake, then you may do so. Do not extend your hand first. Follow their lead.

- Men, dress modestly. Wear long and loose-fitting pants. It's usually best not to wear shorts, gym shorts, or tight jeans. Long sleeved shirts are also good in some places but not necessary in others. And men, be careful of looking a Muslim woman directly in the eyes. In her culture, this is usually not done unless you are a close relative.
- Women, dress modestly. The looser the fit and the less skin showing, the better (no shorts or low-cut tops). Long sleeved, loose fitting blouses and pants are good. We want to help you avoid the stereotype amongst many Muslim people that Christian women are "loose," like "Hollywood movie women" (1 Timothy 2:9).
- At the end of chapter 39, we gave Christian women a very firm warning against dating or marrying a Muslim man. Please heed this wisdom! We sincerely love Muslims, but Islam requires certain things in marriage that no woman should have to live with.
- In Christian witness to Muslims, we strongly, strongly recommend male to male and female to female interaction unless it is in a group. This will prevent the possibility of extremely painful situations down the road, should an unwise marriage (a Christian woman to a Muslim man) take place.

10. *Love, Love, Love*—Each Muslim You Interact With!
- The "Great Commission" (Matthew 28:18–20) without the "Great Commandment" (Mark 12:30-31) can lead to prideful, obnoxious Christians (1 Corinthians 13:1–3; Romans 9:1–3).
- You will make mistakes in reaching out to Muslim people. It's okay! But whatever mistake you might make, don't let it be a lack of Christ-like love!

11. *Pray, Pray, Pray*—for Yourself and for Muslims You Know!
- Prepare by getting right yourself with God: seek forgiveness for all sins and ask for the refilling of the Holy Spirit. Ask for a heart of true humility as a fellow sojourner. (You don't have it all together, do you?)
- Consider fasting for breakthrough in the heart and mind of your Muslim friend so they can see the truth of the gospel.
- Ask other Christians to be praying for you—for you to faithfully obey Jesus's commands to love your neighbor, be a peacemaker,

and make disciples of all nations! Ask them to pray for you to have open doors (Colossians 4:3), clear proclamation of the gospel (Colossians 4:3), and bold, uncompromising proclamation of the gospel (Ephesians 6:19).

- Ask other Christians to be praying for your Muslim friends—that the Father would draw them to Jesus (John 6:44). This is the only way for them—for any of us—to be forgiven of our sins and put in right relationship with our great and loving Creator (Romans 1:16).

APPENDIX 6

HEART-TO-HEART INTERFAITH DIALOGUE QUESTIONS FOR A GROUP OF CHRISTIANS AND MUSLIMS

(from a blog: http://www.iLoveMuslims.net/)

Often, Christians and Muslims talk "head-to-head," and that usually leads to debate. We want to help followers of Jesus engage in "heart-to-heart" conversations with Muslim people. This can assist in preventing defensiveness and arguments but still allow for solid evangelistic witness.

Let's not leave all group interfaith dialogues with Muslims to people from churches who don't really believe in the biblical distinctives of the gospel (this seems to be the norm). As Bible-believing followers of Jesus, we can have good, substantive interfaith dialogue if we use questions that address the heart and life of each person and if we admit from the beginning that, while we have many things in common, we also have important differences in our faiths.

We suggest bringing a group of Muslims and Christians together and then dividing up into groups of two (same gender)—a Muslim and a follower of Jesus. Then simply go through these questions or come up with some of your own if you like. This can be done at a church, at a mosque, in a dorm or college classroom, etc.

The point is, talk to each other. Listen. Get to know each other. From the heart!

- Who has been the most important person in your life as you grew up? Why?
- Outside of Muhammad or Jesus, who would you most want to be like? Why?
- What is your favorite attribute or name of God? (examples: mercy, compassion, power)
- How would you best describe your emotions—your feelings— about God?
- To you, what is the most meaningful verse or story in your Holy Book?
- If you could use one word to describe your own personal prayer experiences (outside of formal prayer times), what would it be?
- What kinds of things do you pray about the most?
- What kinds of thoughts do you have about God when you pray?
- What word best describes your relationship to God?
- Tell about a time when you really experienced God in a positive way. Tell about a hard time when you really struggled with your faith in God or had doubts about Him.
- Who is Isa—Jesus—to you? What does he mean to you?
- If you say that you love Jesus, why? What is it about him that you love?
- When you think about being before God on the Day of Judgment, what thoughts do you have about that? What emotions do you feel?
- What would be the best thing about going to paradise? What would be the worst thing about going to hell fire?
- Why are we here on earth? Besides your general answer, why do you think God specifically put *you* on the earth?
- If you could do anything for God in gratitude for what He has done for you, what would it be?
- If you could give one message of faith to the whole world, what would it be?
- What has this experience been like for you in going through these questions together?
- What do you think would be the single most important thing that could be done to bring Muslims and Christians together in sincere, honest, meaningful dialogue and friendship?

APPENDIX 7

A MULTITUDE OF RESOURCES TO HELP YOU WITH OUTREACH TO MUSLIM PEOPLE

Note: we do not endorse every book or resource in this appendix unreservedly, but we do believe that each of them can definitely help you grow in loving and reaching out to Muslim people.

Books by, or about, Muslims Who Became Followers of Jesus (BMBs—Believers from a Muslim Background; sometimes called MBBs—Muslim Background Believers)

- *Seeking Allah, Finding Jesus: A Devout Muslim Encounters Christianity* by the late Nabeel Qureshi (a BMB). Grand Rapids, MI: Zondervan, 2014.
  This is the best book we have seen, doing two things incredibly well: it combines a phenomenal testimony of a Muslim becoming a follower of Jesus with a helpful and well-written overview of Islam. "Through his faith, though he died, he still speaks" (Hebrews 11:4).
- *I Dared to Call Him Father: The Miraculous Story of a Muslim Woman's Encounter with God* by Bilquis Sheikh (a BMB) and Dick Schneider. Grand Rapids, MI: Chosen, 2003.
  This brilliant autobiography by a prominent Muslim woman in Pakistan was hard for us to put down! Bilquis had dreams from

the Lord that turned her world upside down as she sought answers . . . and found Jesus!

- *From Cairo to Christ: How One Muslim's Faith Journey Shows
the Way for Others* by Abu Atallah (a BMB) and Kent A. Van Til.
Downers Grove, IL: IVP Books, 2017.
This is a captivating story of how one Muslim man was drawn to
the Christian faith in Egypt, and how he later became an ambassador for Christ with a ministry in the Muslim world. Our friend
has personally helped hundreds of Muslims come to Christ and
trained them to lead underground churches in their countries.
We love this man and his wife, and you will love reading his journey to Jesus.

- *The Gospel for Muslims: An Encouragement to Share Christ with
Confidence* by Thabiti Anyabwile (a BMB). Chicago, IL: Moody
Publishers, 2010.
This book by a pastor and Gospel Coalition leader makes excel-
lent points: trusting the power of the Bible when using it with
Muslims; the huge importance of showing hospitality; answering
objections to Christianity; including your church in outreach to
Muslims; and relying on the Holy Spirit. Thabiti also addresses the
"Nation of Islam," the Islamic group made up of African American
people that is rapidly growing in the US.

- *Once an Arafat Man: The True Story of How a PLO Sniper Found a
New Life* by Tass Saada (a BMB). Carol Stream, IL: Tyndale House
Publishers, 2008.
We have spoken with Tass and respect him greatly. This book is
his incredible story. At age 17, Tass ran away to become a PLO
sniper, a one-time chauffeur for Yasser Arafat, and a Muslim who
fought against Israel. Later, he moved to America, started a family, and eventually became a Christian. Then he risked retribution
as he returned home to share his faith with his family—and with
Yasser Arafat!

- *Understanding the Koran: A Quick Christian Guide to the Muslim
Holy Book* by Mateen Elass (a BMB). Grand Rapids, MI: Zonder-
van, 2004.
We have met Mateen and heard this gifted pastor-teacher speak.
In this book, he explains the Koran's historical background and
summarizes its teachings on Allah, sin, the way to paradise, hell,

jihad, Jesus, and much more. Mateen believes that the greatest tool in reaching Muslim people is *love*—yes, love for Muslim people, but also for believers to once again fall gloriously in love with Jesus. Then, he says, "the Muslim world will sit up and take notice."

- *Secret Believers: What Happens When Muslims Believe in Christ* by Brother Andrew and Al Janssen. Grand Rapids, MI: Fleming H. Revell, 2007.

  This book by one of our heroes reads like a page-turner novel, but the stories are true. Brother Andrew says it is his last book. It has a challenging conclusion about how we must be willing to pay any price to see Muslims find Christ—even to the giving of our lives.

- *Which None Can Shut: Remarkable True Stories of God's Miraculous Work in the Muslim World* by Reema Goode. Carol Stream, IL: Tyndale House Publishers, 2010.

  These are fantastic stories from the Arabian Gulf by a missionary—some of the very best stories we have ever read of outreach to Muslim people on the mission field. You will learn much and grow from Reema's experiences.

- *Dreams & Visions: Is Jesus Awakening the Muslim World?* by Tom Doyle. Nashville, TN: Thomas Nelson, 2012.

  Stirring stories of Jesus revealing himself to Muslims in Arab Muslim countries through dreams and visions. This intriguing book reads like the book of Acts!

- *A Wind in the House of Islam: How God Is Drawing Muslims around the World to Faith in Jesus Christ* by David V. Garrison. Monument, CO: WIGTake Resources, 2014.

  David Garrison spent three years traveling a quarter of a million miles through every corner of the Muslim world to investigate reports far and wide of Muslims turning to faith in Jesus Christ. In this amazing odyssey, Garrison gathered the stories of more than a thousand Muslim-background believers, asking them the question: "What did God use to bring you to faith in Jesus Christ? Tell me your story."

Books about What Muslim People Believe—And How to Reach Out to Them with the Gospel

- *Engaging with Muslims: Understanding Their World, Sharing Good*

News by John Klaassen. Croydon, England: Good Book Company, 2015.

This is the book we most highly recommend as a starter for understanding Islam and reaching out to Muslims. It is small but absolutely packed with practical, helpful, compassionate how-to's for sharing the gospel with Muslim people.

- *A Muslim's Heart: What Every Christian Needs to Know to Share Christ with Muslims* by Edward J. Hoskins. Colorado Springs, CO: NavPress, 2005.

  This is a quick, easy read by our doctor friend who has reached out to Muslims and studied Islam for forty years. Ed's book is very practical, with helpful "do's and don'ts" for interacting with Muslims (which we included in Appendix 4).

- *Muslims, Christians, and Jesus: Gaining Understanding and Building Relationships* by Carl Medearis. Minneapolis, MN: Bethany House, 2008.

  This was one of the first books we read when we entered Muslim ministry. Carl was hugely influential in teaching us to focus on Jesus, not "Christianity," with Muslim people. Warren Larson writes about this book, "one that contains several errors about Islam, it nonetheless superbly demonstrates how Christians can and must lovingly interact with Muslims." Carl's stories and spirit will bless you!

- *Ambassadors to Muslims: Building Bridges to the Gospel* by Fouad Masri. LaGrange, GA: Cedar Cross Media, 2011.

  Another practical, quality, easy read by a Lebanese Christian and founder of a superb ministry that we love—the Crescent Project. We have met with Fouad and found his passion for seeing Muslims come to Jesus to be inspirational and contagious! We endorse all of the Crescent Project's resources.

- *Engaging Islam (Study Guide Edition)* by Georges Houssney. Boulder, CO: Treeline Publishing, 2016.

  Georges (silent "s") helped us enter Muslim ministry! This Lebanese evangelist and apostle to Muslims can also help you learn how to engage Muslims, understand them on a personal level, and gain an understanding of the role we have as Christians to boldly share the gospel with them with conviction.

- *Any 3—Anyone, Anywhere, Any Time: Lead Muslims To Christ*

Now! by Mike Shipman. Monument, CO: WIGTake Resources, 2013.

Any 3 introduces Christians to a five-step process that helps them to (1) get connected with Muslims, (2) get to a God conversation, (3) get to lostness, (4) get to the gospel, and (5) get to a decision. Hundreds of Christians have learned to walk this path with Muslims, leading thousands of them to say "Yes" to Jesus in southeast Asia.

- *Breaking the Islam Code: Understanding the Soul Questions of Every Muslim* by J. D. Greear. Eugene, OR: Harvest House Publishers, 2010.
  This book focuses on helping Christians understand what is deep in Muslims' hearts behind their theology of works vs. grace. Greear explains why our gospel of the cross makes no sense to them. His experiences with Muslims in southeast Asia are invaluable as he explains how Muslims think and how you can befriend them and communicate the gospel. Also, we believe that his assessment of the "insider movement" and contextualization is balanced and excellent.

- *Breakthrough: The Return of Hope to the Middle East* by Tom Doyle Bletchley Milton Keynes, England: Authentic Publishing, 2009.
  We have spoken with Tom a few times. He is a master storyteller who loves Muslim people, Jewish people, and the Middle East. This book is a simple overview of Islam and contains compelling stories that will definitely move you.

Books about Christian Women Reaching out to Muslim Women

- *Woman to Woman: Sharing Jesus with a Muslim Friend* by Joy Loewen. Grand Rapids, MI: Chosen Books, 2010.
  Joy was afraid of Muslim women and uninterested in befriending them. But with prayer, wisdom, and a lot of love she overcame these obstacles, found that she actually liked them, and discovered that many of these women are irresistibly attracted to the love of Jesus. Joy shares her insights into befriending Muslim women, along with many helpful stories from her own experiences.

- *Miniskirts, Mothers and Muslims: A Christian Woman in a Muslim Land* by Christine Mallouhi. Oxford, England: Monarch Books/ Lion Hudson, 2015.

Miriam found this to be a very thorough and powerful book. It helps explain the unseen world of Muslim women through personal stories of living in several Middle Eastern countries. Topics include role models, segregation, restrictions, opportunities, family life, unwritten rules, and how Christian Western women are perceived.

- *Ministry to Muslim Women: Longing to Call Them Sisters* edited by Fran Love and Jeleta Eckheart. Pasadena, CA: William Carey Library, 2000.

  Fran is the widow of our late friend Rick Love. This emotionally moving book is a compilation of real-life experiences by women actively involved in reaching Muslim women for Christ. These articles approach the question of the gospel and Islam from a female perspective.

A Book Addressing the All-Important Honor/Shame Culture of Muslims

- *Honor & Shame: Unlocking the Door* by Roland Muller. Los Gatos, CA: Smashwords Edition, 2013.

  It is difficult for Westerners to understand the Muslim culture that is based on shame and honor, not right vs. wrong. To a Westerner, telling the truth is right, and telling a lie is wrong. In an honor/shame culture, the question is "What is honorable?" If a lie protects the honor of the tribe, then it is seen as right. In their worldview, "right" is based on honor, not law. This book gives us a scriptural way to present the gospel to those who live in honor/shame cultures in a way they can hear, understand, and respond to.

Books Addressing the Controversial Israeli/Palestinian Question from a Different Perspective

- *Fresh Vision for the Muslim World* by Mike Kuhn. Downers Grove, IL: InterVarsity Press, 2009.

  Our good friends Mike and Stephanie lived for two decades in the Middle East and know and love the people there. This book will impact how you view the Middle East, patriotism, Muslims, and evangelism. Mike writes from a wise, gentle heart and a scholarly mind. He challenges us to see the Muslim world with new eyes—

eyes not rooted in media lies or personal fears but in the values of Christ's kingdom.

- *Light Force: A Stirring Account of the Church Caught in the Middle East Crossfire* by Brother Andrew and Al Janssen. Grand Rapids, MI: Revell, 2004.
  This is a fascinating book about Brother Andrew's shift from ministry in former Soviet countries to Muslim countries after his life-changing trips to Israel/Palestine. Through God's providential working, Brother Andrew was given favor with Palestinian Muslim leaders—including terrorists. His heart for them to know Jesus and his heart for Palestinian Christians will stretch you.

- *Blood Brothers: The Dramatic Story of a Palestinian Christian Working for Peace in Israel* by Elias Chacour. Grand Rapids, MI: Chosen Books, 2003.
  We were blessed to hear Elias speak and tell his dramatic story. As a child, Elias Chacour lived in a small Palestinian village in Galilee. When tens of thousands of Palestinians were killed and nearly one million forced into refugee camps in 1948, Elias became an exile in his native land. This is his heartbreaking story—a story that Western Christians definitely need to hear.

- *Whose Land? Whose Promise? What Christians Are Not Being Told about Israel and the Palestinians* by Gary M. Burge. Cleveland, OH: The Pilgrim Press, 2013.
  Burge explores difficult questions like these: How do I embrace a commitment to Jewish people when I sense that there is profound injustice in Israel toward the Palestinian people? How do I celebrate the birth of this nation, Israel, when I also mourn the suffering of Palestinian Christians and Muslims?

A Book About Islam and Terrorism

- *The Mind of Terror: A Former Muslim Sniper Explores What Motivates ISIS and Other Extremist Groups (and How Best to Respond)* by Tass Saada (a BMB) and Dean Merrill. Carol Stream, IL: Tyndale House Publishers, 2016.
  In talking with Tass, we would never have known he was formerly a PLO terrorist! This gentle, loving man will help you understand what motivates terrorists, and how we should respond. Tass exposes the underlying factors that fuel terrorism but also does

a skillful job of offering peaceful, practical solutions—all with a great, loving heart for Muslim people.

Books on the Calling for Christians to Go to Dangerous Places in the Muslim World

- *We Died Before We Came Here: A True Story of Sacrifice and Hope* by Emily Foreman. Colorado Spring, CO: NavPress, 2016.
  This is a gripping story written by the wife of a martyr who was killed by al-Qaeda extremists. Emily is a dear friend of ours who still loves Muslims and still goes to the same country where her husband gave his life. She writes of the worthiness of Jesus in following Him wherever He leads.
- *Why God Calls Us to Dangerous Places* by Kate McCord. Chicago, IL: Moody Publishers, 2015.
  Soon after 9/11, Kate left the corporate world and followed God to Afghanistan, where she suffered many losses: comfort, safety, and close friends. Kate considers why God calls us to dangerous places and what going there can mean: death, trauma, and heavy sorrow. But it can also mean a firmer hope, joy unimaginable, and a new closeness to the heart of God.

A Book about Fifty Years of Recruiting Missionaries to the Muslim World

- *You've Got Libya: A Life Serving in the Muslim World* by Greg Livingstone. Grand Rapids, MI: Monarch Press, 2014.
  Born out of wedlock and unwanted at birth, this young man overcame a life of obstacles and later became a pioneer in missions to unreached Muslim people. Greg's burden for the millions of Muslim people who had no opportunity to hear the gospel led him to start—or help to start—three mission agencies and recruit more than 1,400 missionaries to go to over forty Muslim majority countries! This book is a delightful account, full of compelling humor, strange experiences, and self-deprecating honesty. We personally know and love this supremely dedicated man and his incredible wife, Sally!

DVD Courses to Learn about Islam and Reaching Out to Muslim People

- *Bridges: Christians Connecting with Muslims* by Fouad Masri, Crescent Project
  This is an easy to watch and understand overview of Islam and guide for how to share Jesus with Muslims. Fouad is a gifted teacher and communicator. This six-session course is ideal for small groups.
- *Journey to Jesus: Building Christ-Centered Friendships with Muslims* by the Billy Graham Center at Wheaton College.
  Six sessions of realistic dramatizations of Christians sharing their faith with Muslims. Both joys and frustrations are seen. An overview of Islam is also included.
- *Friendship First* by Interserve.
  The Friendship First Course is an interactive course in six sessions. It enables Christians to approach their Muslim friends with confidence by equipping them with the skill and resources needed to be an effective witness for Jesus.
- *Al-Massira*
  This is a spendid DVD course to use with Muslims for either evangelism or discipleship. *Al-Massira* ("The Journey") presents the Christian faith through a chronological overview of the Bible but centers it in its original Middle Eastern context. It is filmed in the Middle East and can be watched using Arabic or Farsi with English subtitles. (One caveat: you have to go through the Al-Massira workshop to get these DVDs. Contact https://www.almassira.org/?Al_Massira_English___The_Journey).

Websites to Learn about Islam and Reaching Out to Muslim People

- *Ethne Outfitters* https://ethneoutfitters.org/.
  This is the website we most highly recommend in this area. It includes an absolute wealth of information to help you engage with and befriend Muslim people through tips about their hospitality, culture, customs, community, and traditions.
- *The Crescent Project* https://www.crescentproject.org/.
  Very helpful tools, articles, and short videos for reaching Muslims by one of our favorite ministries.

- *Say Hello: Serving Muslim Women* https://sayhelloinfo.com/.
This ministry invites Christian women into the beautiful experience of relating Christ to Muslim women through sharing delightful things in common but also addressing differences. Most Muslim women have never once heard that Jesus loves them, and this website helps Christian women know how to tell them. This website is packed with helpful resources—many of which are free.
- *Arab World Media* https://www.arabworldmedia.org/field-guides/.
A plethora of resources for Christians to learn about Islam and reach out to Muslims: prayer guides, articles, videos of former Muslims, etc.
- *Answering Islam* http://www.answering-islam.org/.
Christian site with literally thousands of apologetics articles.
- *YouTube videos by BMBs Abdu Murray and Nabeel Qureshi*—first-rate, practical helps for those who want to share the good news with Muslim people.

Websites to Help in Reaching Out to Muslim International Students

- *International Students Inc.* https://internationalstudents.org/.
International Students, Inc. exists to share Christ's love with international students in cooperation with the local church.
- *Bridges International* https://www.bridgesinternational.com/.
Bridges International is a caring community of Christ-followers committed to serve, promote social connections, and engage in spiritual conversations with international students.

Websites to Help in Reaching Out to Muslim Refugees

- *World Relief* https://worldrelief.org/.
World Relief is a global Christian humanitarian organization that partners with local churches and community leaders in the US to bring hope, healing, and transformation to the most vulnerable.
- *Bethany Christian Services* https://bethany.org/get-help/refugees.
Their mission is to stand up for and give help to vulnerable children, refugees, and families.

Websites of Organizations to Help You Teach English to Muslim People (ESL)

- *ESL Ministries—PCA Mission to North America* https://pcamna. org/ministry/esl-ministries/.
  God has brought the world to our doorstep. English as a Second Language (ESL) Ministry equips churches to reach immigrants, international college students and refugees with the gospel of Jesus Christ.
- *ESL Ministry Resources—*Evangelical Free Church of America https://www.efca.org/resources/document/esl-ministry-collaboration.
  This site offers access to hundreds of free tips, ideas, lesson plans, worksheets, templates, and even a number of free, downloadable books and teaching manuals.

Websites to Learn about Using Discovery Bible Studies (DBS) with Muslim People—Where You Live or Overseas

- *Crossway Discovery Bible Study Method (DBS)* https://intent.org/ wp-content/uploads/2017/04/DBS.pdf.
  Excellent overview of DBS with sample Bible studies, including "Creation to Christ: An Outline for Muslims."
- *InterVarsity International Student Ministry, Discovery Bible Studies* https://ism.intervarsity.org/dbs.
  Helpful explanation of DBS with sample studies.

Websites to Learn about Oral Storytelling of Bible Stories to Muslim People—Where You Live or Overseas

- *StoryRunners* (A Cru Ministry) https://www.storyrunners.org.
  About 7,000 languages exist in the world today. More than half of these languages have no known Scripture. StoryRunners enables people in these unreached language groups to hear the gospel in a way they understand: oral Bible storytelling.
- *Spoken Worldwide* https://spoken.org.
  Two-thirds of the world's population doesn't use a written form of communication. Spoken Worldwide delivers spoken truth to the unreached, isolated, and neglected regions of the world where written words can't go.
- *Simply the Story* http://simplythestory.org/oralbiblestories/.

Simply the Story trains people to orally lead Bible studies. STS offers Oral Bible Schools in which students learn 40–160 stories for evangelism and discipleship.

Websites to Learn about Praying for Muslim People

- *Prayercast* https://www.prayercast.com/love-muslims-home.html. How to pray for Muslims using high quality videos filmed in Muslim countries all over the world. Prayers are beautifully led by former Muslim people.
- *The Joshua Project* https://joshuaproject.net/. Information on least reached peoples of the world with prayer for movements among them.
- *Praying through the Arabian Peninsula* http://www.pray-ap.info/. Praying through the heart of the Muslim World for movements to Christ.
- *30 Days of Prayer* https://www.30daysprayer.com. How to pray for Muslims around the world during Ramadan.

A Website to Help Your Kids Pray for and Reach Out to Muslim Kids

- *Say HELLO—Forever Friends Curriculum* https://sayhelloinfo. com/kids. A curriculum to teach kids how to share Jesus with their Muslim friends. A free downloadable PDF of 35 prayers for kids to pray for Muslim kids is available as well: https://mailchi.mp/eb51d-b429c69/say-hello-forever-friends-prayers-for-kids.

Websites to Recommend to Muslim Seekers

- *A Muslim Journey to Hope* https://muslimjourneytohope.com/. Testimonies of former Muslims—women and men, young and old, rich and poor, from many countries in the world.
- *I Found the Truth* https://www.ifoundthetruth.com/. Inspiring videos and written testimonies of believers from a Muslim background.
- *More than Dreams* http://morethandreams.org/. Five excellent docudramas of former Muslims giving their testimonies of seeing Jesus in a dream or a vision.

- *Who is Isa al Masih?—The Man in White* http://www.isaalmasih. net/.
  Full of excellent articles and resources for a Muslim to examine regarding the true identity of Jesus.
- *Al Injil—Good News for You* https://www.injil.org/.
  Another website with thought-provoking articles for a seeking Muslim.
- *Isa and Islam Religious Dialogue* https://www.isaandislam.com/.
  Another impressive website full of articles and videos.
- *10 Amazing Muslims Touched by God* http://www.amazingmuslims.com/.
  Excerpts from ten BMB testimonies with an invitation to learn more through a free book.
- *Answering Islam: Truth, Love, and Newness of Life—Why Muslims Become Christians* https://www.answering-islam.org/Testimonies/index.html.
  Written testimonies of former Muslims from all over the world.
- *I Love Muslims* http://www.iLoveMuslims.net/
  A blog written for Muslims by a follower of Jesus who passionately loves Muslim people.

A Website for Christian Women Dating or Married to a Muslim Man

- *Loving A Muslim—A Support Group for Christian Women Dating or Married to Muslims* http://www.domini.org/lam/home.html.
  As we strongly warned at the end of chapter 39, dating and marrying a Muslim man can lead to a multitude of problems and suffering for a Christian woman. This website can help with understanding that issue.

Phone Apps to Use and Share with Muslim Seekers

- *The Bible App—YouVersion.*
  2,062 Bible versions in 1,372 languages for free and without advertising.
- *Gideon Bible App* from The Gideons International.
  The Gideon Bible App offers mobile access to Scripture in a multitude of languages, including text and dramatized audio Bibles so

your Muslim friend can read and listen to the Bible in their own language.

- *Jesus Film Project App*
  The Jesus Film Project app is a full digital library of more than 200 full-length movies, miniseries, and short films produced to help the world know Jesus better—in 1800+ languages. Everything on the app is free to watch, download, and share with any Muslim person you meet, wherever you meet them.

Websites to Purchase Bibles or Books to Give to Muslim People and to Purchase Books to Learn about Reaching Out to Muslim People

- *Bibles in Bulk* https://biblesinbulk.com/.
  For bulk purchasing of Arabic/English bilingual New Testaments to give as gifts to your Arab Muslim friends, and Farsi (Persian) New Testaments for your Muslim friends from Iran or Afghanistan.
- *Multilanguage Media* https://multilanguagemedia.org/shop-category/bible/.
  Source for purchasing individual copies of Arabic/English bilingual New Testaments or Bibles (Arabic Contemporary/English NIV). New Testaments and Bibles are also available in Farsi (Persian) and many other languages.
- *Pocket Testament League* https://www.ptl.org/.
  Gospel of John with good news summary in each edition. Arabic and Farsi are available here: https://members.ptl.org/code/join.php.
- *ChristianBook.com* https://www.christianbook.com/.
  Christian books on Islam and other world religions, along with various language materials.

APPENDIX 8

IS ISLAM INHERENTLY A *VIOLENT* RELIGION?

Some believe that in the beginning Muhammad was a sincere seeker of truth and that the revelations he is said to have received in Mecca became the more peaceful verses of the Qur'an. When he fled persecution in Mecca and lived in Medina, the revelations he claimed to receive became more and more violent and were reflected that way in the Qur'an.

Please know that this is a theory from some scholars. Others disagree, saying that we do not have absolute proof of what suras (chapters) in the Qur'an are from Muhammad's time living in Mecca and which are from his later time living in Medina.

But we think that few Christian scholars would disagree that, when one looks at Islam and Muslims in the world today, we see very peaceful Muslims who live their lives according to the more peaceful verses of the Qur'an (regardless of when they were written). They will say, like our friend Khalil, *"Islam absolutely is a peaceful religion!"* These are, by far, *the vast majority* of Muslim people in the world.

You also have violent Muslims in our world—such as the infamous terrorist Osama bin Laden—who live(d) their lives according to the violent verses of the Qur'an (regardless of when they were written). These jihadists maintain that the violent verses reflect true Islam. Thankfully, these are *the small minority* of Muslim people in the world.

To sum up, our belief is that Muslim people vary as to which part of Muhammad's life they emulate and which part of the Qur'an they follow. This is heavily influenced by their spiritual leaders (imams, mullahs, clerics, and sheikhs), their tribe, and the male heads of their family.

These influential people may well determine what kind of Islam a Muslim person will believe in, and thus what kind of Muslim they will be—peaceful . . . or violent.

For the violent Muslim, the ultimate answer to *terrorism* will always be *evangelism*. As the bumper sticker we saw at a missions conference humorously and joyfully proclaimed:

Fight Terrorism!
Support a Missionary!

APPENDIX 9

DIFFERENT EVANGELISTIC STRATEGIES REGARDING OUTREACH TO MUSLIM PEOPLE

If you get very involved in loving your Muslim neighbors, you will learn that there are differing—and sometimes opposing—views on how to reach them with the gospel. Here are some examples of approaches that have both fans and detractors:

1. The *"insider movement"*—In this strategy, missionaries encourage former Muslims to follow Jesus and grow under His Lordship but continue to stay within their pre-existing communities and social networks—their families, their culture, and even their mosque (as much as they can be biblically faithful). Also, in this strategy the BMB—believer from a Muslim background—may still identify as a Muslim in his or her culture, since the word means "one who is submitted to God." The rationale for this is that in living this way a BMB can remain in their Muslim family and culture as a light for Jesus rather than risk immediate expulsion (or worse) if they identify themselves as "Christians."

    Opponents of the insider movement generally hold that any mixing of religious traditions will create confusion and compromise in the mind and lifestyle of the former Muslim. It will lead to an unbiblical syncretism or, as some have called it, *"Chrislam."*

2. The *translation issue*—There are various translation controversies, but perhaps the main one is that some Bible translators translate "Son of God" in other ways (such as "Prince of God," "Beloved of God," or even "Caliph of God") in Bibles for Muslims because the Qur'an specifically says that God has no son. The concept of God having a son is utterly blasphemous to Muslims because they believe it implies sexual procreation. Because of this, some translators have tried to be true to the biblical familial meaning of Father and Son but change the wording so that Muslim people will not be needlessly offended.

    This strategy is strongly opposed by others, who see Muslim-friendly Bible translations as a violation of the integrity of Scripture and a serious compromise.

3. *Using the Qur'an as a "bridge"*—There are books and seminars about how to use verses from the Qur'an as stepping stones toward Jesus for a Muslim. For example, since the Qur'an has many verses about Isa al Masih—Jesus the Messiah—which speak of him favorably, some advocate pointing out these verses to Muslim seekers but then assisting them in moving on to the Gospels. These people do not believe the Qur'an is inspired by God but that He, in His gracious sovereignty, has allowed some truth to be contained in the Qur'an so that genuine seekers can search for still more truth about Jesus and the kingdom of God in the Gospels.

    Others believe that the Qur'an has nothing at all to offer in the way of evangelistic strategies, since it is not inspired by the Holy Spirit and is not a "Holy Book."

4. *Visiting a mosque*—In chapters 23 and 30 we advocated visiting mosques *if* certain precautions have been taken. We believe that Jesus was our example in coming to this planet—a spiritually dark place—to be the Light of the world. In the same way, it is our opinion that followers of Jesus can be used to bring light to the mosque. It is *not* the main place to evangelize, and there are restrictions there, but it is *a* place to be a witness in actions or words.

    A man we deeply respect in ministry to Muslims is very opposed to Christians going into mosques at all. He sees the mosque as a place of spiritual darkness and an unfruitful place for reaching Muslim people. He advocates meeting them in other places where we can be free to share in a more straightforward manner.

5. *Apologetics*—Some are proficient in defending the objective truth of the gospel with Muslim people. Ravi Zacharias, Abdu Murray, Nabeel Qureshi, and others have been extremely gifted in verbal and written answers to common Islamic objections to the Christian faith, such as: the Bible has been changed/corrupted; Jesus did not really die on the cross; viewing Jesus as the Son of God is blasphemous; "Where does Jesus say in the Bible, 'I am God—worship me'"? "Isn't Muhammad mentioned in the Bible?" and so forth. (Nabeel's book, *No God But One: Allah Or Jesus?*, can be very helpful in answering these questions.)

While we believe in the value of apologetics in evangelism with some Muslim people (when used with gentleness and respect—1 Peter 3:15), we still maintain that most Muslims come to faith in Jesus through *relationship* with a genuine follower of Jesus. Apologetics can be a helpful part of that relationship, as it was in the case of Nabeel (*Seeking Allah, Finding Jesus*).

Please keep in mind what the late apologist Ravi Zacharias once said,

"Love is the greatest apologetic."

6. *Polemics*—While apologetics is somewhat *defensive* in its posture—giving *answers* to Islamic objections to the Bible and Christianity—polemics is more *offensive* and is sometimes an *attack* against the teachings of Islam and the person of Muhammad. This can become argumentative and contentious. Probably some of the best-known polemicists are David Wood, Jay Smith, and Father Zakaria Botros—a Coptic priest from Egypt.

Polemics, as led by the Holy Spirit, is usually most effective when working with articulate and zealous Muslims such as those from English speaking South Asia (Pakistan, India, and Bangladesh).

We believe that God can use anything to bring Muslims to Himself, including polemics. Some are called to this ministry, but it is personally not for us, and we don't recommend it for most other followers of Jesus. It requires both an advanced knowledge of Islam and an incredibly thick skin. It can also devolve into mean-spirited interaction with Muslims, which we don't see as a Jesus-like approach to evangelism.

7. *Debate*—We spoke about Muslim-Christian public debates for evangelistic purposes in chapter 20. When done in the right spirit by a Christian debater, we believe that debates can be very educational for a Muslim attendee. Such debates might be the only way some Muslims will hear the essential truths of the good news.

8. The *"Any 3: Anyone, Anywhere, Any Time"* methodology of missionary Mike Shipman—Shipman declares it to be a myth that a relationship or friendship with Muslims has to exist for evangelism to Muslims to bear fruit. He says that the idea that it takes time to build up that kind of relationship before a Muslim will be ready to hear the gospel and make a commitment to Christ is also a myth.

As we were finishing our book and about to send it to the publisher, we read Shipman's book. As we have said, we are personally on an ongoing journey. We are continually learning and growing in our outreach to Muslims. While we continue to maintain that most Muslims come to faith in Jesus through relationship with His followers, which can involve years of investment, we want to learn more about this "faster" approach that is bearing solid, significant fruit in certain places in the world.

To sum up, we want to encourage you: please do not let any of these differences in strategies and models discourage or confuse you. Learn about the approaches above, but prayerfully seek wisdom from the Lord and biblical insight for yourself as you grow in your own unique evangelistic strategies and calling.

Our own personal outreach strategy with Muslims thus far has involved a combination of several approaches that you have mostly seen in this book:

- *First commandment evangelism*—the greatest witness you can have to Muslims, or anyone else, is to love the Lord yourself with your whole heart (Mark 12:30). They will see it and be impacted by it.
- *Paraclete evangelism*—the "Paraclete," of course, is the Helper, the Holy Spirit. To allow Him to help you to think of and use out-of-the-box words or ideas for a specific witnessing situation is

so rewarding. To work together with God Himself is our goal in evangelism!

- *Friendship evangelism*—for us, loving our Muslim neighbor in evangelism is all about relationship, relationship, relationship. We encourage building a warm, genuine relationship with a Muslim person, whether or not they ever choose to follow Jesus. This must include gospel conversations. A truly loving friend shares with the other about Jesus's life, teachings, death, and resurrection and calls for a decision to follow Him when the Spirit leads.

- *Servant evangelism*—helping to meet the practical needs of Muslim people in a no-strings attached way. We have seen this to be significantly impactful with refugees overseas or with refugees very soon after they arrive in the US.

- *Prayer evangelism*—asking a Muslim if they would like prayer for anything, then asking permission to pray for them on the spot, and then finally praying for that Muslim person in their presence: out loud, to the Father in Jesus's name. Think of it: your prayer might be the first time your Muslim acquaintance or friend has ever heard how a follower of Jesus prays to a God who is not distant and aloof!

- *Story evangelism*—while not included in our book to any large degree, we often tell Bible stories to Muslims—stories about what Jesus did in His ministry (power over demons, disease, death, and nature) or stories that Jesus Himself told (parables). When we told a group of Muslim refugees in the Middle East the story of the prodigal son with emotional fervor and animated physical gestures, one man was significantly moved. He said to the others, "Look, the hairs on my arm are standing up!" "Storying" can also be done in a group, and we participated for years in a group where Muslims and Christians came together weekly to hear Bible stories and answer questions together about the text.

- *Discovery Bible Study* evangelism—a very powerful discipleship process centered on opening the Bible with someone who doesn't yet follow Jesus, including Muslim people. We love this kind of study because: it is facilitator, not expert teacher led; it is based on discovery, not teaching; it depends on the Holy Spirit to reveal truth; it involves discipleship into salvation (as we did with Hassan in chapter 50); it emphasizes obedience to what is studied instead of just acquiring knowledge; and it encourages passing on newly learned truth to others.

- *Give a New Testament evangelism*—the best gift you can ever put into the hands of your Muslim friend is the Word of God in their language! We have seen Muslim people everywhere gladly receive this precious gift. If it can be in their language as well as English, all the better. We encourage you to keep bilingual New Testaments or Gospels of John in your car so you can give them away any time the Holy Spirit leads.
- *Hospitality evangelism*—perhaps as many as 75% of international students never make it into the home of a Western Christian! But having a Muslim student, refugee, or immigrant over to your home will open their hearts in untold ways. At our home, we have hosted our Muslim friends and acquaintances to watch the Super Bowl, play board games, do crafts, celebrate holidays (gifts for them at Christmas), watch excerpts from Jesus movies, play games outside, and, of course, . . . eat, eat, and then eat some more!

Whatever methods and strategies you gravitate toward in your outreach to Muslim people, be diligent to love those who differ from you, and do all you can to preserve the unity of the Spirit (Ephesians 4:3).

In conclusion, our thought has been that we can usually learn from almost anyone who genuinely loves Muslim people, regardless of their position on any of these ministry strategies. We believe you can too!

APPENDIX 10

A FEW WORDS ABOUT
VISION AND *CALLING*

Do you have a vision and calling from God for a ministry, but it seems as though God is not coming through to release you from what you are doing now?

Be patient! God does have a good and wise plan—but let *Him* determine the *timing* of that plan.

I, Tim, got my calling from the Lord to evangelism and missions in 1977, my senior year of college. Do you know when God released us to full-time ministry to Muslims? In 2007. Thirty years later! Do you think my heart did not burn many times during those years to be released, to get "out there" and do something "big" for God in reaching the nations? Of course! But God had many, many lessons to teach me in that thirty-year period of waiting: my need of brokenness, humility, and doing ministry *for His glory*. He had a plan of preparation that was very hard and painful—but also very wise.

Think about Abraham. How long did he wait for that little baby boy that God had promised? Twenty-five years. Consider Joseph. How much time elapsed between his vision of leadership and its fulfillment? Thirteen years, which involved both servitude and imprisonment. Look at Moses. How many years of preparation in the desert did he need to endure before he was used by God to deliver the people of Israel from Egypt? Forty years. Look at Jesus Himself. How old was He when He began His public ministry? Thirty. Think of it, thirty years of preparation—for the Son of God! Someone has wisely said, "If God is making you wait, you're in good company!"

We are not saying that God will require you to wait decades for the fulfillment of the calling and vision He has given you. We are saying that normally, after He gives a vision, it must be *refined*. More importantly, *you* must be refined. How does gold get refined? In the fire.

Every vision from God has a God-ordained *timing* for its fulfillment, and the timing of that fulfillment is perhaps as important as the vision itself:

> *"For still the vision awaits its appointed time . . .*
> *If it seems slow, wait for it;*
> *it will surely come; it will not delay."*
> HABAKKUK 2:3

So often God gives us a calling, but He—in His loving wisdom—won't release us to that calling until He deems it best. In the waiting time, sometimes our calling goes through a kind of death. God requires us to give the vision to Him, to put it on His altar—just as Abraham had to put Isaac on the altar. Isaac was the beginning of the vision God gave to Abraham to bless all the nations of the earth, but God wanted to see whether Abraham loved Isaac—and the vision—more than he loved God Himself. There could be no *idolatry*. It had to have been excruciating for Abraham, but he passed the test.

Right now, you may be in a testing time related to your calling. You have a vision from God, but He is asking you to give it back to Him and let Him fulfill it in *His* sovereign, perfect timing. Will you do that? Will you surrender your vision and calling to Him and trust Him with it?

God may send you into your calling soon after you receive it. He sometimes does that. But more often—just as He did with Abraham, Joseph, Moses, His own Son, and with us—He has us wait, learn, prepare, and become ready for the vision and calling He has given us.

Then we will be much more likely to humbly give Him the glory rather than take it for ourselves.

> *"Not to us, O LORD, not to us,*
> *but to your name goes all the glory*
> *for your unfailing love and faithfulness."*
> PSALM 115:1, NLT

> *"Be still, and know that I am God.*

I will be exalted among the nations,
I will be exalted in the earth!"
PSALM 46:10

"Trust in the LORD and do good;
Dwell in the land and cultivate faithfulness.
Delight yourself in the LORD;
And He will give you the desires of your heart.
Commit your way to the LORD,
Trust also in Him, and He will do it.
Rest in the LORD and wait patiently for Him . . ."
PSALM 37:3–5, 7, NASB

ACKNOWLEDGMENTS

The authors would like to thank all who helped with their input in this book, especially those who worked diligently in the editing process: Mike and Stephanie Kuhn, Donna Huisjen, and our patient publisher, Tim Beals, at Credo House Publishers. You have each helped us "publish" God's glorious deeds!

"Sing to the LORD; praise his name.
Each day proclaim the good news that he saves.
Publish his glorious deeds among the nations.
Tell everyone about the amazing things he does."
PSALM 96:2-3, NLT

Made in the USA
Las Vegas, NV
08 December 2020